ASCEND

LEADERSHIP LESSONS
AT 28,000 FEET

To Catherine!
May God Bless You
in everything you
do.

the publishing CIRCLE

For permission requests, write to the publisher, addressed "Attention: Permissions Coordinator," at the address below.

admin@ThePublishingCircle.com

or

THE PUBLISHING CIRCLE, LLC
Regarding: Mark Carr
19215 SE 34th Street
Suite 106-347
Camas, Washington 98607

ASCEND / Mark Carr
ISBN 978-1-947398-62-7 Paperback
ISBN 978-1-947398-71-9 Hardcover
ISBN 978-1-947398-65-8 Large print paperback
ISBN 978-1-947398-72-6 eBook
FIRST EDITION

CREDITS:
Front cover photo © Mark Carr
Book design by Michele Uplinger

Author's Note

I have recreated events, locales, and conversations as best as possible from my memories of them.

In some instances, I have changed the names of individuals to maintain anonymity for various reasons. I may have also changed some identifying characteristics and details, such as physical properties, occupations, and places of residence.

If you are interested in learning more about how you can hire Mark for speaking engagements or as an executive/leadership coach please visit my website at:

www.summitparadigm.com
or email me at
mark@summitparadigm.com

For bonus chapters about my climbs on Mount Fuji and Mount Kinabalu, go to:
summitparadigm.com/bonus.

Dedication

THIS IS DEDICATED TO ALL THE SHERPAS AND PORTERS throughout the world who risk their lives to enable people like me to achieve their far-flung dreams.

I would like to encourage you to donate to the Himalyanstoveproject.org whose mission is to transform the lives of individuals and families living in the Mt. Everest region and in other remote villages in Nepal who currently cook with traditional, rudimentary stoves or over open fire-pits inside their homes. By donating, you'll provide clean, vented, fuel-efficient Envirofit cookstoves.

Contents

ASCEND

LEADERSHIP LESSONS
AT 28,000 FEET

MARK CARR

the publishing CIRCLE

CHAPTER 1

The Mother of Mountains

O N THE DOORSTEP OF OUTER SPACE, I MARVEL AT where I lie. I am literally at the edge of Earth's atmosphere where the surrounding sky glows a strange, endless deep blue. I lie in the infamous "Death Zone" at 26,300 feet above sea level. In the deathly still air, I quietly thank God for bringing me safely to this point. I pray a long, solemn prayer for safety for the remaining and most difficult part of the journey. I am a single day away from summiting Mount Everest, the highest peak on Earth; the ultimate prize for most climbers; the pinnacle of my dreams.

We reach Camp Four on the South Col of the Tibetan side around one in the afternoon. The South Col is a sharp-edged saddle that stretches between Everest and Lhotse, with the landscape belonging more on the moon than anywhere you'd find on Earth. There is little snow as the constant, gale-force winds ravage the Col and sweep it clear of any form of life. When we arrive at camp, I am awestruck by Everest's majestic yet ominous summit pyramid looming right above me, casting a long, deep shadow over our intended route.

Upon settling into the camp, I hydrate and force down some noodles. Eating is monumentally difficult at this altitude, as your body uses less energy to burn muscle and what little fat you carry instead of digesting new food. In the Death Zone, your body literally cannibalizes itself. Minute by minute, you are actually dying. This is the reason it is only possible to remain at that height for about two days at most.

I hope to get a little sleep, but I don't count on it. I know if the weather holds, the guides will get us up around midnight to prepare for our final push to the summit. I'm both tired and thrilled, but don't expect to get any sleep. Probably because I don't worry about it, I doze off and on for a few hours, even with the discomfort of wearing an oxygen mask. I wake around 8:00 p.m., and although I am incredibly anxious to get out of my tent and get going, I lie in bed, becoming more nervous with each passing hour. I know what lies ahead.

The next few hours feel like an eternity. I want the day to be over. I badly need to know what the outcome will be. Will I make it to the summit? Or will it be too much? After exposure to such brutal conditions for so many days, I just want the climb to be over. Thankfully, there is no wind, and the temperature is only about ten below zero. In my down suit, it is not uncomfortable.

Around 11:00 p.m., I can't remain in bed and get up and begin to pack my gear. Before long, the Sherpas have roused everyone, and it is time to go. Michael, our lead guide—a powerful, sunbaked Montanan with strawberry-blond hair—makes one final, diligent check with the help of our ever-grinning Sherpas. They ensure our crampons are tight, our regulators work, and they set our oxygen flow to the correct level. Too little, and we won't have the energy to make the climb. Too much, and we'll run out and die on the mountain. With our headlamps glowing, we begin our trudge out and up the southeast ridge of Everest.

They have assigned each of us a Sherpa. We form a sort of conga line, heading up with Michael at the front, our personal Sherpas with each of us in the line, and one lone, extra-strong Sherpa bringing up the rear. The going is incredibly slow. We have to take one step and breathe for thirty seconds, then another step and breathe for thirty seconds. Even so, I wonder if my oxygen bottle is open enough since it is already all I can do to evenly measure my breaths. Eventually, the line spreads out a little, but I often have to wait for the climber ahead of me to take another step, then wait again.

We are all clipped on to a fixed-line, and sometimes there is just no way to go around a slower climber. Although I consider myself fairly fit and experienced, some climbers pass me going up the mountain. Now and then, I overtake a climber who is slower than I am. I also move by those who have turned back to head down. As we cross paths, they wish me "good luck," and I notice the relief in their eyes. They focus only on escaping this treacherous peak. I fend off doubts that try to creep into my head, wondering if they are smarter than me or if they know something I don't.

I try not to dwell on how extremely steep and painfully cold the mountain face is and the complete exposure I face at the literal edge of the atmosphere. Every time I pause for more than a couple of minutes, the bone-chilling cold penetrates deeper and deeper, like a slow, icy knife. We keep pushing upward and my thighs, arms, and lungs burn, while my skin and bones seem frozen. I tap into reserves I did not know I had, yet I feel like I am running on pure adrenaline. A ghostly, yellow moon begins to ascend far below, but I am too tired to appreciate its foreboding beauty. The stars above are spectacular, but I really don't care, since looking up takes far too much energy. I keep my head down and focus on my next step.

We continue to climb up and up and up, as the ice turns slick and hard and very, very scary. When I look up, I peer at the horizon, searching for the first rays of dawn. The smallest hope of warmth, or any small comfort, would be enough to convince me to keep going for another hundred feet. Even with double-insulated plastic boots, my feet are literally freezing, and I worry about frostbite. I really don't want to lose any toes. Finally, we reach the landmark called The Balcony at 27,700 feet. We stop to rest. I welcome the respite, and it's much needed, but I am growing colder and colder. I long to be back in the searing heat of my hometown of

Phoenix. My Sherpa changes me to a new oxygen bottle, and we set our sights on the southeast ridge—1,000 feet of entirely exposed terrain that leads to the South Summit.

We continue upward and, just barely, I sense the sky lightening. The first rays of dawn are breaking through, and I am blessed with a little surge of energy. We navigate over a ridge, and suddenly, right above us looms the majestic South Summit. As the sky lightens, the enormous shadow of Everest's summit pyramid stretches out toward the horizon. I look behind us, and the entire Earth lies far, far below. I smile at the wonder of such a privilege, my joy momentarily eclipsing the struggle. But my grin fades as I see clouds beginning to swirl in the valley thousands of feet below. My thoughts immediately fly to Jon Krakauer and his book *Into Thin Air*[1], which chronicles the 1996 tragedy on Everest where many people died after getting caught in a storm that suddenly ascends from the valley below. This worries me. Soon we step up onto the small plateau that is the South Summit. Everest's true summit is just around the corner, only 300 vertical feet above us. But getting there is the most difficult part of the climb.

What stands in the way is a knife-edged ridge, where being clipped on to the fixed rope is a must, unless you wish to tumble 8,000 feet or 10,000 feet to your death. Suddenly, my foot slips, and I claw frantically at the line to keep from sliding down the ridge. The other climbers

---

[1] Krakauer, Jon. *Into Thin Air: A Personal Account of the Mount Everest Disaster*. Villard Books, 1997.

brace and steady themselves as I regain my footing, which I thankfully do. I use up precious oxygen with my panicked breathing, and now every step requires focus—something my oxygen-starved brain refuses to do.

Ahead, I see another line of climbers. They are too close. Something is wrong. Many climbers are standing below the step, and when I inquire, I am told the Sherpas, who were supposed to secure the lines up the step, arrived late. This has delayed everything, and I am far back in the queue. The problem is the cold. While you're moving, it's almost tolerable, but as we wait and wait on the exposed side of the frozen peak, it feels like my blood is turning to ice. I sigh in frustration as the Sherpas struggle to untangle lines at the top of the step. I look down, and the clouds below continue to rise menacingly. My feet are now totally numb, and I am sure frostbite has set in. Precious minutes pass, and my uneasiness increases. I continue to fixate on the swirling clouds below. How quickly are they rising?

A climber in front of me decides to turn back. Gingerly, we do a kind of one-two-you-go-I-go dance to clip and unclip so he can go around me without one of us falling thousands of feet into Tibet. This climber's decision does little for my confidence. Finally, the climbers begin to go up, but will still be a while for me. The waiting continues. Is it my imagination, or are the clouds below becoming darker? I am now shivering uncontrollably and am, without a doubt, in the first stages of hypothermia. What follows will be incoordination, confusion, weakness, and apathy.

I am engaged in the greatest mental battle I have ever faced. I have come this far . . . yet I feel like I have nothing left. Do I truly have the remaining strength necessary to summit Everest? Or will it cost me my life?

More importantly, do I even care?

CHAPTER 2

Embrace Challenge

I GREW UP IN A TOWN CALLED LONGMONT, COLORADO, named after the mountain that dominates the skyline, thirty miles to the west. At just over 14,000 feet, Longs Peak would not be considered a difficult climb for an experienced mountaineer, but for the amateur, believe me, it should not be underestimated.

Since childhood this mountain fascinated me. It truly is one of the monarchs of Colorado, stretching across the western horizon from northern Denver all the way to Fort Collins. My bedroom window directly faced Longs Peak, so for as long as I can remember, this majestic morning vision greeted and called to me. Perhaps I am biased, but I include it in my pantheon of the greatest peaks in the lower forty-eight states: Rainier, Shasta, Whitney, the Grand Teton, and Longs.

I dreamed of climbing Longs Peak and vowed

someday I would embrace the challenge. Climbing that mountain became my first major focus—a goal that eclipsed all others. One small problem: I had a deathly fear of heights. At age eleven, my family and I visited Tokyo, and my dad took us on a trip to the top of the Tokyo Tower. Despite the completely enclosed observation deck, nothing could convince me to walk to the windows and look down. I wasn't afraid of much, but heights paralyzed me. When we arrived home, however, Longs continued to greet me each morning with a regal smile, beckoning me to her summit. I knew she could feel the passion in my heart, but I couldn't find the determination to answer her call.

Soon after graduating from high school, Todd—one of my closest buddies—asked me if I wanted to climb Longs with him and his older brother, Bill. Todd was 6-foot 3-inches and weighed around 185 pounds, with thighs the size of tree trunks. Born missing one ear, surgeons constructed Todd a facsimile out of the skin so it didn't look unnatural, but if you looked closely past his curly blond hair, you could see it. It didn't faze Todd in the least. He was an adventurer.

The brothers lost both of their parents to cancer just a couple of years before, so Todd had to rely on Bill, who was nine years older. Likely due to this life cataclysm, Todd and Bill were ardent atheists, revering logic and science above all else. Predictably, they were also extremely close. When their emotional scars became apparent, my heart broke for them because they were two of the funniest, most fun, and most brilliant people

I have ever met. It seemed likely that their intense grief and confusion had contributed to their dry wit and compounded Todd's hilariously contrarian nature.

Bill stood about the same height as Todd, except he had long hair and sported a thick, luxurious mustache. Bill had always been an exercise fanatic, constantly running, cycling, and lifting weights. He got Todd into running and cycling, so both were incredibly fit, but tennis constituted our mutual athletic ground. Overall, though, I'd have to say Todd could claim title to being the best athlete out of all of us.

When Todd asked me if I wanted to join them to climb Longs, the request provided one of those moments in which destiny blindsides you with a decision. All my life I had wanted to climb Longs, but to this point, I had never faced my incapacitating fear of heights. That day, without hesitation, I said, "Yes!"

None of us had a clue about what climbing Longs entailed. We only knew what everyone else in the area did: you needed to start early to avoid rainstorms and lightning, and a Longs climb didn't require any technical gear like crampons or ropes. At least it *shouldn't*. Though nervous, I was committed. My lifelong dream lay before me, and I knew if I backed out now, I would probably never embrace the challenge again. Determination drove me forward.

In early July 1980, we left Longmont at 2:30 a.m. so we could reach the trailhead by 4:00 a.m. Thinking back, I shake my head at how ill-prepared we were. We all wore tennis shoes, each of us carried only a couple bottles of water (not nearly enough), and we hiked in blue jeans, cotton T-shirts, and cotton hoodies tied around our waists. We had no idea that getting soaked high up on the mountain, wearing all that cotton would almost certainly result in hypothermia.

Dawn broke just as we got going, which was good since we didn't have a flashlight and could barely see the forest trail that stretched up the trailhead. Once it became lighter, Todd suggested we "put on a display of physical fitness," so we started huffing it up the trail, trying to pass as many other hikers as we could. We did well for a while, but as we gained altitude, our oxygen and youthful exuberance thinned, and we were soon hiking up at a reasonable walking pace.

Before long, we were out of the forest and hiking above timberline. Blessed with a gorgeous day, we couldn't see a cloud in the sky. Beyond the timberline, the trail felt easy to follow and many other people were heading up, so we had little chance of getting lost. After a couple of hours of hiking, we reached a large area called The Boulder Field, right below the actual peak of Longs. Aptly named, large and small boulders littered the two-acre plateau. Some people had set up tents in the middle of the field to spend a night or two, and we nodded as we passed them and other climbers. Many quickly glanced at our tennis shoes and cotton clothing and nodded back with, what I realize now was, a look of concern or bemusement. We didn't think much of it at the time.

Our first sign of trouble began when Bill complained

of a headache, but he said he was determined to continue. "Are you sure?" we asked, and he said "of course" and waved us off. We followed the trail through the boulders and headed to a feature of Longs called The Keyhole. The Keyhole is a gap in a flowing ridge that allows you to pass conveniently from the east side of the mountain to the west side. When the trail petered out below The Keyhole, we just followed the route we saw other hikers taking up to the feature, unaware the climb would soon change drastically.

Passing through The Keyhole was mindboggling. To that point, we had followed a gentle, upward slope for about four miles, but I now stared down a straight drop, hundreds of feet into Glacier Gorge. Suddenly, my stomach lurched, and I desperately fought off a panic attack. I looked to Todd, who sensed my fear. He told me not to look down. I looked to my left instead and found the route the other hikers were following. They were heading south, traversing a series of narrow ledges, each about three-foot to five-foot wide, marked only by red-and-yellow bullseyes. My stomach flipped again.

At the same time, Bill announced his headache had become severe and too distracting for him to continue. I'd heard altitude sickness could cause headaches like this, so I wondered if it would only get worse the higher we climbed. Bill had been very strong on the hike since he was so fit, and I knew he'd been powering through the pain so far, but we all knew it was not a good idea to traverse the narrow ledge in his state. For the first time, I became a little concerned that we may have bitten off more than we could chew. After a few minutes of contemplation and persuasion, Bill decided to turn back. Although disappointed at losing his company, I suppose Bill's dilemma provided a distraction to my acrophobia, so Todd and I bid him adieu and continued.

I didn't realize it at the time, but lessons of leadership began to form. Sometimes people have outlying situations or simply don't have the skills to do what is asked of them. It would have been risky for all of us had we pressured Bill to keep going, so we placed no unrealistic demands on him. This would turn out to be a crucial decision.

We turned to face the ridge and carefully started navigating the slabs. I kept my left hand on the rock wall above the ledges to reassure myself, and as we walked across, I desperately tried not to look down into Glacier Gorge. Step by painstaking step, yard by yard, we eventually stepped across the last ledge and heaved a sigh of relief. Our relief vanished, however, as we looked up at the next challenge—The Trough.

The Trough is a 600-foot couloir (or steep, narrow gully on the mountainside) going straight up the face. To that point, we had been faithfully following the red-and-yellow bullseyes. Suddenly, we faced a dilemma. The people above us had abandoned this marked trail into the middle of the couloir and instead headed up the left side. Being naïve eighteen-year-olds, we kept going, following the conventional trail markers, heading right into the middle of the deep trough.

Before long, we realized why taking the middle

hadn't been our best idea—the incline steepened, and we found ourselves climbing on rock mixed with snow. We had been unaware that, despite it being early July, when you get above 13,000 feet, the mountain would still show spring-like conditions. In a couple of weeks, the ice and snow in the couloir would melt, but at that time, the red-and-yellow bullseyes led us directly into a steep climb on ice. We realized we were in big trouble.

Todd moved directly above me, kicking footholds into the ice and snow with his tennis shoes. He repeatedly told me to not look down, but of course, I eventually did. When I did, I could see that if either of us slipped, we would fall hundreds of feet to our deaths at the bottom of the rocky Glacier Gorge. When Todd said, "Mark, if I slip, don't try to catch me, okay? I'll just take you along with me," I began to panic. Seeing the fear in my eyes, Todd reassured me he wasn't going to slip. He also remained calm, which did the most to somewhat abate my anxiety.

A strong temptation was that safety lay only ten feet away on the rocks to our left. Thankfully, we were smart enough to know trying to traverse that ten feet of ice sideways in our tennis shoes would be suicide. Going back down seemed even more dangerous, so we had only one option left: continue to climb upward and slightly angle left, when possible, to eventually reach the safety of the rocks. My stomach knotted up, and I began to pray like the prophet Daniel in the lions' den.

Gingerly, Todd continued to punch handholds and then footholds into the icy snow as we inched our way upward.

My muscles began to burn, and my exposed hands grew numb. Soon my legs shook uncontrollably, which scared me even more. Fear's icy fingers gripped me firmly as I realized one wrong move or muscle failure would mean certain death. I'd never been so afraid in my life. From the bottom of my heart, I begged God to deliver us out of the mess we had gotten ourselves into.

Six inches by freezing, aching six inches at a time, we meticulously made our way up the slope. I kept telling myself to take deep breaths and stay calm but remaining calm became more difficult with each foot traveled. At this point, I had to have a pep talk with myself. I had envisioned climbing Longs my entire life, and specifically had envisioned what it would be like to stand on the summit, looking down on my teeny house from the "monarch of the front range." In the middle of crazy fear, numbing pain, and exhaustion, I had to dig deep to keep that vision in front of me. I steeled my resolve and tried to focus all my energy on reaching the rocks.

Finally, after what seemed like an eternity, Todd reached out with his left foot and gained purchase on a protruding piece of granite. He pushed up higher with his right foot and could then grab a solid hold with his left hand. He pulled himself over and took a huge breath of relief from the safety of this rock. Todd then turned himself around, anchored his feet and legs, and reached down to me with his hand. As I inched up to where he had been, I grabbed his forearm and he pulled me to safety. As I collapsed on the slab, I looked at how far we'd come. In total, we had only climbed about twenty feet up and fifteen feet to the left.

After about five minutes, the shaking stopped, and I calmed down a little. After another five minutes, I gathered the courage to look down to where we would have fallen. I was utterly mesmerized. Dropping hundreds of feet to land on a rocky bottom would have been a terrifying, painful way to go. Neither of us said a word. We simply sat there for a long while, lost in our thoughts of how foolish we had been and how blessed our escapade hadn't turned fatal. I thanked God over and over and over for protecting us.

Sitting there gathering myself, I reflected on how and why we had made it. I concluded that Todd's leadership with a slow and steady pace, as opposed to fast and erratic, made the crucial difference. I shuddered to think of the outcome had I been with a less even-tempered or hasty climber. More importantly, my vision of seeing my house from the summit kept me going. I wanted that so badly. Holding that vision allowed me to push through my fears and aching muscles. That desire had likely saved my life, too.

After sitting silently for about ten minutes, we gave each other a knowing glance and started to laugh uncontrollably. Slowly, the tension coursing through our bodies released like steam from a pressure cooker. It amazed us how naïve we'd been, ignoring the other hikers' path and blindly following the bullseyes onto the ice. We marveled at how ill-prepared we were, too, climbing the ice in our tennis shoes. We laughed as only eighteen-year-old kids who think they are indestructible would. This gallows-humor moment may seem strange, but it helped tremendously, and after a few minutes we were in good enough spirits to move on.

We trekked up The Trough, finding our own sketchy route through the rocks on the left side. Our improvised route required slow and cautious movement—not to mention we were now climbing in pretty thin air. But we finally made it to the top of that stretch. Well, almost. We had one tricky maneuver left: up and around a giant boulder that marked the end of The Trough. Thankfully, the move up and around the boulder wasn't too difficult, but I didn't look down once.

I became a little somber as I realized the next challenge would be The Narrows. This part of the climb worried me the most.

I had heard about The Narrows, and what I'd heard troubled me. The Narrows is a thin, exposed ledge that crosses the south side of the mountain. At certain points, it is only a foot wide with a drop of 200 feet to 300 feet off the right side of the mountain. Once again, I gathered all the courage I could muster and told myself if I could climb a face of ice in tennis shoes, I could navigate The Narrows. The trouble was, I had expended a ton of energy so far.

We set off, and our first challenge loomed: we needed to climb our way around a couple of badly positioned rocks. Again, I kept my left hand on the rock face to the left as a means of feeling some kind of security as I warily traversed this ledge. This time, I actually looked down a few times, since I wanted to really see and feel what the exposure was like. A feeling of both exhilaration and terror filled me.

Todd had no problem with this section and went across much faster than I did. Even so, after only a few minutes, we were both across and ready for the final pitch of the climb. This section is creatively called The Homestretch. I had heard The Narrows was scary, but this looked ridiculously daunting, especially after all we had endured. Three hundred feet of steep, smooth rock slabs lay between us and the summit. I had no idea how we could scale this in tennis shoes.

Despite my misgivings, we began the steep ascent up the slabs and basically friction-climbed, using our hands and feet. Friction climbing is a method that sort of comes naturally—you keep your arms flexible, elbows slightly bent, with your fingers stretched out to the sides. You also keep your butt out, which places your center of gravity over your feet, increasing the pressure of your feet and fingers on the rock.

To my surprise, The Homestretch became a straightforward climb, as we simply followed the cracks on up to the summit. To my relief, the rock had no ice or moisture—a good thing, since the steepness of the slope meant if you slipped at all, you would slide and tumble hundreds of feet down, with no way to stop.

After what seemed like ten minutes or so—but may have been longer—we pulled ourselves victoriously up onto the summit. What I saw stunned me. The summit was *huge!* Longs' summit is about the size of a couple of football fields and it's completely flat. I didn't expect it to be so big. Or so flat! Todd came prepared and had a small football in his backpack, so, feeling elated and giddy at having just summited Longs, we threw a few passes to each other. Energized by our success, we even tried to run a few pass patterns, but soon conceded the rocky terrain prohibited safe footwork. When we sat down to relax awhile, we saw five marmots, which are large members of the squirrel family that look a lot like the groundhog in the *Caddyshack* movie. I found it astonishing they could live at such high altitudes.

I couldn't see my house, but that did not bother me. I had achieved my dream!

After basking in our victorious conquest of the summit (and after we'd recovered), the time to head down arrived. Not caring in the slightest about appearances, I slid down most of Homestretch on my butt, using the friction of my blue jeans and sneakers on the granite to control my descent. My reverse trip wasn't pretty, but it worked and made me feel safer.

Next, we crossed The Narrows, and this time I wasn't completely terrified. We made it back into The Trough and then descended the right side of the couloir, giving the ice a wide, wary berth. We traversed The Ledges, and when I stepped across The Keyhole onto the east side of the mountain, I exhaled a huge sigh of relief with the knowledge I wouldn't face more exposure for the rest of the way down. The hike down felt like a breeze. When we reached the car, I looked at my watch—it had been an eleven-hour day. More exhaustion than I'd ever felt in my life suddenly overwhelmed me.

But I reveled in the knowledge I had smiled back at the peak that had been so majestically prominent in my youth and had accepted her long-standing invitation. I had finally summited Longs.

Climbing Longs marked a milestone. A life-altering day. When I ponder what had driven me to face my acrophobia, I concluded my goal and desire to climb this mountain overrode my fear. At that young age, I learned in dramatic fashion just how powerful a dream or goal can be. Dreams and goals can literally overcome mountains, and I am so grateful to God for protecting us that day on the ice field. Even now, almost forty years later, I still shake my head at our stupidity.

The most remarkable and significant thing about my first real climb, however, is that Longs caused my fear of heights to greatly diminish. I suppose I learned that even when you don't know all the details and make stupid mistakes, when you embrace the challenge, using as much wisdom as you have in that moment, God's protection will cover you.

From this initial summit of Longs, I went forth to climb some of the greatest mountains in the world. This, of course, included nostalgically and fondly climbing Longs over and over again.

CHAPTER 3

No Man Is an Island

WHEN I WAS STILL A NEW CLIMBER, THE COMPANY I worked for purchased a semiconductor manufacturing facility in Portland, Oregon. As a result, I made several work-related trips to Portland each year. Before one of those trips, I had an idea. Mount Hood is a gorgeous 11,237-foot mountain located about fifty miles east of Portland in the Cascade Range. The peak dominates the city's skyline on a clear day. Mount Hood is permanently snowcapped, adding to its beauty. Hood is a dormant volcano—one of a string of several, stretching down the West Coast of the U.S. These dormant volcanoes include Rainier, St. Helens, and Shasta, to name a few.

I had wanted to climb this stunning mountain for a long time but realized if I did, I would have to do it solo.

Climbing a mountain alone may not raise cause

for concern at first thought, but to a climber, it could well be a life and death decision. There is an interesting phenomenon little known to the general public, which is explored in a series of books called *Missing 411*[2]. These books outline stories of hikers and other people who have mysteriously disappeared in the wilderness. Hundreds and hundreds of people have disappeared—many of them in our national parks—which is a secret the parks never communicate as they obviously do not want to affect tourism. So, the phenomenon continues, and in about eighty percent of these cases, the person who disappeared traveled solo.

With my career in full bloom at the time I considered climbing Mount Hood solo, I pondered many of the lessons I might take from the corporate world into my climb. In business, as with climbing, there are countless potential obstacles, dangers, and pitfalls. If you are operating solo and you encounter any of these—and you will—there is no one to help you. Aside from the danger, from many standpoints there is more power in a team: motivation, camaraderie, emotional support, diversity of thinking, and sharing the workload. These all reduce burnout and exhaustion while adding healthy competition, better communication, and the pure potential of fun. The bottom line is that the best way to mitigate risk is to have someone with you on the journey, whether in climbing or in business.

On my next business trip, I arrived two days early

---

2   Paulides, David. *Missing 411*. CreateSpace Independent Publishing Platform; First Edition, 2012.

so I could attempt to climb Mount Hood. Despite my thoughts about the preference to climb with a team, I'd weighed the information I had and decided the factors surrounding this climb would mitigate the risk of climbing it solo. The key would be to pick a time when the weather cooperated, as Mount Hood turns dangerous in bad weather and the weather can change quickly. Having arrived at the end of July, I soon discovered a high-pressure system had stalled over the Northwest, which meant the area would be warm. In fact, Portland weather forecasts predicted a sweltering 102 degrees Fahrenheit on the day I picked to climb. I figured the weather should be just fine, so I began planning my adventure.

I decided to start my ascent around three in the morning, both due to the route and the fact rockfalls pose a real hazard in the summer. The danger is reduced by starting in the early hours of the morning, since rockfalls are more likely due to melting ice once the sun comes out. (Icefalls, on the other hand, happen more often in the winter.) Since I would be climbing on an extremely hot day, I definitely did not want to be climbing when the ice began to melt.

I left my hotel room at about 1:30 a.m. and drove to an idyllic, alpine-esque village called Government Camp, which is the informal base camp for all sorts of outdoor activities on Mount Hood. From there, I turned down an access road until I reached a huge structure called Timberline Lodge, a historic hotel right at the base of the ski area. This is where the trail starts. The path up the mountain is easy to find; you just walk to the east of the ski trails, where a climber's trail is well marked with yellow disks mounted on poles.

As I began the journey, excitement coursed through me. Being alone, I had a lot of time to think. I thought about the many business leaders I'd watched try to go it alone and mulled over why they did. I concluded that many are afraid to delegate, afraid to look at alternative ideas, and afraid to relinquish control. These traits don't serve them and are actually risky, because these leaders face burnout, resentment from their employees, lack of engagement from their employees, retention issues, and worst of all, they may miss out on genuinely better or more profitable ways of doing things. A leader who tends to fly solo may eventually get to where he or she wants to go, but are the incredibly high risks worth it? And how much longer does it take that leader to reach the summit (whatever that is) than if he or she took others on the journey? These thoughts sifted through my mind, causing me to begin to have doubts about climbing alone. I thought I might as well make the most of the trip and trekked on.

I climbed in the dark for about two miles up a steep trail to the top of the ski lift at 8,600 feet. The key to not getting lost was to head up a ridge until I reached a geological feature called Crater Rock. Before long, I saw it over to my left and headed up the snow slope, working my way toward it. I vigilantly kept left of another feature called the Devil's Kitchen, which is a series of steam vents that emit highly toxic sulfur. If I stumbled into that series of vents, I would almost certainly become one of the missing persons in the national park phenomenon.

Finding a steep saddle called the Hogsback, between Crater Rock and Mount Hood's summit, became the next objective. Besides the dangers of falling rocks and shifting snow, fumaroles loomed as another potential liability. A fumarole is an opening in the Earth's crust that releases the poisonous gases of a volcano. If I slipped and slid into the wrong fumarole, I would be burned alive and asphyxiated in moments.

Yet, as treacherous as the Hogsback is, beyond it lies the greatest danger of Mount Hood: the Bergschrund. The Bergschrund is a deep, wide crevasse that in the winter months is covered with snow. If I'd scheduled during a colder time, I could have potentially hiked over the Bergschrund on a snow bridge, but the bridge had already collapsed. I would have to trek around the crevasse.

Past the Bergschrund is an even steeper climb through a thin chute, ominously known as the Pearly Gates. This area has been the site of many falls and fatalities. Falling rocks and ice are more likely here than elsewhere on the mountain and, coupled with the steep climb, if you fall in this section, you would likely slide long and fast right into the Bergschrund. After the Pearly Gates, a short summit ridge leads to the true summit.

The going up Crater Rock became intense. Despite being experienced and having ice gear with me, I began to think again of my business life. Leadership was on my mind, and as I meditated on various aspects of my career,

I thought about the single most significant attribute I'd observed, one that differentiates the strongest leaders from the rest. It is amazing how clearly one thinks on the upper sections of these mountains. I suppose it is because every other concern in the world pales compared to each moment of the climb since your life literally depends on almost every step. Everything is reduced to its most basic "no-nonsense" form. As my legs began to ache a little, and the cold began to sink through my clothing, the conclusion was clear: *self-awareness is the most significant attribute of truly strong leaders.*

Self-aware leaders tend to delegate, communicate, motivate, and engage their employees in a much more effective manner than other leaders. This is because they are able to perceive how their words, actions, body language, tone of voice, and attitude impact the people who work for them and with them. Because of this, they instinctively adjust their style, their tone, and their words to adapt to the situation or person. This automatically results in far superior organizational energy and more engaged employees. Leaders who have no self-awareness tend to just march blindly forward, often bluntly, doing, saying, and being the same person they always are, regardless of the impact on the personal styles of others.

Aside from work relationships, self-aware leaders also constantly consider their environment and adapt accordingly. This is more than a data-driven assessment. Rather, it's an awareness of one's current skills, goals, and the conditions in which you and your team are operating, and the ability to instinctively adapt to any changes.

By the time I made it up to the Hogsback at 10,600 feet, I knew why these leadership concepts had been playing on my mind. It suddenly became clear that it would be enormously risky to continue without the security of being roped to someone else. The exposure going forward appeared far more frightening than I had realized during planning . . . but I wrestled with a mild case of summit fever, which is something that happens to climbers where the desire to reach the summit overrides everything else including safety and weather concerns. It can prove fatal as it causes climbers to throw caution to the wind in their desire to reach their summit goal. I desperately wanted to summit this beautiful peak, and I knew I had the skills. I sat for several minutes, debating whether to go on or not. Thankfully, I did the most important thing I could. I prayed. The answer soon became clear. Although reluctant to accept the answer, the rest of the climb posed too much risk to undertake the climb solo. I would have to descend and live to play another day.

Unenthusiastically trudging back down, I decided to focus on the positive. I had gained valuable experience. I thought about how my day could also be a metaphor for trying to walk alone, either in spiritual faith or in business. If we attempt to walk solo, it may go okay for a long period of time and we may reach decent heights, but at some point, things are bound to get dicey. The challenges we face (like the ridge above the Hogsback) may simply be too difficult and too scary to tackle alone. Our solo journey will suddenly turn risky, which may mean we have to then turn back and reattempt our mission later. I smiled as I grasped the valuable lesson— we absolutely need to be "roped" to others as we journey through life.

In business, in almost all cases, the team is better for the many reasons I have mentioned. Obviously, many entrepreneurs have little choice but to go solo in their business ventures, but even then, they will find power in having a support system behind them, whether that is a spouse, family, friends, vendors, or even friendly competitors in the same space.

In climbing, the only time I could think of when going solo might be better is if you are doing a speed climb, and there is no one with you who can keep up. But even then, you need to ask yourself *what's the point of the speed climb?* Is it to set a record, to complete the climb before bad weather sets in, or is it for ego gratification? Whatever your reason, you should have a valid reason to do it without at least one teammate. The same holds true in business. The reward *must* outweigh the risk, and the risk is significant.

I once saw an amazing demonstration of this principle in nature. One day in Phoenix, the temperature hit 122 degrees Fahrenheit, which made me wonder how my body would respond to hiking in that kind of heat. I decided to head up a local mountain at 1:00 p.m. (Ironically, I hiked as a lone wolf once more which, again, was not smart.) But I came upon a Mesquite tree and saw the most amazing thing: a collection of honeybees had gathered in a clump on one of the branches. The clump had the circumference of a beehive, and all the bees furiously beat their wings so the group could remain cool in the clump. What was most fascinating, however, is the bees rotated positions from the center to the outside of the clump, and then back to the center again. This kept them cool.

The bees would take their turn being on the outside in the scorching heat, then rotate inward, where it was cooler, so as a collective, they could all stay cool and survive. In the intense heat, my guess is that if any bees tried to go it alone, they would perish.

I have seen many executives take on huge projects and try to do them by themselves, then fall flat on their faces. The project stalls, fails, or collapses because of their unwillingness to ask for help or form a team. This is why coaching is so valuable—it allows the executive to partner up with someone who is unbiased but can provide a neutral but honest perspective as a sounding board. The leadership coach also provides support.

Similarly, the most important lesson I took away from my attempt to summit Mount Hood was the potential to go higher with a team. I had become hooked on 14,000-footers in my home state of Colorado and had underestimated Mount Hood. Even though it is just over 11,000 feet, I realized that if climbing alone, it is not a peak to be trifled with.

What would it take, I wondered, *to go higher? Much higher.* The answer would be found in a mountain that, for many years, claimed the title of being the highest summit in the world. I didn't know it that day, but on Chimborazo, an equally valuable lesson lay in store.

CHAPTER 4

Touching the Sky

A T 20,564 FEET, CHIMBORAZO, THE MAJESTY OF Ecuador, long considered to be the highest mountain on the planet, was dethroned by the much higher mountains in the Himalayas when measured at sea level. What is interesting, however, is, due to the equatorial bulge at the Earth's equator, the true summit of Chimborazo is actually the farthest point from the Earth's center. This also means Chimborazo's summit is Earth's closest point to outer space.

I climbed Longs Peak in 1980 and spent the following six years hopelessly hooked on climbing Colorado's numerous 14,000-footers (fourteeners). After about five years, I had gained enough experience to feel ready to go higher. With the air already thin at around 14,000 feet, I couldn't imagine what it would feel like at 20,000 feet or higher. But with all my heart, I wanted to find out.

In 1986, the time arrived to push my limits and try for a much higher mountain.

I started researching peaks over 20,000 feet that seemed doable. Several piqued my interest, but quickly, Chimborazo stood out as the obvious choice. In 1986, the cost was a primary factor, and although Chimborazo is a *huge* mountain, it is located in the Western Hemisphere, so I could fly there rather affordably. Despite the significant jump from 14,000-footers to over 20,000 feet, I reasoned it would not be unmanageably dangerous if I hired an expert guide. I had a strong feeling about this as I knew the climb involved crossing crevasses and climbing ice fields, but I figured a guide with enough experience would know how to navigate through the safest routes.

My mind raced with curiosity. *How would my body react at such enormous heights? Would I experience altitude sickness? Would I even be able to breathe? Realistically, can I summit a mountain this tall?* I pondered these questions and decided I had done my due diligence. Technically, Chimborazo, despite being such a high peak, appeared safer than some other choices, even if I could afford them. Starting out on fourteeners, I'd gained a lot of experience since my adventure up the icy slopes of Longs Peak in tennis shoes. I'd spent the necessary time learning on smaller, but by no means insignificant, mountains.

Thinking the choice over, I remembered the Biblical story of David and Goliath, where David is infuriated that a Philistine—no matter his size—is blaspheming his

God and challenging his army, while no one is stepping up to put him in his place. After David's brothers try to dissuade him, he convinces King Saul to allow him to face the giant, saying he has defended his father's sheep successfully against a bear and lion. The point is, David dealt with what scared him in smaller doses until he became ready to tackle something truly scary.

I decided to go. Climbing the fourteeners had given me confidence. I applied for a passport and started the exciting business of planning a climbing trip to Ecuador. I had no idea this step would propel me into what would become my life's dominant theme.

Looking back, I'm amazed at my naiveté. A more experienced climber asked how I planned to train for the trip, and I stared at him blankly. The concept had previously been unconsidered. In Colorado, I just hiked and climbed, never thinking about actually "training" for any of the mountains. I replied, "I'm just going to prepare by doing what I've always done—get up into my beloved Colorado Rockies and climb!" But a nervous knot twisted in my stomach. Ignoring it, I reasoned spending as much time as possible above 10,000 feet would adequately prepare me for Chimborazo.

I then realized I had no idea about the gear I'd need. (At least I suspected it would be something more than sneakers and a cotton hoody.) I found a reputable guiding company in Quito, Ecuador, that I felt comfortable with after talking with them on the phone. I asked what I should bring and was overjoyed to hear they could provide me with all the requisite equipment, even clothing for the frigid temperatures I would face in the ice fields and beyond.

In the months before my trip, I hiked as many of the 14,000-foot peaks as my body would allow as a final piece of so-called training for Chimborazo. Right before the trip, I spent four days in Leadville, Colorado, which sits at over 10,000 feet. I thought that would help acclimatize my body and respiratory system to the heights. As the time to leave approached, I felt strong and fit.

My mind, however, spun another story. To be frank, fear began to creep in. Intense fear. Not so much of climbing the mountain; that part I couldn't have been more excited about. The fear evolved around venturing into a foreign country alone, without even knowing the language. I had no idea what to expect from Quito, other than I knew they spoke Spanish. Would it be dangerous there? I would be completely out of my element and extremely vulnerable. The more I thought, the more I began to have serious second thoughts. I considered canceling the trip.

But something inside me wouldn't allow that. I knew my life needed more than living a boring, "sterile" life like so many people around me. Somehow, deep inside, I knew this trip held the key to unlocking a life that felt different, bigger. I didn't know how or why, but I knew. I desperately gathered the little courage I had and focused on taking the first small steps. I paid for my trip. I researched. I packed. I drove up to Leadville and acclimated to the thinner air. I did the easy stuff. I did what I could.

These smaller steps, I discovered, easily gave me the confidence to take that big milestone step. I drove to the airport, boarded the plane, and flew to Quito, Ecuador. Not that the fear evaporated, but I had prepared. I knew I had, and the rest I decided to entrust to God.

This process is actually based on the psychological concept of systematic desensitization. When I was in psychology graduate school, the first "patient" I saw was a successful lawyer in Phoenix who had an irrational fear of using public restrooms. I discovered the fear emanated from an incident from his childhood: he was on a car trip with his parents, and they kept stopping at gas stations so he could "go," but for some reason, he couldn't. His dad became more and more frustrated, which made him more nervous. He ended up wetting his pants and soiling the car's back seat, causing his dad to erupt in anger.

When he got into law school, he started experiencing this irrational fear of using public bathrooms. My guess is the stress of law school triggered the repressed emotions around this childhood incident. This severely hampered his life. I mean, think about it. He had to monitor how much he ate and drank when out in public for extended periods of time. He could not go to public sporting events because of this fear. He could not use the restroom in his law office and would have to run home whenever nature called. His dream of taking a rafting trip down the Grand Canyon seemed unreachable because the fear of needing to use a restroom loomed over his thoughts.

So, he came in for help.

The life lesson I used to undertake the Chimborazo climb mirrored the treatment I prescribed: he had to face his fear a little at a time. First, I had him stand outside a public restroom and practice relaxation techniques. Over time, I then instructed him to stand just inside the restroom with the door open. Then he moved completely inside while he practiced progressive relaxation techniques. Finally, after about six months, he got to the point where he could "go" in the restroom if no one else was in there, and eventually, after about nine months, he could urinate regardless of anyone else's presence.

This happy success story strongly reinforced this method in my mind as a tool for approaching scary obstacles.

•   •   •

As the plane banked to land at *Aeropuerto Internacional de Quito*, the view floored me. The enormous city sprawled across a giant bowl encircled by the regal Andes. Three colossal, snowcapped volcanoes loomed over the city: Antisana, Cotopaxi, and Cayambe. I had never been so excited in my life.

I disembarked and walked into the terminal, my head still spinning and my heart fluttering from the view. The airport buzzed with travelers and tourists, most of whom spoke Spanish, so I had no idea what they were saying, though everyone sounded like they were having a really good time. As I exited the arrivals' lounge, I noticed a man holding a sign with my name on it. In my naiveté, I hadn't given any thought to how I would reach the guide company when I arrived. I figured I'd just phone them from the airport or something. Never in my wildest dreams did I expect anyone to meet me at the airport. This seemed like the coolest thing in the world. I felt like some kind of important executive as I grinned at the guy and nodded.

As we drove out of the airport, the sights both mesmerized and appalled me. I had visited the Philippines as a kid, so I had seen horrible scarcity, but as an adult, the squalor and abject poverty of the Quito slums hit me like a sledgehammer. It instantly struck me how much I took for granted, living a comparatively privileged life in the United States. I went from feeling like an executive to feeling humbled.

As we continued driving through the city, I was also, however, utterly blown away by the beauty of Quito. Wonderful parks were a common theme. In fact, one magnificent park in Quito is *fifteen times* the size of New York's Central Park. Myriad fascinating seventeenth-century colonial buildings everywhere added greatly to the historic charm of the city. As we drove, I felt my apprehension dissipating. The charm of this unique city captured my heart instantly, allaying all fears and doubts. Had I never pushed past my fear, I would never have experienced the incredible scenery. I became incredibly excited.

Quito is nestled in the Andes at a soaring altitude

of over 9,300 feet, so I planned to spend two days there to acclimatize. When we arrived at the company headquarters, I met Sergio Delgadillo, my expert guide for the climb. Sergio, an Ecuadorian native in his mid to late twenties, stood about five-feet ten-inches tall and weighed a stocky 180 pounds. He had jet-black hair and an excellent sense of humor. I liked him immediately.

He spoke English well, which made sense—he'd need to as a full-time guide on the volcanoes of Ecuador. He also told me that about twice a year he guided on the famed Aconcagua in Argentina as well. As your typically cocky, macho, Hispanic male, I could quickly tell he'd fashioned himself to be quite the ladies' man. In each moment, my trip was becoming more and more fun.

Everyone had told me to go to Old Town, so I asked if anyone could take me to visit. Old Town bears the prestigious title of being the first place in the world to be designated as a UNESCO World Heritage Site. This fascinated me. The town is full of colonial churches, museums, historical buildings, and uncountable cultural sights. What really touched me the most, however, was the sweet nature of the people of Quito. Everyone smiled and helped when possible. I got the sense they'd literally give me the shirt off their back if I needed it, which humbled me even more. Prices in Old Town blew me away. A scrumptious, five-course dinner cost little more than two dollars! *I could get used to this.* I grinned to myself.

On the second day, we took an acclimatization hike to 14,000 feet. I couldn't have been more ready to climb.

My body felt good, and I was chomping at the bit to get to Chimborazo. Still, I thoroughly enjoyed the climb and took the opportunity to get to know Sergio a little better. Boy, what a character! When I asked him if he had a girlfriend, he explained he did not, he had "multiple ladies." I laughed and inquired if this ever presented problems. "It's like climbing," he said, shaking his head with a wicked grin. "No problems if you're smart and careful." I chuckled even more, seeing why he was such a sought-after guide.

I nicknamed Sergio "The Ultimate Hiking Machine" because he had such a high opinion of his abilities, albeit in a lighthearted, amusing way. His abilities, however, held up to his boasting. Sergio proved to be a powerful climber. His "ice-breaking" teasing meant we soon had a relationship where we playfully "talked smack" with each other in a comfortable manner. I learned Sergio came from a large family but no one else had been bitten by the climbing bug. As we hiked up the slopes, he shared that he had grown up in Quito and that his father was a doctor. Once I started climbing with him, I knew I'd made a sound decision hiring such an experienced guide. I had no idea how important that decision would become.

Sergio, after sharing his background, wanted to know everything about me, Colorado, and Arizona, too. To my surprise, he revealed he was a huge American football fan. His favorite team? The Dallas Cowboys. I chuckled at how American culture had spread to even this remote, picturesque corner of the globe. He knew his stats, too. We chatted a great deal about football during the climb. Later that day, I asked Sergio what his ultimate dream was. "To become a climbing guide in Nepal, especially on Mount Everest," he replied with an intent gaze. I could tell he was serious, and he impressed me. My new friend's goals were even loftier than mine.

After a great dinner and a good night of rest, I woke to my third day in Quito. Finally, I could head to the mountain. Both thrilled and nervous at the same time, I tried to focus on the beauty around me. We headed south out of Quito to La Reserva de Producción Faunistica Chimborazo, which gets its name from the hundreds of vicunas that make their home there. Vicunas are a type of South American camelid, related to the llama, and native to the Andes. Quito to La Reserva de Producción Faunistica Chimborazo heralds the unofficial entrance to the mountain.

We began our climb with our destination being the Whymper Refuge, at 16,400 feet. This would be 2,000 feet higher than I had ever been in my life. Eager to get going, I nevertheless made a point of looking around to drink in the mind-blowing beauty. As we began, I felt confident and I completely trusted Sergio. I had also never felt stronger. The initial stretch didn't present much of a challenge, so I continued the friendly banter with Sergio. He smiled and joked back but had shifted to a sharp focus on the climb. His professionalism, confidence, and skill began to shine, and he seemed to know every inch of Chimborazo.

As we climbed higher and higher, I felt totally alive

and loved every minute of the experience. After a while, Sergio told me we had passed the 15,000-foot mark—higher than I'd ever been before. I pulled in lungfuls of thin, crisp air, but still felt great. *I must have done something right in Colorado.* I smiled to myself.

We reached the Whymper Refuge around four in the afternoon, with no issues. We ate a quick meal and then tried to get some sleep as we needed to leave for the summit around midnight. The refuge had room for over thirty climbers. With all the new and first-time experiences, my mind raced. Way too hyped up to sleep, I just lay there and tried to rest my body and control my breathing. It also didn't help that experienced climbers surrounded me, snoring loudly and contentedly. I think I finally dozed off at around 10:00 p.m., and in what felt like minutes, the guides began waking everyone up just before midnight. The excitement kicked in again. We had a quick meal and geared up to head up the mountain.

As we stepped out of the refuge, the frozen air bit into my lungs with each breath. *This is new*, I thought, a little startled. I had hoped to be wowed by an incredible sky filled with stars at that height, but to my dismay, the sky stayed overcast. This probably served us well, because it wasn't as cold as it would have been with clear skies. Still, I shivered for the first half-hour or so until exertion got my heart rate up and warmed my body.

We climbed slowly and steadily upward in the dark. I'd never worn crampons before, and they felt strange. I had never been on a true glacier either, so my nerves began to surface again. I didn't want to do something stupid with the crampons on, so I stayed hyper-focused, which, combined with my lack of sleep, began to drain my energy. Thankfully, Sergio reassured me. He showed endless patience, and I suddenly realized the true value of paying more for a good guide. Sergio had a fun personality, and I recognized his strength as a climber, but where the rubber met the road—or rather the crampon met the ice—he led effectively. This was invaluable. His soothing voice flipped my stress to calm confidence.

Soon we came to a heavily crevassed section, and Sergio told us to rope up. Another first. I'd never been roped to someone else on a mountainside, and the gravity of our endeavor suddenly struck me harder than I would have liked. I was no longer casually climbing up a fourteener in Colorado. I was mountaineering, climbing one of the great volcanoes in the world, one on which many people had lost their lives. I again experienced a rush of anxiety until Sergio's steady glance caught mine. The slightest narrowing of his eyes and a confident nod both conveyed the question *"Are you okay?"* and informed me I *was* okay at the same moment. My panic abated. I realized my choice to hire a guide may well have been the difference between life and death, as Sergio knew exactly what route we should follow to minimize our risk—a route I would never have intuitively taken.

We continued upward. The air grew even thinner. Sergio may have been humorously talkative about his climbing skills, but his methodical leadership shone above all else. He assessed the conditions, weighed his options, then led us forward with an educated decision. This gave me tremendous assurance on my first big mountain. We climbed long and hard for a good stretch, then took a short break at 18,500 feet I looked around but couldn't see much because of the overcast weather. I couldn't believe I was so high. I had blasted past my record highs by over 4,000 feet.

It became a little harder to breathe, but I still felt really good. In my youthful exuberance, I thought, *Bring it on, Chimborazo!* A mental image of Rocky Balboa yelling at Clubber Lang (played by Mr. T) flashed across my mind. "Bring it on! You ain't so bad!" I smiled because that's exactly how I felt—like I could conquer the world . . . but we were still 2,000 feet from the summit.

The thing about mountains is they almost always get steeper the closer you are to the summit. Chimborazo was no exception. After only 500 more vertical feet, I began to tire. You see, the situation compounds the higher you go—the air is thinner, you've been climbing longer, and the mountain is steeper. This adds up to an exponential drain in energy and strength. No one else in our party showed any signs of turning back, though, so I tried my best not to slow down. We continued upward, upward . . . constantly upward. I started to breathe heavily.

Finally, Sergio told me we'd passed 20,000 feet. *Only a few hundred feet to go*, I thought wearily. *Keep pushing. You have to make it.* My exuberance had long ago worn off. So had any ability to hide my exhaustion. I focused on putting one foot in front of the other so I could reach the summit and rest. Light sifted through the clouds, so I knew the sun was coming up, but I couldn't see a thing. Still, the dim sunlight heartened me a little.

After about seven hours of climbing, we reached the summit. I'd looked forward to an incredible view, but clouds and mist sheathed the summit. I couldn't really see anything through the mist beyond a few yards in front of me. Though disappointing, I also felt satisfied. I also felt somewhat relieved to have made it to the summit, but I began to get extremely nervous again when I thought about heading down. I knew most accidents happened on the way down. I also knew we had to navigate through a dangerous rockfall corridor right at the glacier's entrance called "El Corredor." This was fine on the way up, but by now, the sun had begun to warm the ice. I prayed and hoped with the cloudy sky that the warming of the glacier might not be that intense, reducing the chance for any rockfall.

I suppose my anxiety showed on my face because Sergio cast me a broad smile. "It's beautiful, isn't it?" He laughed, spreading his arms wide to show the dramatic splendor of the ten-yard circumference we could see. The irony in his statement made me laugh, too, and somehow filled me with the comfort of knowing that he had done this many times and we would be okay.

We had planned to stay on the summit for about thirty minutes, but the cloud covering had me ready to leave in fifteen. Standing around caused the cold to bite into my exposed skin and anything that did not have down clothing directly above it. We left after spending only a few minutes. After the climb up, I'd become more comfortable with the crampons. The nervousness, however, hadn't dissipated, and I remained hyperaware, not wanting to make a mistake. Finally, after a few hours of down-climbing, we pushed through "El Corredor." This was especially grueling because the fatigue, combined with my hyper focus through the area of rockfall had begun to take its toll. But soon enough, we were off the glacier without incident, and I could finally, and with great relief, take the crampons off. We continued hiking down right away.

Eventually, we made it off the mountain. A rush of energizing joy I had never experienced before filled me completely! I felt prouder of myself than I'd been in my life. I had successfully climbed my first big mountain and, in so doing, had pushed out of my comfort zone to travel to Quito, Ecuador. I had never been so happy. *What a wonderfully enlightening growth experience this has been.*

The experience completely filled me with a wanderlust to travel the world—not even necessarily always to climb, but for the adventure. *How did I do this?* I mused. I thought back to the moment it all moved forward. I decided to measure each step carefully, then did what scared me in little doses, slowly building confidence to do more than I thought I could. *That's how you did it!* I made a mental note. This method allowed me to summon the courage to push past the fear of the biggest step—boarding the plane.

Small steps. Slow and steady. Sergio was a godsend. Opting to pay more for an experienced guide made all the difference, a lesson I would carry on every big mountain. I vowed to always spend the extra money to hire an experienced guide.

This all added up to my first big step toward living an extraordinary life. Chimborazo had been the experience of a lifetime. Not every climb would be as silky smooth as Chimborazo. As the cliché goes, "You can plan a pretty picnic, but you can't predict the weather."

CHAPTER 5

Russian Hospitality

THERE IS A COMMON MISCONCEPTION THAT THE highest mountain in Europe is Mont Blanc, located on the French and Italian borders. Mont Blanc is the highest mountain in Western Europe at over 15,000 feet and the highest mountain in the Alps, but technically, the highest mountain in Europe is an extinct volcano, just inside the Russian border. Mount Elbrus is, without a doubt, king of the Caucasus Mountain Range and dominates any other peaks in sight. Elbrus last erupted in 50 A.D., and its caldera (volcanic crater) is now completely filled with snow. Mount Elbrus has two main summits: the western summit towers at 18,513 feet, while the eastern summit does so at 18,442 feet. In 1829 a Russian army team achieved the first ascent of the western peak and the many years later, in 1874, an English team took the honor of being the first to summit the eastern peak. If I hadn't been determined to climb the seven summits, I would never have considered traveling to Russia to climb a mountain, especially in 1998 with political and criminal violence rife in the region, and the Russian border region under siege and total control of the Russian military.

At the time, I worked for Motorola, who had acquired a company in the Czech Republic. Flying to the Czech Republic every few weeks anyway, I soon realized this presented the perfect opportunity to climb Elbrus. I started reading up on the mountain and found the climbing route from the south offered one of the easiest technical routes of any high mountain on the continent. I also discovered, however, that despite its relatively low technicality, Elbrus remains one of the deadliest mountains in the world with an average of over twenty-five deaths per year. In 2004 alone, forty-eight people lost their lives on Elbrus. The danger arises from climbers underestimating the altitude and sudden and severe weather changes that cause people to go off route. They end up dying from exposure or disappearing into the many crevasses that litter the mountain. Some are never seen again.

I always try to be wise about when deciding to climb a significant mountain, so I weighed the pros and cons. On the one hand, the mountain posed an obvious danger and the region itself held no less danger. On the other hand, climbing Elbrus fulfilled one goal towards climbing the seven continental summits I had on my list. Then, too, I had the opportunity to do so. Weighing everything, I had to go. I tacked an extra week on to a September trip to the Czech Republic.

That didn't mean I wouldn't be wise about the climb. As with all major mountains, I knew I needed to hire an expert guide service. In this case, I desired someone who would not only know and follow the safety procedures essential for this particular climb but someone who knew how to navigate the tricky political climate. I eventually chose a U.S.-based guiding service that had operations in Russia. With their assistance, I secured my Russian and Ukrainian visas. (I had to travel through Ukraine to get there.) The company also helped me secure the permits and everything I would need to enter the region. Or so I thought.

September rolled around. I felt excited yet unexplainably more nervous than usual. I finished up my work week in the little town of Roznov, Czech Republic and had my driver take me to Prague, where I would stay overnight, then fly to Kiev, Ukraine the next day. I'll admit Prague is one of my favorite cities in the world, so I felt extremely blessed to spend the evening walking around. I thoroughly enjoyed the sites like the Charles Bridge, the Old Town Square with its Astronomical Clock installed there in 1410, and, the Prague Castle.

Feeling cultured, fulfilled, and happy, the next day I flew to Kiev, not knowing what to expect of the capital city of Ukraine. Kiev appeared even lovelier than I imagined. I spent the afternoon visiting magnificent Russian Orthodox churches, then went to an opera at the Kiev Opera House that evening. This being my first time at the opera, I wasn't sure what to expect, but I felt pleasantly surprised to really enjoy it. The next day, I took a train from Kiev through Donetsk, then traveled into Russia to the city of Sochi. I don't mind my own company, so I'd been really enjoying my adventure. In fact, the trip had been perfect so far.

From Sochi, I traveled by bus to a town called Nalchik to meet my guide, Peter. Peter was in his mid-thirties, stood about six-feet one-inch, and weighed maybe 175 pounds. He had a shock of curly, black hair with a dark olive complexion, which made him look like he could be from the Mediterranean, maybe Greece or even Sicily. Friendly and affable, I could tell immediately Peter possessed a keen intelligence. His wife, Daniella, was so sweet and hospitable. They had the most adorable two-year-old girl, and Peter proudly showed me all the pictures since her birth. Daniella was pregnant with their second child, and Peter told me, with a gleam in his eye, he hoped they'd have a boy. I told him I hoped his wish came true as I sat back, taking in the warm culture of my new friends. I felt at home right away.

Peter spoke English well, although he sometimes found the nuances of the language challenging. His blunders were small but endearing things, like instead of saying, "Out of the frying pan and into the fire," he might say something like, "Out of pot and into heat." Or instead of "The pot calling the kettle black," he would utter, "The pot calls the other pot dark."

He told me he was studying to be an engineer, so

he didn't have long-term ambitions as a guide. I always find it fascinating to hear the various motivations and scenarios that lead people to guide. I contrasted Peter's inspiration to Sergio's, on Chimborazo. For Peter, guiding served as a means to an end, but for Sergio, his entire life's ambition was to guide on Everest, the granddaddy of them all.

Peter, again in contrast to Sergio, was an introvert with a calm, soft-spoken demeanor. He didn't have much of a sense of humor, at least from what I could tell, but tended to be a highly logical thinker who spoke in a sort of methodical way. As we chatted, Peter explained he'd grown up in Sochi and really had no desire to leave Russia. Though content to guide on Elbrus so he could be with his wife and daughter while working on his engineering degree, he confessed he didn't know much about America but someday hoped to take his children to Disney World. I grinned at the universal appeal of the cartoon mouse—even at the edges of the world.

That night, Peter checked all my gear and equipment and pronounced me ready to go. The next morning, we got up early and headed out in a strange, Russian-made van, similar to the classic Volkswagen "hippy" vans. We drove and talked for a couple of hours until we reached a Russian Army checkpoint. Sudden, unusual anxiety churned in my stomach even though I knew Peter had to have all the red tape figured out since he'd guided fifty climbs up Elbrus and had been doing this for years. Peter got out of the van and started talking to the Russian soldier. Suddenly, the conversation became animated.

My heart sank. For some reason, I instinctively looked behind the van to ensure we had a clear route of escape. Of course, not speaking the language, I didn't understand what was going on but tried to make out what I could from their lively gesturing. As the conversation became even more heated, a second Russian soldier walked over to the van from the checkpoint office. I began to panic. The soldier opened the door, pointed his rifle at me, and snarled an order that I figured meant I should get out.

I climbed out of the van. As I did, the soldier began shouting and pointing aggressively toward the ground, while his other hand kept the rifle trained on my chest. Peter yelled at me to kneel on the ground with my hands behind my head. Instantly, I dropped to my knees, raised my hands, and placed them behind my head. The Russian soldier screamed, "Passport! PASSPORT!" I slowly lowered my hands and, with two fingers, gingerly retrieved the passport out of my pants pocket and offered it up to him. He snatched it away and handed it to the other soldier, who remained engaged with Peter. I stayed on my knees with my hands behind my head for several minutes as the guard kept his rifle trained on me. Peter continued arguing with the other soldier.

After what seemed like hours, Peter turned to me and explained the situation. Unbeknownst to me, in the mid to late 1990s, it was common practice to pay a bribe to the presiding army unit to gain access to the Elbrus region. The fact that I had a permit from the Russian government to enter the region meant absolutely nothing to the soldiers with AK47s. They insisted on payment.

Without the bribe, I would not make it to Elbrus. It didn't take much intuition to realize I could easily "disappear" if I tried to play the obstinate foreigner, demanding my legal rights to enter. Peter knew about the practice of paying bribes and had made this payment a few days earlier. Unbeknownst to Peter, however, the army unit he'd paid had just been rotated out, and these pleasant gentlemen had taken its place.

One doesn't typically climb a mountain carrying tons of cash, so I had secured most of my money in a safe at Peter's office. I asked Peter how much I needed to pay, and when he told me, I knew I did not have enough on me. Neither did Peter. The problem was, now that they had discussed the bribe, the soldiers weren't about to let us leave. This presented quite the dilemma. Peter then told me the only option he could negotiate would be for him to drive back to Nalchik to pick up more money, while I would stay as a guest of the Russian army until he returned.

I've been in some hairy situations, but I never thought I'd face my demise at the end of a Russian machine gun. Peter apologized profusely, promised he would be back as soon as possible, then gave me one last helpless glance and left. That glance disturbed me the most, yet I had no choice but to believe him. He got back into the van, turned around, and drove off.

As the van disappeared in a cloud of dust, I turned to the two soldiers with a "What now?" expression. The soldier who had been screaming at me motioned with his rifle that I needed to move to the edge of the road and pantomimed I should sit down, keeping my hands behind my head. This guy was about six-feet tall and weighed what looked like a sinewy-tough 180 pounds. He had short, brown hair, balding in the front, and appeared to be in about his mid-thirties. He looked strongly Slavic, his face angular and sharp with a vivid scar dividing his left eyebrow. He must have also had bad acne growing up, as pockmarks peppered his face. Besides his general cruel and menacing manner, the soldier's voice held a deep harshness with a disturbing undertone of cruel anger.

He walked up to me, training his malicious eyes on mine without blinking, and slowly raised his rifle. As he got close, the stench of cheap cigarettes filled my nose. When he jammed his rifle's muzzle between my eyes, still not breaking his gaze, my breathing became ragged and raspy. As I tried to lean back from the gun barrel, he followed me, keeping the muzzle firmly pressed into my head. I felt sure my heart would break out of my rib cage.

"BANG!" he shouted suddenly, causing me to jump and almost lose control of my bowels. The sadist cackled maniacally with laughter, doubling over, holding his knees. I thought I might lose my mind. *This guy is insane*, I thought. The other soldier quickly barked a reprimand to the sadist, and, to my relief, he slowed his cackles and backed up a little. As he did, though, he made his eyes big and crazy, and with a wicked grin out of the view of his compatriot, he mouthed "BANG!" again, which caused him to break into another volley of laughter. In all sincerity—and I am not one for exaggeration—I felt an aloneness at that moment I had never experienced in all my life.

As I sat on the side of a muddy road in the middle of nowhere-Russia with my hands locked behind my head and a crazy, vicious Russian soldier taunting me with a loaded, automatic weapon, I could not believe what was happening. I did the only thing I could do—tightly shut my eyes, pray, and ask God to extricate me safely from the situation. After a minute or two, despite the heartless soldier's constant, menacing gaze, my heart rate slowed, and I tried to think logically. My lone consolation was that my parents could not see me in this situation. I had to believe Peter would return, but that didn't stop the anxiety from soaring. Try as I might to thwart them, horrible thoughts began to race through my mind. Visions of being imprisoned in a Russian gulag filled my head: sitting nearly naked on a cold, dirt floor, starving, filthy, never to be seen again. Perhaps the only public mention of my demise would be a story on the back page of an Arizona newspaper about a local man who had disappeared during an attempted climb of some Russian mountain, while his family grieved but could only wonder about his terrible fate. I fought desperately to keep my mind under control and kept praying, trying not to allow these thoughts to take a foothold within me.

Finally, I forced myself to think rationally. *What is the worst thing that could happen, besides getting "accidentally" shot by this lunatic pointing an AK47 at my head?* I figured even if Peter didn't come back, these soldiers would not want the death or serious harm of an American citizen on their watch, no matter how much they seemed to revile me for my nationality. The more I thought about it, the more I believed if it came down to imprisonment, I could get the U.S. Embassy to intervene and, hopefully, would not be imprisoned for long. I felt good about this scenario for a little while, but before long, I wondered what would happen if they decided I could not make a phone call. Visions of being forgotten in a Siberian gulag kept creeping into my head. I tried to focus on the positive possibilities as opposed to negative ones and continued to pray silently. After some time, my arms began to ache, so I motioned to the guards to see if I could slowly let them down. My sadistic buddy growled "Nyet!" (meaning "No!") but the other soldier nodded okay. The sadistic one scowled, surely thinking of a new way to torment me.

I checked my watch, knowing it would take Peter at least four hours to make the round-trip. Dismayed to see it had only been thirty minutes since he left, I sighed and resigned myself to waiting. I just kept my head down, determined not to make eye contact with the cruel soldier. Soon the other guy walked into the office, so the sadist seized the opportunity and tried taunting me with the rifle again, but I didn't react or show any emotion. Somewhat heartened, I realized he always stopped short of striking me or actually hurting me, but I definitely didn't want to test his resolve. After a few minutes, he got bored and left me alone. I continued to pray and pray, asking God for the strength to get through the scariest situation I'd ever experienced.

After a while, the heat of the day began to get to me. We were only at an altitude of about 4,000 feet, being not quite in the mountains, so soon sweat started dripping down my face. I also began to get thirsty, and after only about an hour, my nerves started to get on edge again. All I could think about was just getting out of Russia. I tried to meditate, but every time I heard a noise, I expected to see the evil soldier's rifle muzzle stuck in my face again. My mind kept reeling with thoughts of my predicament, and time crawled along. Once in a while, a vehicle broke the monotony as it approached, the occupants curiously studying me before proceeding through the checkpoint. Each time, as the vehicle drew near, both soldiers sternly motioned for me to stay seated. With each vehicle that passed, I felt slightly more hopeless.

As the minutes dragged into hours, I began to freak out internally. My back and butt started to hurt from sitting in the same position, and crazy thoughts started to roll through my head. *Maybe I could get up and run? Sneak off and hide while they were preoccupied with another vehicle? Will they really shoot me if I run?* Eventually, I decided I didn't want to find out. As deflating as it felt, I had to just sit and wait, possibly until these guards' shift changed, at which point, I would be at their mercy to call the U.S. Embassy. Or perhaps, until a friendlier group arrived. If they were friendlier.

At the three-hour mark, I couldn't help but scan the horizon for any sign of Peter, even though I knew he would be at least an hour longer. Hopefully, he would try to break the land speed record. Around 3:45, I finally saw the dust from a vehicle in the distance. My hopes soared as I prayed fervently it would be Peter. Rubbing my face, I prepared myself to be done with this entire nightmare. But it wasn't Peter. My heart sank, and I felt a stab of frustration. Another van, full of climbers headed to Elbrus, stopped at the checkpoint. Like the other travelers, they all stared at me through the windows, seeming a little unnerved and surely wondering what was going on. I contemplated running up to the van, screaming, "HELP! HELP ME!" but I couldn't get up the nerve. I thought about gesturing to them but didn't know what they could really do to help—if they would even help—and what the soldiers would do if they saw me. The driver stopped, showed the soldier some paperwork, then visibly palmed him some money, which the soldier counted, and then waved them through. The sadist turned to me, glaring with a wicked grin, knowing each time a vehicle went through, my emotions jerked around like a Yo-Yo.

At the four-hour mark, there was still no sign of Peter. Suddenly the reality that he may have decided to keep all my money and abandon me to the Russian army made me nauseous. I continued to pray fervently but couldn't help but feel discouraged. Still, I begged God to end this terrible situation. From what I knew of Peter, I couldn't imagine he would just leave me, but I had to admit, I really knew nothing about the regional culture or what was likely or even possible. What would the soldiers do if Peter didn't show up in the next couple hours? One thing for certain: it would be open season for the crazy one.

Thoughts tore through my head faster and faster, and my prayers became desperate. I began to frantically consider whether I should try to befriend the soldiers, promising them huge bribes of cash and gear if they took me back to Peter's house (if I could even find the way there). Or should I just try to make a run for it, looking to hitch a ride in the wilderness of the Caucasus Mountains? My anxiety reached fever pitch at around the four-and-a-half-hour mark as I saw another vehicle approach. I couldn't handle the disappointment if it was not Peter. Frantic, I began to seriously consider jumping up and running back into the European territory. *Surely the guards won't shoot me in the back with a vehicle full of witnesses. Would they?*

I watched both soldiers, who seemed preoccupied with the approaching vehicle. I shifted in my seat and stretched my legs a little so they wouldn't be numb when I ran. I put my hands on the ground next to me to boost myself up but tried to maintain an air of compliance and subservience.

I cannot—I will not—sit here for who knows how much longer.

CHAPTER 6

====================

Overcoming Challenges
to Take on Your Primary Challenge

O NE OF THE THINGS I SO OFTEN HAVE TO DEAL
with in Human Resources is leaders who use
the power of their position to bully, embarrass,
and harass other people. At the time of this writing, I
am dealing with a case where a high-level manager was
brought in to change the culture of a manufacturing
plant. This guy has a strong personality and is very
driven. His philosophy is that of "storming, forming, and
norming," a philosophy developed by Bruce Tuckman
in 1965.

This manager came into the site and definitely shook
things up, which I agree was necessary. The problem is,
he began to use the power of his position to humiliate
people in front of others, even belittling staff and verbally

abusing subordinates. He had the right intentions in terms of shaking things up, but he let the power go to his head and he really hurt a number of people.

The issue he now faces is people are tuning him out because he understandably doesn't have their buy-in. The result is he is now having difficulty transitioning out of the storming phase and into the forming phase. As John Emerich Edward Dalberg-Acton stated way back in 1887, "Power corrupts, and absolute power corrupts absolutely." This error is the polar opposite of a leader who puts his people first—a leader who won't ask his people to do anything that he wouldn't do, and one who treats his people in the way he would like to be treated.

· · ·

I nearly shouted with joy when I saw the van was Peter's. As he pulled up to the checkpoint, Peter's face registered alarm when he saw my expression. I watched as he pulled up to the checkpoint, got out, and again apologized profusely to me. Despite the growls of the sadistic soldier, I leapt up and hugged Peter, thanking him for coming back. He quickly handed the payment over to the soldier he had been dealing with, who began counting the bills. I was still a little in shock, so I watched, wide-eyed, afraid these guys would demand more money or try to torment us further simply for sport. Peter motioned with his eyes and through clenched teeth said, "Just get in the van now." I wasted no time in obeying and pulled myself up into the vehicle. Once satisfied with his payment, the guard nodded and waved us through. As Peter cranked the van's engine, my other "buddy" glared at me, a final, wicked laugh rippling across his face as he pointed his thumb and forefinger at me, mouthing "BANG!" and pulling the imaginary trigger. I turned, stared ahead, and never looked back.

At that point, I didn't care about the trip. The last thing I wanted to do was climb Elbrus. My thoughts revolved only around getting the heck out of Russia and heading home. As the checkpoint disappeared behind us, I told Peter this, hoping he would turn the van around and head back. Peter assured me he understood how I felt but said it might not be a good idea to go back through the checkpoint right away. He suggested we head to a little town called Terskol at the base of the mountain. There, I could spend the night gathering my thoughts, and if I still wanted to go home the next day, he would gladly take me. What he said made sense, since it had already been such a long day, and waves of hunger assaulted me. So, despite my determination to go home and abandon the Elbrus climb, I agreed. We stayed at a dumpy little hotel in Terskol and enjoyed a simple yet tasty Russian dinner that night.

When I awoke the next morning, I thought about how close I was to Elbrus and casually checked the weather on the hotel TV. The forecast looked favorable for the next five days. Strangely—probably because the immediate danger had passed—anger bubbled inside me at my treatment by the Russian soldiers. I had done nothing wrong. Their corruption had caused my dilemma. I had the legitimate documents and they could have let me travel back with Peter, but they didn't because they wanted to ensure they got their dirty money. Even the halfway-decent soldier angered me. I considered that my goal was to climb the seven summits, Elbrus being one of them, and that would never change. Realistically, I might never have this chance again, or maybe not for many years. *Why should I let those soldiers intimidate me and ruin my lifelong goal?* I asked myself with a frown. I immediately decided to stay. When I met Peter at breakfast, I let him know I wanted to do the climb. He smiled and said he was not surprised. I realized then how wise his advice to stay the night had been.

As we drove from Terskol, heading three miles up the valley to a cable-car station at the 7,700-foot elevation, I once again pondered how similar my situation had been to some I'd experienced in my career. The anxiety and fear echoed certain experiences in the corporate world of leadership. Well . . . sure, I'd never had a machine gun stuck in my face at work, but the concrete jungles can seem nearly as intimidating at times. What I *had* experienced, in no small amount, people actively standing in the way of my dreams and goals—maliciously even—trying to stop me from achieving them. True, I had faced an extreme situation at the checkpoint, pretty much one of the worst nightmares for a climber, but the bottom line remained the same: *sometimes you have to overcome challenges to take on your primary challenge.*

The truth is, there will always be people standing in the way of living a different life. There will be an endless array of people you could use as an excuse to turn back from your dream. I realized then that although we sometimes have to endure seasons of severe loneliness— those brutal experiences we can only endure alone—one of the keys is to heed the advice of trusted allies when we are at our wit's end. Our allies will speak rationally, while we are frazzled and determined to quit. Their wisdom can save your dream.

We parked and rode the cable car up 12,800 feet to Garboshi Station. Garboshi Station is where "The Barrel Huts" are located. These are a dozen barrel-shaped bungalows, one of which would be our home for three days while acclimatizing for the summit bid. Each hut can sleep four people, but they're still pretty small and bare bones. While the huts were nothing to write home about, the area around them, however, came as a shock. The place looked like a dystopian industrial complex, with power lines and electrical wires scattered everywhere. A huge trash dump lay just east of the huts, while the toilet facilities were the worst I had ever experienced. "Gross" didn't give them justice. Also, the huts kept out the weather, but they were still freezing. Each hut had a heater, but the one we had didn't seem to put out much heat. Still, this is where the climb of Elbrus begins, so I had to man up and deal with it. But I couldn't wait to start the climb. The one upside— and a significant upside at that—was the spectacular mountain scenery.

Once settled in, we cooked some food and introduced ourselves to other climbers. The familiar, communal spirit of climbers encouraged me greatly as I shrugged off the last of my negative experience entering Russia. I once again met people from all over the world, a testament to the global attraction of climbing one of the seven summits. Yet, I knew, without a doubt, that if Elbrus had not been considered the highest mountain in Europe, ninety percent of those climbers would not have been there.

With the day still relatively early, we decided to hike up to another stone hut a thousand feet higher called the Diesel Hut. We hung out for a bit, taking in the remarkable view, then hiked back down for the evening.

Mount Elbrus is considered a moderately high mountain at over 18,000 feet, so I already knew how important acclimatization was. Underestimating the potential for altitude sickness is common on Elbrus, and many climbers have perished from pulmonary or cerebral edemas. In fact, Peter assured me we would encounter several climbers who would either be staggering or have to be carried down the mountain due to altitude sickness. He said he saw them every time he guided. It stunned me that people wouldn't take the time to acclimatize for the altitude. How can you risk your life because of impatience? We had spent one night at Terskol at 7,700 feet and the Barrels were at almost 13,000 feet, so we were doing our best to acclimatize. I hoped after enduring all the drama with the soldiers, I wouldn't be defeated by the altitude.

The next day, we hiked up to a feature called the Pashtuhova Rocks at 15,300 feet to acclimatize even more. As are most guides, Peter seemed quite fit, but I noticed Peter possessed a nimbleness, too. Sure-footed as a mountain ram, he sprung agilely over tricky terrain. Happily, I felt strong that day, too, and had no issues with the altitude. Peter planned for us to do this hike, go back to the Barrels, then take the next day off as an acclimatization/rest day. I knew deep down this would be best, but I felt strong and suddenly eager to attempt the summit so we could get off the mountain and I could get out of Russia. Perhaps we could skip the extra acclimatization day?

Unsure at first, Peter eventually let me convince him to move our summit bid to the next morning.

We woke at 2:30 a.m. and prepared to depart. I ate some cold black bread, drank some water, put on my crampons, and we headed out into the dark. One of the first groups to leave, I could only see a few other headlamps slowly heading up the mountain. As I mentioned, Elbrus is not a technical climb, but it is a snow and ice climb up a moderate slope. Again, it is not to be underestimated, despite the route being clearly marked by wands. The only real dangers on our route were the weather—admittedly notorious on Elbrus—or going off route and falling into a crevasse. Once again, my time spent researching and selecting quality guides paid off, since Peter knew the route like the back of his hand. But honestly, in this case, with the route marked so well, it would have been easy to find my way to the summit. Still, I couldn't have known that from my living room in the U.S., and just having the assurance of a guide brought priceless confidence. I knew a long climb stretched ahead, though, with the total elevation gain from the Barrels to the summit being almost 6,000 feet, so I braced myself for what would certainly be a ten- to thirteen-hour day.

We made it to the Pashtuhova Rocks in what seemed like no time at all and continued our push upward. A high-pressure system had locked into the region, so we were pleased about the perfect weather. Once the sun rose over the eastern sky, I could see a brilliant sky with not a cloud in sight. As we got higher, the view of the Caucasus Mountains took my breath away. One might think you'd become used to these views after several mountains, but this is not the case. In fact, the wonder grows each time.

Even after my ordeal with the Russian soldiers, I felt blessed to be on that mountain, climbing on such a perfect day. Things, so far, had seemed to balance themselves out. Yes, I'd had a rough entry to Elbrus, but the climb had been smooth so far and extremely beautiful. I thanked God profusely, drinking in the wonder and majesty of His creation. At those elevations, it always gives me a personal and intimate sense of His omnipotence. As we climbed higher, and the views got even better, I shook my head and muttered, "Life is so good."

Despite the low technicality of the climb, Peter insisted that we "rope up" in some sections in case one of us fell into a crevasse. The method behind roping up is if one person falls into a snow-covered crevasse, the other instantly falls on their ice ax, digging it into the ice and stopping the other person from falling into the abyss. For most of the climb, though, Peter did not find this precaution necessary, as the route avoided the majority of the crevasses.

After a long stretch of climbing, we finally reached the saddle between the east and west summits. I could hardly believe the view. Russia and Europe stretched in opposite directions before us. I once again had that sense of incredible privilege. Our goal was the west summit, which is higher and, therefore, truly the highest spot in Europe. About halfway through this section, Peter wanted to rope up again as we crossed another open area scattered with crevasses. I doubt he would have mentioned it if the skies were not so clear above us, but Peter proceeded to tell me about many climbers who'd died in this area due to storms. I could see why. Had it been snowing, it would have been utterly treacherous without an experienced guide. I gave thanks for the good weather. Under the surface of this gorgeous mountain, she had an undeniable air of foreboding.

I thought I might surprise myself and maintain my energy all the way to the top, but with only about a thousand feet to go, I began to feel the altitude. I didn't experience the hangover-like feeling, which is mild nausea and a slight headache, but definitely began to feel less energetic. My legs still felt strong, though, so we pressed on at the same pace. Peter's stamina, poise, and professionalism impressed me. After a tough push that left me winded, we finally reached the western summit's plateau. From this vantage point, you could really tell just how high Elbrus was. It absolutely dominated the surrounding mountains.

From the summit plateau, a short, twenty-minute walk took us to a flat area leading to the final fifty feet up to a small summit. As I stepped up to a large rock and a sign in Russian that marked the spot, I smiled happily. I had done it. I stood atop the highest point in Europe. Peter and I congratulated each other and then sat down to admire the view. *Wow* is all I can say. As we took it all in, Peter pointed out the various mountains and regions on the horizon: Russia to the north, Georgia sprawled out to the south, the Caspian Sea to the east, and the Black Sea to the west. I marveled at the clarity of the view and again thanked God for the blessing of being able to witness this. What a mind-blowing experience!

It's probably to be expected, if even a happy cliché, that one becomes contemplative at moments like this. Not deviating from the expectation, I once again ruminated over how not all climbs bring what you expect. In this case, the climb up was straightforward and blessed with spectacular views, yet I faced other daunting challenges. I wondered if the loneliness and fear from my time at the checkpoint had perhaps been amplified because it had been so unexpected. I determined in my heart to learn from the experience and to always do my best to "ride the wave" of a bad situation, believing things will always work out for the best as long as I trust in God.

The temperature on the summit sat at about fifteen degrees Fahrenheit, but with no wind and a strong sun, it really didn't seem bad at all. We lingered for about thirty minutes and then, reluctantly, started the climb down. I made sure to take in as much of the view as possible, as the return journey surely would be faster. It only took us about four-and-a-half hours to get back to the Barrels, which we left as quickly as possible, taking the cable car down the mountain to our car and finally driving into Terskol. The easy descent felt like God had rewarded my tenacity to climb the mountain. Yet I knew we had to pass through the checkpoint again, and a small pang of anxiety flickered in my stomach.

We stopped in Terskol and got something to eat, with both of us in good spirits after an amazingly successful summit day. As we ate, we decided not to stay the night in Terskol but to instead undertake the long drive back to Nalchik into the night.

We left Terskol and soon approached the security checkpoint. I couldn't help but become nervous, despite being annoyed at myself because of it, since I resolved on the mountain to get better at "riding the wave" of anxiety. I wasn't too hard on myself, though, as it's not every day you have a soldier jam a machine gun's muzzle into your head in the middle of rural Russia. I considered how the Russian guard had complete power over me on Elbrus, and he had abused that power, just as weak leaders do every day in the corporate world. I can almost guarantee you, however, that the Russian guard never went far in leadership. That style of bullying doesn't work and creates more problems for those you report to than it solves for you.

I compulsively scanned the checkpoint for the

sadistic soldier, but he was nowhere to be seen. A different group of soldiers stood on duty that night. They waved us through without even a second glance. I breathed a sigh of relief, while Peter chuckled at my nervousness. I was just thankful I had not only summited Elbrus but could safely head back home. As Peter maneuvered the road back, I thought about how good God is. He had truly been my rock and my shield through the entire experience. Looking back, it is one of those times for which I am so grateful to Him for every aspect of the experience, the good and the bad. Mount Elbrus remains one of the most memorable climbs of my life.

CHAPTER 7

Finding Strength in Weakness

THE SEVEN SUMMITS: A GIANT, HAIRY, AUDACIOUS goal. That means climbing the highest mountain on every continent: North America, South America, Antarctica, Africa, Asia, Europe, and . . . what is the seventh continent? Is it Australia, Greenland, or something else? Well, in climbing circles, a region called *Oceania* is considered the seventh continent. Oceania includes Australia but not New Zealand—which makes no sense—and may encompass parts of Indonesia.

The idea of climbing the seven summits became popular after a wealthy man named Dick Bass wrote a book called *The Seven Summits*[3]. In fact, that book is what caused me to become completely enthralled with the idea. What is interesting is Bass was not a

---

3   Bass, Dick, Wells, Frank, and Ridgeway, Rick. *The Seven Summits*. Grand Central Publishing, November 1, 1988.

climber, so he strategically hired the best climbers in the world (he could afford it) to lead him up all the tallest mountains. And his plan worked beautifully. Dick Bass succeeded in climbing what he proclaimed to be the seven summits. One of the peaks he climbed is the highest spot in Australia—a simple walk up a mountain called Kosciuszko, which stands at just over 7,000 feet. I have never been there, but it seems to be about a two-hour hike up a well-maintained trail.

But controversy soon ensued over Dick Bass's claim. A man named Reinhold Meissner, (whom I consider the greatest climber in history), challenged Bass's assertion that Kosciuszko is one of the seven summits. Reinhold claimed the seventh continent was called Oceania, and that New Guinea, Australia, Timor, *and the submerged continental shelf* combine to form the continent of Oceania. Therefore, he contended that an obscure peak called the Carstensz Pyramid on the Indonesian territory of the island of Papua, New Guinea is the true seventh summit.

Carstensz Pyramid, known locally as Puncak Jaya, is a 16,024-foot limestone behemoth first sighted in 1623 by the Dutch explorer Jan Carstensz. It sits close to the equator but at 16,024 feet can receive snow. In fact, people ridiculed Carstensz when he reported seeing a snow-covered peak setting on the equator since no one at the time believed that possible. Carstensz Pyramid is also the highest point between the Himalayas and the Andes and is the highest island mountain in the world. What's even more interesting is, despite Carstensz being the lowest in elevation of all the seven summits, it is the hardest climb in terms of technical rating. It is, however, not the most physically demanding since the actual climb is done in one day. But, as you'll come to see, this largely depends on how you get to base camp. The idea that Carstensz is one of the seven summits soon caught on and was first conquered by an Austrian team in 1962.

I subscribed to the notion that Carstensz held the honor of being the seventh summit, so I knew someday I would attempt to scale it. In the spring of 2013, that day presented itself. When I learned my company wanted to send me to Bali for a week-long manufacturing conference, that familiar thrill of a new climb kicked into overdrive. As always, I contracted with a guiding company to take me up the mountain. I picked a company that seemed experienced and arranged to meet their representatives in Timika, a mining town close to the peak. In fact, the world's biggest copper and gold mine, owned by the Fremont Mining Company, is only about four miles away from the mountain, on the other side of a dense jungle. This, as I'm sure you can imagine, creates a unique environmental situation.

When I arrived in Bali, I had to endure some rough duty: I stayed in a lush, green golf resort set on a cliff, overlooking the tranquil ocean. Such a challenge, but I guess someone had to do it. With work complete, the time to head to Carstensz arrived and my excitement kicked into high gear. Since Bali is part of Indonesia, it is the most convenient place to catch a flight to Timika and from there begins the journey to the mountain.

When I landed, I met my guide, Robert. Hailing from Christchurch on the South Island of New Zealand, he was unique in that he guided both mountain climbing and white-water rafting expeditions. About twenty-five years old, with dark brown hair, and fairly tall, at about six-feet 3-inches, Robert lived for the freedom of his lifestyle. He didn't talk a lot but commanded respect when he did. I concluded that since he did both mountain expeditions and white-water rafting, he must truly be the ultimate outdoor guide.

I chatted with him for some time and immediately felt comfortable that I had made the right choice in choosing this guide company. As we talked, Robert shared a familiar dream I'd discovered in talking to my guides—he wanted to transition into high-altitude guiding in the Himalayas, which would be more the ultimate challenge and far more lucrative.

Robert told me I had choices in how I got from Timika to Carstensz Base Camp. One could use a helicopter to fly into base camp, which means one day in and one day out. Another way is to take an aircraft over the mountain range and land on a makeshift runway at a local village called Llaga, then do a five-day trek through the jungle up to base camp. This meant a four-day trek out after the climb. I always try to immerse myself in the full environment, and for reasons I'll explain in a bit, I really desired the experience of the jungle. I also wanted to meet the famed Papua New Guinea tribes as they lived day-to-day.

Three other climbers were going on the expedition,

so we all booked the same flight out of Bali. We easily cleared customs, then spent the night at a hotel in central Timika. We flew to Llaga the next day on a small propeller plane and landed on the dodgy runway. My imagination had painted a picture more vivid than the actual experience. Once in Llaga, we joined the guides and porters and, with little ado, began the trek into the jungle.

In my childhood, I lived for several years on the island of Guam and spent plenty of time playing in the island's jungle. From this experience, I knew trekking through the jungle would not be easy, but I expected it to be similar to the fond memories I had of the jungle on Guam. Boy, I could not have been more wrong. Like Guam, the New Guinea jungle was hot and intolerably humid, but that's where the similarity ended. The density of the New Guinea jungle and the spongy marsh bogs, which were tremendously difficult to traverse, held little similarity. Add to that the blood-sucking leeches that dropped from the trees as soon as they sensed your body heat, and sharp, thorny plants that shredded your legs, plus all manner of insects buzzing around your head constantly, especially mosquitos, and you have what amounted to a difficult start. It also rained every afternoon like clockwork, starting around 1:00 to 1:30 p.m. and ending around 7:00 p.m. This made the terrain constantly slick and treacherous, and every one of us fell numerous times. I thought to myself, *If it is this tough hiking on our way to base camp, what will it be like descending the mountain while tired and trying to control our hiking speed?* Needless to say, I became concerned.

I could write an entire book about it, but the simplest way to describe this trek through the jungle is "utterly miserable." The worst part, by far, were the leeches. The disgusting creatures would constantly drop from the overhead branches, trying to find a place to latch onto my skin to suck my blood. I came prepared, wearing long pants and a long-sleeved top (even in the sweltering heat) to minimize the bare skin they could latch onto, but those only helped so much. These things had a millennium of learning to find a way to wriggle onto one's skin, and when one attached itself, one of the guides would have to hold the flame of a butane lighter up to it, after which it would soon detach and you could fling it to the ground. What an entirely nasty, painful, uncomfortable experience.

The trek had a bright side, though. The rich variety of fascinating wildlife eclipsed that of any on Guam. We must have seen at least thirty different species of exotic birds, different kinds of marsupials, and a wide variety of rats. Yes, rats. (They were not part of the bright side.) New Guinea even has a species of tree kangaroo, although these don't live on this part of the island. Robert also emphatically told us to be on alert for wild boar. Extremely dangerous, these animals can rush and gore a man to death in seconds. I had encountered wild boar on Guam, so I knew to steer clear of them. We encountered a few, but at a far enough distance that we could avoid them.

The highlight of the trek was a remarkable animal

we heard but never saw—the New Guinea singing dog. These wild dogs are related to the Australian dingo but are known for harmonizing with each other when they howl. We only heard them singing one night, but the sound mesmerized us. They actually sing in perfect harmonies, their voices creating a beautiful melodic backdrop to the jungle night. Seeing New Guinea's large number of bats form giant swarms each night created another incredible experience. We watched in amazement as they soared out in a huge group against the night sky, feeding on the myriad insects that populate the jungle.

Before long, Robert told us we were approaching the first tribal village. The rumor persisted that some of these jungle tribes were still head-hunting cannibals. When we asked Robert and the other guides, they assured us the tribes we would encounter were not cannibals, but we couldn't really tell if they said this to placate us tourists. Perhaps to make myself feel better, I reasoned that Robert and the other guides would not be taking routes that would risk their own lives. Even so, this gave me shallow comfort.

After trekking for about five hours, we came into a clearing that edged the tribal village. Awe surpassed any fear. As we walked up to the entrance of the village, I felt like I had gone back eons in time to the Stone Age. As soon as our presence became known, all the villagers came out to greet us with a reserved curiosity. I knew I wasn't "in Kansas anymore" when I couldn't help but notice the men of the tribe proudly sporting the ubiquitous penis gourds. Most of the women were topless, too, and the children were basically naked. I had truly stepped into the pages of a *National Geographic* magazine and it had me spellbound.

Suddenly, the mob of villagers parted submissively, and a short, squat man, decked out in colorful regalia, marched through the crowd. The man sported a giant headdress of brilliant green, red, and yellow feathers and wore several necklaces adorned with multi-colored stones and shells. I guessed him to be in his forties, but he appeared much more weathered because of the difficult life the tribes live. Around five-feet eight-inches, he looked to be over 200 pounds. He looked like a solid bowling ball. No doubt he was muscular and strong, but he had a distended gut and his muscles appeared to be turning into fat as he aged.

Robert nodded respectfully, deferring to the man who stood proudly as he surveyed our motley crew. We all imitated Robert and nodded in the same manner as the chief's inquisitive eyes fell upon each of us. After visually inspecting our entire group, the chief suddenly erupted in laughter and welcomed us to his village. I heaved a small sigh of relief, likely the intended effect, and cast a guarded smile at one of my companions.

Robert chuckled back at the chief and shook his hand as we all stepped forward to meet him and his wives. Though seeming quite full of himself, he also laughed a lot. My people analysis instincts kicked in despite his gregariousness, and I could tell the man was shrewd. In fact, Robert warned us his welcome would become extortion the next day when we would have to pay a bribe to leave the village. I marveled at the anthropology experienced firsthand in all its wonder.

I saw two wives standing behind the chief, but he may have had more. We were told he had fathered many children in the village. He had a large forehead, and his ebony skin accentuated the huge whites of his eyes. When he spoke in a deep voice, I could tell a few of his yellow teeth were missing. One thing was certain: he commanded the respect of everyone in the village and led with a strong presence. I also got the distinct feeling he could be ruthless if necessary.

After the initial meet-and-greet, our team set up camp in a designated open space and our porters began to cook dinner. The meals were basic—lots of rice, beans, eggs, and bread. I am not an egg person, so I opted to subsist on rice and beans for the entire journey. I always try to get to know the people on my climbs, so I took time to chat with our porters, all of whom I really liked. They treated us well and were also good at their jobs, which is always a relief on a climb. We heard rumors, however, that porters commonly went on strike on the second or third day of a trek and refused to go on without being paid more. I'd prepared for this to happen, but thankfully, it did not. I did make sure I tipped our porters generously, though, which is always a good idea.

After a night of rest in the village, we woke early and ate breakfast. Our guide then proceeded with the business of negotiating the chief's extortion fee so we could leave in time. This casual tradition of ultra-friendly yet expected bribery amused me on one level, but what if someone couldn't or wouldn't pay? Or what if a dispute arose over the fee? After bidding our hosts farewell, we tried to hustle to reach our next stop before the full torrent of the afternoon rains set in. By this point, I have to admit it took a lot to remain positive. The jungle's humidity, insects, leeches, and brutal terrain overwhelmed everyone. And this was only day two.

I would find no immediate relief, as this would be the procedure for the next four days. We'd battle our way through the dense, wet jungle and endure leeches, insects, and rain to reach a village as a stopping point, each time going through the semi-tense motions of either a warm, friendly welcome followed by firm extortion the following morning, or in one case, a bribe up front before receiving the warm, friendly welcome. One night, we simply camped in a clearing in the jungle and had to pay the nearest village's chief for permission to do so (I assume to avoid being attacked, and who knows what, in our sleep). I had seen a lot in my tenure in human resources, but it really began to sink in just how cultures differed and what seemed "normal" varied so greatly around the world.

By the fifth day, we felt beaten up and mentally exhausted from dealing with the bogs, leeches, insects, the suffocating, damp heat, the background threat of potentially hostile tribes, and the endless, drenching rain. When we came within sight of our base camp in the

Yellow Valley, marooned survivors seeing a rescue ship on the horizon couldn't have been more thankful. We stopped for the night. Just as I was strongly regretting my decision to do the jungle trek (and desperately trying to avoid the thought of the journey back) a porter told me of the possibility of hitching a ride out after the climb. It would have to be on one of the other climbing team's helicopters if they had extra room, and it would carry a hefty price tag. Without hesitation, I knew I would be on that chopper if at all possible.

We set up our camp at about 14,000 feet and rested for the next day and a half with Carstensz's north face looming above us. Two other expeditions had arrived at the camp ahead of us, so both my tentmate and I asked Robert to see if he could arrange a helicopter trip back with one of the other teams (the other two climbers in our group were determined to make the return trek back out for some unimaginable reason). When Robert returned, he told us he could secure spots on their helicopters for $600 U.S. each. Overjoyed, we instantly agreed, and my spirits soared. Knowing I would not have to face that trek out of the jungle afterward gave me the boost I needed for the climb. As I settled in for the night, I thought about how each climb brings its own challenges. If something unexpected or excessively challenging comes up, you just have to keep trying to find a solution or trust God will help you find one. The bottom line is this: it's crucial to remain stable, no matter how you feel.

We rested the next day, taking in the stunning scenery

around us. Seeing snow on the surrounding peaks, since we were virtually on the equator, surrounded by hot, humid jungle, felt amazing. I took a short walk to where our route would start up the mountain, just to scout it out a little. We had been told to bring extra-thick, durable gloves to use on the climb, and after exploring the limestone rock at the base of Carstensz, I could immediately see why. The limestone was almost as sharp as obsidian!

We went to bed early, the rain still pattering down around us, as we had a wake-up call at 1:00 a.m. I slept well due to the lingering exertion from the prior few days, and awoke to a chilly, nighttime temperature. Everyone wolfed down a little bread and drank some tea to warm us up, then prepared for the climb. I wore the same type of clothing I would use for a fourteener in Colorado: high-top boots, a wool top, sturdy hiking pants, wool socks, a climbing helmet, thick gloves, an ultralight shell, and a heavier Gore-Tex shell in my pack for when we got higher. My additional technical gear consisted of a harness, a jumar (a clamp attached to a rope that automatically tightens when weight is applied and relaxes when weight is removed), and carabiners (a rope coupling link with a safety closure).

The start of the climb began only ten minutes from our camp, and soon we were climbing on a fixed rope up solid rock. I mused again over how every climb is different, and the best you can do is research, get an excellent guide, and be prepared according to that guide's advice. Much like business, of course. The other two groups were starting at about the same time, so a line of headlamps already snaked up the mountain. Since Carstensz had only recently become popular, I was thankful the fixed ropes and anchors were solid, which I learned in my research had not always been the case.

We climbed rapidly and reached a relatively flat spot where we took a quick, five-minute breather, after which the climb became vertical again. Every climber has strengths and weaknesses, and if you plan to climb the seven summits, every one of your strengths and every one of your weaknesses will be tested. Rock climbing is admittedly not my forte, and in a couple of spots the required technique didn't come easy. Thankfully, I'd prepared for these spots with my jumar, which was attached to my harness and greatly aided me in pulling myself up the fixed-line. Before long, and without incident, we passed these difficult stretches.

The final long pitch took us up a chimney at about a sixty-degree angle with plenty of hand and footholds, a climb I found to be comparatively easy and quite fun. I began to feel the cold. The sun slowly rose above the ridge as I put my heavy Gore-Tex on to stay warm. After the chimney, we arrived at the most famous (or infamous) part of Carstensz—a fifty-foot gap in the rock with a 2,000-foot drop along both faces. A heavy steel cable had been secured across the gap, with a pulley attached to the cable. Using a device that looks like a figure eight, we would have to execute what is known as a Tyrolean traverse, a maneuver in which we attach ourselves and our gear to the pulley and traverse the gap. Fixed-lines are anchored across the gap, too, so for extra security, we attached ourselves to them as well.

In an awkward maneuver, we had to step out from the ledge and turn our bodies to face upward, looking at the sky as we hung from the cable. Then we had to pull ourselves and our packs headfirst along the steel cable to the other side. Since we were going toward the summit, the cable slanted slightly uphill, which was a little tough. I, however, felt glad to be facing upward, as I did not want to look down at the 2,000-foot drop, even for a moment. I suppose it could have been fun if I had allowed myself to relax, but I just wanted to get across. Thankfully, after only a minute, which feels much longer when you're suspended 2,000 feet in the air, my feet hit solid ground. With Robert's help, I pulled myself up and disengaged from the pulley and the ropes. I heaved a sigh of relief. I had made it!

Probably because of the prior trek through the jungle, greater fatigue than I usually experience at this altitude set in. I found myself hoping the summit might be just around the corner. Unfortunately, we still had to navigate an additional two shorter gaps, which required some tricky down-climbing that I did not like at all (thank God we were roped together). We then had some up-climbing to do, which in itself didn't bother me, except we were at almost 16,000 feet so the incredibly thin air had everyone struggling to breathe.

After a difficult, tricky, and mentally exhausting stretch, we eventually reached the final summit pitch.

Maybe because I had come to expect something more dramatic from previous tough climbs, this summit seemed kind of anticlimactic. A simple plaque marked the spot. I stood there and looked around, grinning, but felt somewhat underwhelmed. But that only lasted for a moment. The expedition so far had been strenuous, the trek through the jungle miserably so, but the now-familiar glow of conquering one of the seven summits made it all worth it.

We each got our requisite pictures and prepared to head down. The joy of summiting soon faded, as I began to feel a great deal of unease, knowing we would be taking the same route down. Frankly, parts of the climb outright scared me. The descent would involve multiple rappels and some serious down-climbing. But I had no choice. Every serious mountain climber has these moments—moments where you are physically and mentally drained—yet you know you still have to safely complete parts of a climb at a time when you are at your weakest. In fact, taken to the extreme, this is where many climbers die. They cannot mentally face what they know is ahead, so they sit down and rest, some never to get back up. On Everest, people will stop and rest in the Death Zone, just before the summit, after which they cannot get back up.

The problem with focusing too far ahead is you risk not taking the steps immediately in front of you. I knew if I concentrated too long on how I felt and on what lay ahead, I could become dangerous to myself and my team. I had to remind myself of a maxim I'd learned as a leader in the corporate world: a leader—or even a teammate, as I was in this situation—has to be aware that people are always watching him and how he reacts to adversity. As a member of a team, you must consider how your actions will encourage or discourage other team members. As a leader, it also becomes crucial that you model what you preach.

I quickly gave myself a little pep talk and remind myself I had secured a spot on a chopper so I wouldn't have to endure the brutal jungle on the way out. I didn't even want to imagine how I would have felt if I had to trek back out. We began our descent, and I decided the best thing I could do was down-climb even *slightly* tricky sections slowly and carefully. The professionalism of Robert and the other guides meant they knew to allow any climber the time necessary to descend safely, even when under time constraints. As the adage goes, "Slow is smooth, smooth is fast."

Even after many climbs, I still had to battle a fear of heights, and mountains with long sections of vertical up or down-climbing still sparked my anxiety. Yet, I fought to remain stable and unshakeable. After a little mental battling, I discovered something remarkable: I *enjoyed* rappelling. In fact, I would even say rappelling became the most enjoyable part of the Carstensz climb.

After a long, tense descent, I breathed a huge sigh of relief when we finally made it back without incident. I had done trickier, even tougher climbs before, but I have to admit, Carstensz is a unique blend of tricky and tough—especially if you do the jungle trek. This meant

I would *really* enjoy my first ride in a helicopter over that treacherous jungle!

The helicopter ride did not disappoint. Incredible views shimmered beneath us, although I also got an up-close-and-personal view of the Freemont Mine. The scope and scale of the environmental destruction appalled me, and to be perfectly honest, it made me terribly sad for some time after the flight. I couldn't help but think about how much beauty could be found right next to such devastation. I thought I'd have a long time to think over the entire climb, but faster than seemed possible, especially compared to the five miserable days of trekking through the interminable jungle, we landed in Timika. When I discovered one of the tribes we had encountered on the way in had engaged in cannibalism as recently as fifteen years before, I knew I'd made the right decision.

When we arrived, I easily changed my ticket and caught a flight out to Bali only two days later. From Bali, I caught a flight to Sydney, Australia and, for a moment, entertained the thought of hiking up Kosciuszko. I quickly came to my senses, though, and decided to enjoy a couple of days exploring Sydney instead. I went to the famed Sydney Opera House, did the Sydney Bridge walk, and relaxed on the beach, reveling in the knowledge I had conquered the highest peak in Oceania. Life was good.

The trip to Sydney and the long journey back to Phoenix gave me time to reflect on my latest adventure. I pondered how, in some ways, that trip reflects our life here on Earth. The jungle trek was long, arduous, and a little dangerous, but also entirely and uniquely rewarding. I had seen rare and fascinating wildlife and experienced the unusual cultures of New Guinea's Stone Age people. Similarly, the difficulty of the climb, though sometimes scary, ended up being rewarding.

I also thought about how, in much the same way, life as a Christian can be similar. God may allow us to go through long, arduous, and difficult trials or afflictions, and we will undoubtedly experience highs and lows. And yes, sometimes it can be downright scary. But if we persevere in our faith and keep putting one foot in front of the other without giving up in our walk with the Lord, He has guaranteed us we will triumph. The key is consistency—remaining stable and unshakeable, even in the face of exhaustion and weakness. I smiled at the thought of how, when we've truly given our best and we're still facing a grim struggle, God always sends a proverbial "helicopter" to make our journey bearable.

As I learned on Carstensz, sometimes circumstances around a climb add to the climb's difficulty but also present unique rewards. And sometimes these circumstances are what make the climb entirely special— like climbing a peak on the most remote, deserted place on the planet.

CHAPTER 8

The Mountain
I Did Not Want to Climb

WHEN I SET THE GOAL OF CLIMBING THE SEVEN summits, I knew at some point my journey would involve a ridiculously expensive trip to Antarctica to attempt a summit of Mount Vinson. Mount Vinson—or Vinson Massif as it is also known— is the highest point on the continent of Antarctica at 16,067 feet. Out of the seven summits, this was the mountain I least wanted to climb.

The first detractor was the cost. Because of the logistics and difficulty of getting to Antarctica, and traveling and staying on the ice shelf, only an attempt on Mount Everest is more expensive. To put it in perspective, Mount Vinson would cost five to six times more than I had paid for any other non-Everest expedition.

Second, time off from work meant a substantial

investment in both time and income. The time needed for the trip would be three weeks, but because of the risk of sudden and severe weather changes, I had to block out *five weeks*. That meant I would have to get permission to take an unpaid leave of absence. In fact, when I began researching in the spring of 2010, the most promising guide company specifically told mountaineers to book the return flight two weeks later than the scheduled end of the trip. If all went well with the climb, the guide company would then reschedule the return flight on the exact date we could fly home. Of course, rescheduling meant additional ticket fees, an added expense to an already outrageously expensive trip.

Finally, if I went, I would have to leave on December 10th and would not return home until after the New Year. That meant missing Christmas with my family.

But Vinson is an intriguing mountain with a fascinating history. Located 600 miles from the South Pole, it was first climbed in 1966 by climbers from the American Alpine Club. Named after a U.S. Senator, Carl G. Vinson, an avid supporter of all Antarctic research, and despite only Carstensz being lower (by only forty-four feet), Vinson claimed the honor of being the last of the seven summits to be climbed. Vinson is statistically the least dangerous of the seven, with 1,200 people having climbed Vinson since 1966 and it has no recorded deaths. Vinson Massif is not a technical climb; it just involves tough trekking up long snowfields. The threat comes from the weather. Climbing teams have been stopped in their tracks for days on end by some of the worst weather on the planet. That can be a concern if you run out of supplies, have an injury, or experience altitude sickness.

That spring of 2010, I debated back and forth continually about whether to embark on such a journey. To be frank, I simply did not want to go. Vinson didn't offer intriguing scenery, the climb wouldn't be technically challenging, and the trip itself would be long and arduous. Not to mention insanely expensive. I faced a dilemma. One would think a major upside of the goal of climbing the seven summits is the exciting sense of adventure and risk, but with Vinson, the challenge just didn't seem to be there. Vinson was, to me, just a checkmark, the least exciting notch out of seven to make on my proverbial belt. Mount Vinson, however, was indisputably one of the seven summits. So, the question became, "How badly do I want to conquer all seven summits?"

Somewhere inside, I knew the answer all along. "Badly. Desperately even." Climbing the seven was my dream. My lifelong goal. Yet, I had to wrestle with all these negatives suddenly piling up. I struggled with apathy and had to really "look myself in the face," so to speak. Yet, no real decision remained once I acknowledged that my goal of climbing all seven summits would never be complete without Vinson. And, when honest with myself, the financial timing worked. I could afford it (just barely). Almost grudgingly, I booked the trip.

I decided to go with a mountain guiding company based in the Pacific Northwest that had plenty of experience on Vinson. The lead guide had summited Vinson over thirty times, which made me comfortable under his leadership. Now to start the increasingly familiar training to prepare for the journey.

Although physically ready, when the calendar pages hit December, I could hardly believe the time to depart for South America had arrived. Still not wildly enthused about the trip, nevertheless my excitement to see Antarctica began to grow. I kissed my family goodbye, wished them a Merry Christmas, and with a secretly sad smile told them not to open the presents I'd bought them before December twenty-fifth. I departed Phoenix and flew to Miami. From Miami, I flew to Santiago, Chile, and then onward to a little seaside town called Punta Arenas, Chile, located at the tip of South America.

I took a taxi from the airport to the Hotel Diego De Almagro, where I met the other climbers who were part of my expedition. There were eight of us in total—six men and two women—all from various parts of the U.S. I immediately clicked with one guy named Jay, a San Francisco Bay Area native and a huge college football fan, just like I am.

Jay primarily loved to hike and especially loved to spend time in Yosemite and the Sierra Nevada Mountains. He owned a cabin outside of Lake Tahoe, where he would spend many weekends—undoubtedly an outdoors kind of guy like me. Jay had climbed Whitney and two of the other fourteeners in California and decided he wanted to do Denali. He next climbed Mount Rainier to get a feel for bigger challenges and absolutely loved it. Jay then decided to do Vinson as a precursor to Denali. He wanted to see how he would deal with the extreme cold he would find on Denali, but on an easier mountain. Vinson naturally presented the perfect choice. If all went well, he would do Denali the following summer.

At the hotel, I also met Dave, the main guide for our trip. Dave had quite the reputation as one of the top climbers in the world and as a world-class guide (probably in the top twenty-five on the planet). He was about 6' tall, lean, and extremely powerful. His sandy-brown hair had started to thin a little. He had a friendly but firm face. Dave instantly commanded everyone's respect, but not because he acted like a prima donna. A genuine and down-to-earth guy, he began to take the time to get to know each of us individually as we all talked and mingled.

We spent the next day in Punta Arenas, as our guides went through our gear to be sure we had everything we needed. We also had a briefing with an organization called Antarctica Logistics and Expeditions (ALE) that provided flights and various trips to Western Antarctica. The briefing room was large and filled with not just climbers, but people who had various "Antarctica goals," like skiing to the South Pole or visiting a penguin colony. The briefing lasted for about an hour and a half and primarily covered our responsibility to protect the environment of Antarctica.

After that, we relaxed a little. We were scheduled to depart Punta the next day, weather permitting. The two-day forecast looked positive, so our team felt optimistic about arriving in Antarctica the following evening.

At about noon the next day, we received word our flight was a go. We would fly over the Drake Passage on a Russian Ilyushin IL-76 aircraft, which had been built to fly in the Siberian Arctic. This plane has four gigantic engines and can carry seriously heavy payloads. The ALE uses this jet in the summer months to service their base camp in a place they call Union Glacier and, of course, to transport explorers like me.

Since the Ilyushin IL-76 is really a cargo plane, we were told the flight would be frigid, so we dressed in literally all our cold-weather gear for the flight. This included parkas, down pants, clunky plastic climbing boots, hats, gloves, and even goggles. That evening, we boarded the plane and sat three-wide in each row, each of us decked out and looking like the Stay Puft Marshmallow Man. They served us a little food—a cheese sandwich and a cookie.

Jay and I chatted for the duration of the flight, and before long, we heard it announced that we would be landing. The lack of windows meant we could not tell how close we were to landing until we felt the wheels of the plane hit the ice. The plane is designed to land on blue ice, which means it is pointless to use brakes. As soon as we touched down on the ice, the pilot slammed on the reverse thrusters, trying to reduce speed that way. After several minutes, we finally came to a stop on the three-mile-long runway. For the first time, the rush hit me: I was in *Antarctica*.

As I cautiously stepped onto the ice, I looked around in awe. The remote, barren beauty of the continent struck me hard. The air felt brisk and dry. Looking at my watch, I could see one a.m. approached, but since there is no real night that far south in the Antarctic summer, I could see the legendary Ellsworth Mountains in the distance. The sun hovered overhead, adding to the "soft" and beautiful, light blue-green tint of the sky. Snow and ice stretched as far as the eye could see until the sky and ice met on the hazy horizon.

For several seconds, I took in the overwhelming sites and the sensation of being in the remotest place on the planet, thanking God for giving me this once-in-a-lifetime opportunity—and persuading me to go. It felt entirely surreal. I was actually on the Southern Pole of the Earth!

We'd planned to spend the day at the ALE's Union Glacier Camp, and if the weather held, we'd fly to Vinson Base Camp the following night (although *night* was an arbitrary term). The Union Camp amazed me. About twenty-five full-time residents, employed by the ALE, lived there. The camp could also house up to seventy-five guests. The buildings, called "weather ports", looked like Quonset huts—lightweight buildings made of corrugated galvanized steel with a semicircular shape. Guests resided in tents lined up in rows. We tried to get some sleep, but the sunlight made that a challenge. We all waited anxiously for news to see if we could fly out the following night.

Once again, the weather held, and we left around six

that evening. For this journey, we would fly on a Twin Otter Osprey, a small plane specifically designed for short takeoffs and landings—perfect for a remote place like this. We packed our gear and boarded the Osprey. After a quick forty-five-minute flight, we arrived at Vinson Base Camp, which is located on the Branscomb Glacier. This time, the plane had portholes! The views were honestly some of the most incredible I have ever seen. A brilliant blue sky shimmered over a sea of white clouds, with only the black granite peaks of the Ellsworth Range peeping through in startling contrast. I had my face glued to the window for most of the flight.

As we circled base camp preparing to land, I saw several other climbing groups with tents already set up on the glacier. I watched, mesmerized, as the plane approached the glacier. We came in for a bumpy landing. Another surreal rush hit me as I realized the base of Vinson Massif lay before me. As I got off the plane, I could see Vinson to the south. I'll be honest, from that vantage point, it did not look that impressive, but Vison took the title of being the highest in the range. We quickly unloaded the gear and began setting up our rugged North Face tents, built for use on high-altitude mountains like Everest and K2. After setting them up and securing them, we built snow walls out of blocks of ice carved using a saw. We would then place the ice blocks around the tents to protect them from the gale-force winds that could come up anytime.

Dining proved interesting. We dug a pit in the snow and created four snow "benches," with three of the benches for seating, while the fourth became a "table" for our stoves. We did all our cooking on these stoves, which included melting all our drinking water. A pyramid-shaped piece of canvas, supported by one pole sticking out of the middle of the pit, provided cover. We not only ate at the "dining pit", we gathered there for team meetings, regardless of the weather.

Dave explained we would stay at three camps to climb Vinson: base camp at 7,700 feet of elevation, Camp 1 at 9,100 feet of elevation, and Camp 2 at 13,000 feet. Each camp would be set up the same way, with tents, a dining pit, and latrine facilities. Weather, however, guided us. Every day at 9:30 p.m., ALE meteorologists stationed at the Union Camp provided a two-day forecast. All the expeditions on Vinson tuned their radios in to receive this forecast. Every decision to advance or not revolved around these two-day forecasts.

With the weather forecast once again positive, the next day we packed our first load to carry to Camp 1, taking all the gear we wouldn't need for the night. As is typical, everyone carried their personal gear plus a portion of the group gear. We carried our backpacks, and each of us also pulled an orange, plastic sled roped to our body. Between the backpack and the sled, which equaled about seventy pounds of gear apiece, we could only gradually move up the mountain. We were also roped to each other as we climbed, in case one of us fell into a crevasse.

The climb became a fairly strenuous five-mile hike to Camp 1. When we arrived, we found a spot to dump our gear, piled it into several protective bags, and headed straight back to base camp to listen to the next day's forecast. The forecast for the next day predicted extreme wind, so we decided to take a day off as an acclimatization day and move to Camp 1 the following day. After hearing the forecast, we hunkered down in our sleeping bags for some well-earned rest.

The next morning started out windy, as predicted, so we just hung out in our tents and Jay and I got into the deeper stuff of life, like the nature of God, getting older, life in the corporate world, and more. It became clear Jay possessed a keen mind. We also discussed sports, especially football, which caused us to bond instantly.

The wind died down in the afternoon, so we emerged from our tents to practice falling onto our ice axes. We also practiced "self-arresting," which means using the ice ax to stop from falling down a steep, icy slope if you lose your footing. The reality of being on an extremely icy mountain hit home, and I remembered I should never, ever, underestimate any peak. I definitely did not want to be Vinson's first victim.

The following day, clear skies stretched above, but everything felt *freezing* cold. Regardless, we needed to move to Camp 1. We broke down base camp and loaded everything into our backpacks and onto our sleds. We climbed the five miles back up the glacier, sleds in tow. When we arrived, we set up our new camp, repeating the process from base camp. By the end of the "day," we had earned our rest.

Just before we settled in for the night, Dave called

us to the dining pit and discussed the plan. The next morning, he wanted us to take a load of stuff up to Camp 2 (or "High Camp" as it is known), and then return to Camp 1. Unfortunately, when the weather forecast came through that night, it didn't look good. The weather was supposed to deteriorate drastically over the next couple days, and although I knew we'd had a good run with the weather so far, I still couldn't help feeling a little frustrated. I'd been looking forward to climbing again and going as high as possible, as quickly as possible. Regardless, we could do nothing but resign ourselves to waiting out the bad weather.

The next day, time dragged by because we didn't have much to do. The wind blew so hard at times that we had to repair the snow walls around our tents or dig snow from the entrance. Jay and I ended up playing numerous games of cards, trying to pass the time however we could. That evening, the weather forecast still looked bad, as it did the evening after that. For three days, we endured the terrible weather. I came to realize one of the significant challenges of Mount Vinson—dealing with the unexpected.

Jay and I played more cards, until we couldn't anymore, then competed against each other in all kinds of sports trivia. Finally, on the third night, we heard the news we had all been waiting for: a prediction of clear weather. We were ecstatic!

The next day revealed clear skies and ridiculously cold weather—the coldest by far since landing in Antarctica. We bundled up, then loaded our gear and started along the fixed safety rope lines that had been put in place on the glacier. Like on other mountains, each climber is always attached to these fixed-lines to prevent a fall. We headed out to High Camp, near the crest of Vinson's dramatic western escarpment.

When we arrived, although we were only at 13,000 feet, the camp felt much higher. When you are at really high latitudes like in northern Alaska or Antarctica, the altitude feels higher than it actually is. On Vinson, 13,000 feet felt like 16,000 feet on a mountain like Aconcagua. The thin, dry air and brutal cold made it feel like the first day we were doing actual climbing, despite the slope only being about forty degrees. Thus, by the time we reached High Camp, I felt winded and tired. We quickly ditched our loads, then spent about forty-five minutes resting and admiring a spectacular view of the surrounding white wasteland, juxtaposed against that soft, shimmery, blue-green sky. I thanked God for the amazing opportunity, and even apologized for snubbing the trip a little at first. It humbled me that an expedition I viewed as a "requirement" would turn out to be so exhilarating. As always, on any big mountain, I continued to learn a lot about myself. After we'd caught our breath and rested, we headed back down to Camp 1.

Normally, the plan would be to spend a rest day at Camp 1 before heading back up to Camp 2 for the final summit push, but since we had just rested for three days and had a two-day window of decent weather, Dave suggested we head back up to Camp 2 the next morning, then summit the following day. Everyone felt strong enough, so we agreed. At this point I realized, out of all the guides I had ever climbed with, I had the most confidence and respect for Dave. He had a no-nonsense attitude whether we were climbing, digging snow, or putting up tents, but when all the work wrapped up, he had a relaxed and personable manner. I had the thought that Dave would have made a great platoon leader in wartime.

Despite being afraid I might feel a little fatigued the next day, I felt stronger as we pushed back up to High Camp. Jay experienced the same phenomenon. The climb takes about seven hours, but it seemed to fly by that day. I figured it might be due to the excitement of summit day being less than twenty-four hours away, but we climbed like beasts.

We arrived at High Camp and immediately began setting up tents and building snow walls. Because of the reduced amount of oxygen in the air, I quickly discovered the challenge of digging at that altitude. In fact, I became winded after only a minute or so. *So much for beast mode*, I thought, and pushed through the exhaustion. Soon enough, we had the camp erected and the dining pit dug. The team gathered eagerly around the radio for the nightly forecast, hoping we still had a clear weather window. I said a quick prayer as we waited for the meteorologist, then the radio crackled with the news: the good weather would hold!

Excitement kept me awake that night, which is a common occurrence before summit day. We left promptly at 8:30 a.m., our roped teams starting out slowly and meandering up the glacier. Probably because my energy had been spent the night before, I hadn't really paid attention to the views of the surrounding mountains. Utterly awe-inspiring, they rose majestically out of a pure-white ocean of ice that stretched to the horizon, slowly uniting with the washed-out, watercolor-blue sky. Thankfully, there was no wind, and even at around fifteen or twenty degrees below zero, I did not feel cold. We would, however, gain about 3,600 feet in altitude before we summited, so I reined in my optimism about staying warm, while Dave kept a slow but steady pace.

As we climbed, a smile rose to my lips. I'd soon summit the famed Mount Vinson. Even though the mountain might prove to be the least challenging of the seven I had climbed so far, it still had a strong "adventurer" quality, as if we were all pioneers, exploring the remotest part of the planet for the first time. Of course, this wasn't the first time Vinson had been summited by any stretch of the imagination, but there is something other-worldly about the mountain. Maybe because of the almost nonexistent life in the area, it feels like an accomplishment just to survive and climb the continent's highest mountain. As I climb, once again I am struck by the blessing God has bestowed on me. But in that moment, I feel as though He is saying I am experiencing what so few others ever would *because* I embraced the challenge of living an extraordinary life through faith . . . especially when I hadn't wanted to accept the challenge of this mountain. Hours away from conquering the summit I least wanted to climb, I have made a great new friend and am thoroughly enjoying the expedition as well as what the trip is teaching me about myself.

The feeling I experienced reminds me of a time I worked for a large semiconductor company, and they announced plans to acquire Sanyo Semiconductor—a huge Japanese semiconductor company with manufacturing sites in Japan, Thailand, Vietnam, China, and the Philippines. It would be the largest acquisition of a Japanese semiconductor company ever attempted by an American company.

To say the acquisition would be challenging would have been an understatement. Sanyo Semiconductor was a proud, conservative Japanese company whose leadership felt shame for being in the position where they had to be acquired by an American company to survive. In addition, many of their executives did not speak English. Topping it off, they had manufacturing issues at several of their plants. Culturally, the two companies seemed universes apart.

I led the Human Resources part of the acquisition. Like climbing Mount Vinson, I dreaded it, mainly because I knew that for at least a year and a half, I would have to spend most of my time in Asia, mainly in Japan but also in Thailand, Vietnam, China and the Philippines (where Sanyo had manufacturing facilities), first doing the due diligence, then helping with the integration. Don't get me wrong, I love to visit Asia, but only for short periods at a time. I quickly get homesick for Western food and culture. This acquisition made me fear I would have to spend months at a time in Asia, which ended up being the case.

I racked up over 200,000 frequent flier miles during the first year of the acquisition, the travel predictably brutal on me. Working with the Japanese posed a challenge because of the cultural differences in trying to integrate the conservative Japanese into American culture. Just getting them to share information with us presented a chore.

Still, that was probably the most rewarding project I have ever worked on in my entire career. I decided to embrace the challenge, and the moment I did, I began to feel invigorated by the goal of making this giant acquisition a success. Before long, I grew to love working in Vietnam and Thailand—a wonderful first in my career. I also found myself thoroughly enjoying my work with the Sanyo HR teams I inherited as part of the acquisition.

To this day, if I am interviewing for a new role, when I am asked what accomplishment I am most proud of in my career, without hesitation, I say it is the successful acquisition and integration of Sanyo.

This is purely because I decided to adjust my attitude to embrace the challenge.

• • •

After many hours, the slope suddenly trailed away, and Dave announced we had reached the summit. Unlike other major mountains I have climbed, there was no dramatic obstacle before the summit, no tricky maneuvers to get to the peak, and nothing spectacular about the summit, aside from the view. But Vinson turned out to be a special summit because I had conquered one of the toughest and most insidious foes we'll face—apathy.

Each of us took turns stepping up to the true summit, posing for pictures in triumph, and yelling out whoops of congratulations. We stayed up there for about thirty minutes, gazing at the unparalleled views of the Ellsworth Range, the Ronne Ice Shelf, and what seemed like the entire continent of Antarctica. I silently thanked God again for allowing me to be there and nudging me to go. I prayed for the safety of all the climbers on the mountain, specifically asking for us to have a safe descent.

On some mountains, I leapt at the chance to leave the summit quickly, but on Vinson, much too soon, the time to head down arrived. Nevertheless, I knew we had to head back because of the unpredictable weather. We formed into our rope teams and proceeded back down the slope. It only took us about three hours to make it back to High Camp, after which we melted snow, cooked our dinner, and listened to the weather forecast. The weather would be good enough to continue descending, so with great satisfaction, we climbed into our tents to rest for the night. I immediately fell asleep from the quality kind of exhaustion caused by stretching one's limits, reaching for one's goals, and pushing through the obstacles. Man, it felt great.

The next day, we returned all the way to base camp,

grabbing our sleds at Camp 1 and redistributing the loads. Once again, we set up our camp and dug out the dining pit. We planned to fly to Union Camp the following day, but the weather forecast was sketchy. We hoped it would be solid enough to fly the next day, but as it turned out, we had to spend an additional day at base camp. Such is life in the Antarctic.

After a day of rest, we flew out on the Osprey to Union Camp. When we arrived, we heard the excellent news we could fly out to Punta Arenas that same day. The big Russian jet had not been able to fly for three days, so when we heard it was flying in, we joyfully hopped onto snowcats and traveled the five miles to the landing zone. As we arrived, we saw the plane make its final approach and watched, mesmerized, as it landed on the ice, then immediately reversed power to try to stop.

A whole new crew of adventurers got off the plane, some of whom were going to climb Vinson and were eager to hear our stories about how it went. We jovially shared our experiences and cautioned the group to heed the weather forecasts, especially the wind alerts. I gave them some tips on building and maintaining the snow walls.

Despite my great exhilaration at having conquered the most remote of the seven summits, when I climbed aboard the big Russian plane, I felt relieved to be on the last leg of this journey instead of just starting it. Soon, we were fully loaded and heading back to Punta Arenas for a welcome night of sleep at the Hotel Diego

De Almagro.

Tired but happy, I thought again about what a great trip it had been—no drama, no real danger, just wonderful people, incredible views, a physically challenging climb, and the best part, of course—summit success. Vinson had pushed me out of any remaining comfort zones, which I suppose is the most valuable thing about embracing the challenge to live differently, to live extraordinarily. The joy and fulfillment cannot be described, it can only be experienced.

Jay and I stayed in frequent contact. I now consider him one of my best friends. He did attempt Denali that next summer but had to abandon his climb at 14,000 feet because of severe altitude sickness. He was wise to do so. There will always be another opportunity if you really want it.

When I think back on Mount Vinson, what stays with me is that not every mountain is dramatic and sensational . . . but every mountain offers a lesson. There is always something in your character that needs conquering, and sometimes, like on Vinson, it is the subtle, insidious enemy you don't see, like apathy or disregard. I found that overcoming these hidden obstacles can be rewarding.

Not every climb is as unexpectedly rewarding . . . sometimes, they're unexpectedly brutal.

CHAPTER 9

The Forty-Percent Rule

IN JUNE 2017, I HAD THE OPPORTUNITY TO DO A climbing/tennis trip with Mark Reed, one of my oldest friends from high school and college. Mark is a year older than I am and is the same guy who climbed Longs Peak with Bill, Todd, and me. Mark and I have been friends for forty-two years, which is so rare in life, and like me, Mark is uber-competitive. In fact, we still compete like crazy with each other. The Pikes Peak trip would be no different.

This trip had me incredibly excited, since I could not only climb, I could hang out with my old buddy, too. We met at the Denver Airport, arrived in Denver around midnight, and got to the hotel at around 1:30 a.m. I quickly discovered Mark snored loud enough to shake the roof, so I only got a couple of hours of sleep when we woke up at 5:00 a.m. to play tennis at an indoor facility.

Our competitive nature compelled us to make our game of tennis more challenging by adding an element. If one of us attempted a drop shot and missed, he had to do twenty push-ups on the spot. If the drop shot was made and the other guy couldn't get to it, he had to do thirty push-ups. I do push-ups as part of my workout routine, so I did not have to train, but Mark actually trained for the trip by doing push-ups to compete in this game (that's scratching the surface of how competitive Mark is). The people on the court next to us thought we were crazy, but that was nothing new to us and we cared little. It makes tennis much more challenging from a fitness standpoint when you throw in push-ups—especially at Denver's altitude. Adding to that, Mark has bone-on-bone in one knee, so even the game of tennis presented difficulties. But Mark never shies away from a challenge.

To give you an idea of Mark's mental toughness, he, Todd, and Bill planned to do a rim-to-rim hike of the Grand Canyon in less than twenty-four hours in the middle of June (I'd torn my Achilles tendon and couldn't go). To put the hike in perspective, it would be over forty miles, with over 12,000 total feet of elevation gain in under a day. The Grand Canyon is one of the toughest hikes in the world if you do it in the middle of June when the temperature at the bottom can be over 110 degrees Fahrenheit. It's no joke, even for ultra-athletic, seasoned climbers.

Since I couldn't go, Todd and Bill brought along a

friend who is one of the fittest cyclists in Phoenix. Mark and the three of them started out at the South Rim, hiked down to the bottom, then crossed over to the trail going up the North Rim. When they reached the North Rim, they had hiked over twenty miles and gained 7,000 feet in elevation in less than nine hours. By the time they finished, they had only the stars to light the path, and they were all exhausted. Todd, Bill, and their fit buddy felt they were too tired to continue and decided to stay the night on the North Rim and take a four-hour bus ride back to the South Rim in the morning. Mark wouldn't accept that. He decided to do the hike back to the South Rim alone and completed the entire hike in less than twenty-four hours, doing half of it solo. The man is all heart.

Neither of us had played tennis in a while, but we both started off crushing the ball and played at a high level for a couple of hours and, of course, did more push-ups than either of us cared to do. We weren't used to playing at that altitude, so we both felt a little winded when we called it quits. We then took off and headed for the mountains.

We ate lunch at Beau Jo's Pizza in Idaho Springs, which is a mountain tradition for me, then we did an easy fourteener (a 14,000-foot peak) to acclimatize. We saw a number of bighorn sheep and mountain goats on the trail, making the climb even more glorious. We then drove to a town called Dillon where we spent the night, and the next day, we did two more easy fourteeners called Grays and Torreys. This nine-mile round-trip hike should have been our "easy day", but a gorgeous summer Saturday with two easy fourteeners close to Denver meant huge crowds. Not expecting this, we had to park two miles from the trailhead. This added four miles round-trip to the hike.

Despite the extra four miles, I felt strong that Saturday, and since I'm a far more experienced climber and my hip arthritis wasn't nearly as bad as Mark's knee (at that point), I could have really hurt Mark if I wanted to, especially once we got above 13,500 feet. I always fall back on my leadership experience in any challenge I undertake, and this one was no different. Leaders play hard to win, but they know their own and their team's boundaries and are willing to step back when necessary. Leaders also anticipate instead of reacting, and I'd already made the mistake of not anticipating the crowds, so I did not want to make any more errors.

The key is self-awareness and awareness of your team's strengths and weaknesses. One of my mottos is, "Never expect your team to endure something you are not willing to endure." In business, people sometimes really don't have the skills, time, or budget to do what is asked of them. Often, unrealistic demands have been placed on them, and because of this, it is important to create an environment where people can be free to ask for help without fear of recrimination. It is the wisest approach to take because you may lose a good person for lack of insight. That happens all the time. In climbing, the same general rule is true: being blind to your team's limitations can be dangerous—if not fatal. Even though

I wouldn't have thought Mark any weaker if he needed to slow down or stop, I knew *I* had to take responsibility, slow down, and consider Mark.

We made it back down in decent time, but I found myself a little cranky at having to do the extra two miles beyond the trailhead. We had lunch in Dillon, then drove to Manitou Springs at the base of Pikes Peak to prepare for a long day on Sunday. At 14,115 feet, Pikes Peak—known as "America's Mountain"—is one of the monarchs of the front range of the Rocky Mountains of Colorado. It looms over Colorado Springs and is intricately woven into the fabric of that city, with bicycle racers, car racers, and climbers all jockeying for faster times in their respective sports.

There are three ways to reach the top of Pikes Peak: by a winding (primarily) dirt road with hairpin turns and precipitous drop-offs, by cog railway, or by foot. The most popular hiking route up Pikes Peak is the Barr Trail, which starts in Manitou Springs. The Barr Trail is thirteen miles one way, with 8,000 feet of elevation gain.

The Barr Trail is one of my favorite hikes in the entire world. There are many reasons for this. First and foremost, the trail is magnificently beautiful, especially at the lower levels. It is honestly one of the best-groomed trails in Colorado, which boasts generally well-groomed trails. Second, it is a true physical fitness challenge. The trail starts at around 6,000 feet elevation and climbs to 14,115 feet. No other fourteener in Colorado can boast such a feature. The best part is after doing the thirteen-mile hike up, we could take the train down, saving thirteen miles of downhill wear and tear on our aching knees (downhill is always tougher on your joints).

Months before, I had made a train reservation for the two of us, as it fills up fast in the summer. Without reservations, there is no room to take hikers down. This meant, however, we had to make it to the summit in time to catch the train or hike the thirteen downhill miles back. I knew this shouldn't be a problem, short of any unexpected issues.

When we arrived at our motel in Manitou, I felt beyond excited. I was already having a blast catching up with my buddy and being outdoors in my home state. I'll admit, though, when we looked up at Pikes looming over the city, the task seemed daunting, even though we had done it many times before (I wasn't yet ready to admit that age affects us all). The summit seemed so far away; it seemed unbelievable that it could be only thirteen miles and around five hours to the top.

We set the goal of getting on the trail by 5:30 a.m. because we had to be on the summit by noon to catch the 12:30 p.m. train down. By being on the trail that early, we had just over six hours to make the train. We hoped to do the climb in five hours to give ourselves a little cushion to chill at the summit, but we would have to see what the day would bring.

I took the lead and set a nice three-miles-per-hour pace for the first three miles, which climb quickly out of Manitou Springs in a series of switchbacks (zigzag trails up the mountain that are more resistant to erosion). I felt good for the first three miles, then suddenly, around mile four, hiking just ahead of Mark on a flat session, I became so light-headed, I truly thought I would faint.

I steadied my legs and mentally willed myself not to go down. After about twenty seconds, the sensation of almost blacking out passed, but I still felt extremely light-headed. I also began to feel warm and started sweating profusely. Mark soon noticed my entire back and legs were soaked, and by mile five, I realized I had standing water in the pockets of my pants. *What is going on?* I wondered.

I kept pushing but soon began to feel weak and nauseous. My entire body started to ache. I didn't want to admit this to Mark. I thought the previous day's thirteen-mile hike might have taken too much out of me, causing me to struggle on Pikes. *Surely time has not been* that *cruel to me*, I thought. I concluded that maybe I hadn't trained enough, or maybe multiple-day fourteener trips were too many. Regardless, I had committed and felt determined not to let Mark see my weakness, even though he kept asking why I kept my heavy Gore-Tex jacket on when I was "sweating buckets." The truth was, I had chills and couldn't stop shivering uncontrollably.

I tried my best to keep the three-miles-per-hour pace going. I didn't want to let my friend down. I knew if we didn't keep the pace, we would not make the train, and Mark would have to hike an excruciating thirteen miles back down with a bone-on-bone knee. But I had a decision to make. Reaching mile six, in my mind, would be the point of no return since, at that milestone, it is just as far to go down as to go up. If we turned back, Mark would still have to hike six miles *downhill*. If we pushed on, we'd *have to* make the train, or we'd be hiking thirteen miles back down.

In 2001, due to various circumstances, the semiconductor industry completely crashed, almost overnight. The company I worked for found themselves in a severe cash-flow bind, resulting in only enough cash to survive for about five weeks. This meant we had to take some drastic actions, one of which was to eliminate 300 jobs at corporate headquarters in the space of a week.

They chose me as the lucky guy tasked with managing it.

I had to coordinate facilities, security, finance, legal, our occupational health nurses, and the police department (we had them on-site for extra security). I also had to organize and oversee outplacement, severance payouts, exit packages, escorts, notifiers, the purchase of boxes and tape (to pack up belongings), and much more.

I had a week to pull it all off.

This task elicited much the same feeling as trying to make the train while brutally sick on Pikes Peak. I ended up doing three all-nighters during that week, and when I could sleep, it meant only a few hours at a time on a cot I kept in my office. For four days, I did not go home.

The toughest part in challenges like this and Pikes Peak are those that came right before the end. In both instances, overwhelmed with exhaustion, but not quite at the finish line, they both presented all-or-nothing tasks. We pulled it off at the semiconductor company and, sadly but successfully, exited over 300 people in a single day.

What a miserable experience all around—the stress, the exhaustion, and, most of all, the lousy feeling of having to let all these people go. But with the company's survival at stake, it had to be done. Every single leader will have those moments and, more often than not, they will happen at the worst time.

I already knew in my heart that no matter how bad I felt, I would make it to the top of Pikes Peak in time to make that train. I also knew for the next two to three hours, I would have to dig deeper than I had in a long time. For as far back as I could remember, I had never felt so weak. As Mark describes it, I would have to go "deep into the belly of the beast."

I prayed to God for the strength to make it in time to catch the train. But we were rapidly reaching a higher altitude with the air becoming thinner, and thus, hiking became much, *much* harder. We somehow made it to mile nine at the three-hour mark, so I knew the three-miles-per-hour pace I'd set still held. But the worst was yet to come. We faced the "crunch" part of the trail. That meant hiking up the east face of Pikes in a series of long, arduous switchbacks.

Physically, my energy began to drain like a sieve, but besides never wanting to let a climbing partner down, I had learned another survival skill that had served me well in the past: *have a clear and measurable goal.* I'm not exaggerating when I call this a survival skill. Navy Seals operate by what they call the "forty-percent rule," which they've discovered is when your mind is telling you you're completely done—and I mean you think you have nothing left—you're only forty percent done. You still have sixty percent left in reserve until you physically cannot do any more. The only thing that keeps you from tapping into your reserve is failing to have a clear and measurable goal. In extreme mountaineering, this level of mental toughness—a survival skill—can literally mean the difference between life and death.

Still, by that point, this was by far the most miserable hike or climb I'd ever experienced. I kept telling myself, "One more step, Mark, one more step," as I continued to focus on just making the train. I kept that mantra in my head, not only because all I wanted to do was collapse on a seat and be transported down the mountain, but also because my second measurable goal meant that under virtually no circumstances would I let my friend Mark down because of my weakness.

I continued to pray for strength, and we kept pushing higher and higher. Soon, however, at that altitude and in my weakened state, I could no longer maintain the three-miles-per-hour pace. My fallback objective aimed at two miles per hour. By then, Mark had become fully aware something was wrong, but he (perhaps naïvely) still didn't seem worried at all about making the train. I, on the other hand, had started to panic. A few times I had to force my anxiety down.

We eventually hit mile eleven and, instead of any relief, things became brutal. While doing all I could to keep pushing upward, this became even tougher when we hit snowfields covering the trail. Most of them were not difficult to traverse but crossing them added a little more exertion and a little more time to the hike. Then, at almost the twelve-mile mark, the trail disappeared into a large snowfield. Adding to that, beyond the snowfield loomed a series of sheer cliffs. The mental strain of this perfect example of Murphy's Law caused me to ask Mark if he wouldn't mind doubling back about a quarter mile to see if, somehow, we'd missed a turnoff. He readily agreed, and I sat down to rest for a precious few minutes. Mark soon returned, saying he was sure we hadn't missed any turnoffs. I then realized the trail must switch back in the middle of the snowfield. That meant we had to climb straight up the snowfield to try to find the trail again.

This was the last thing I needed in my physical state. I had to decide right there on that snowfield, cold, shivering, sweating, and in aching pain. *How much do I have left?* I sat for a moment while Mark's expression betrayed his concern. *Sixty percent!* I shouted in my own mind. *You have sixty percent left! Get up.* I stood on my feet and nodded to Mark, who raised an eyebrow but knew if I thought I was okay, I was okay. Every muscle and joint in my body screamed, but I climbed step after step, about a hundred vertical feet, straight up the snowfield at 13,000 feet of elevation. At the top, I discovered the trail and breathed a sigh of relief.

Once I found the trail, Mark joined me, and I kept pushing myself. Soon we escaped the snowfields, which told me we had a mile to go and over two hours to reach the train. A surge of confidence filled me despite being totally spent and sick. (As it turned out, I had come down with a wicked case of the flu before the hike without realizing it.)

I knew I had around 2,000 steps in the last mile, so going back to my mantra, I started counting each step as a way of measuring progress and keeping my mind focused on *how* I could make it to the top. By that point, our pace had trickled to a feeble one-and-a-half-miles-per-hour pace. I kept pushing by counting steps—one, two, three, four . . . up to one hundred. Then I started over again. I broke it down into twenty sets of 100 and worked my way through each set. My body felt like hell, so I decided not to leave it there and push through, if not to Heaven, at least to the summit.

Finally, agonizingly, we crested the summit and could see the buildings on the top. We also saw there was a road race on Pikes Peak that day (it's a popular location for sports car racing), so race cars and race drivers packed the summit. We hobbled into the little cafe so I could collapse into a booth and wait for the train. Too tired and sick to eat or drink anything, I finally admitted to Mark that I thought I had come down with the flu. He told me he wasn't surprised but gave me a look that said he knew how mentally tough it must have been to push up that mountain.

As we waited, I marveled at the power of having a

measurable goal and doing whatever it takes to achieve that goal. I had just hiked thirteen miles and 8,000 vertical feet to reach 14,000 feet of elevation, all with a severe case of the flu. Obviously, this is something you never want to do in such a weakened state, but I really had no choice. By the time I realized it would have been just a little easier going back down, through prayer and through a laser-like focus on that one goal of making the train, I pushed through the extreme physical suffering to achieve that goal. I closed my eyes and thanked God for giving me strength and for the good weather. Looking at Mark, I smiled, feeling great satisfaction. I had not let my friend down.

CHAPTER 10

The Wonder
of Embracing a Challenge

FRICA! AN EXOTIC CONTINENT FILLED WITH magnificent animals, people of fascinating cultures, and . . . Mount Kilimanjaro! Climbing this iconic 19,340-foot volcano to the roof of Africa had long been a goal of mine, way before I ever thought of doing the seven summits. As a young man, I'd been captured by the dream of climbing Kilimanjaro, then adding a wildlife safari after summiting. Something about Africa's wild, raw freedom had always called to me.

In late August 2011, I would leave one company and start a job at another. I quickly realized this gave me the perfect three-week window to do a Kilimanjaro/safari trip. I could hardly believe I might finally make my dream a reality. I began to make plans, first by deciding which trekking company I would use to lead me up the mountain. Kilimanjaro is unique in that it stands in a national park, and park rules require you to hire local guides and porters. This is to ensure protection of the wildlife and flora while also stimulating the local economy, which I'm always happy to do. It's a good deal, in fact, because the porters carry all the gear up the mountain for you. All I would need to carry would be a daypack with water, snacks, and extra layers of clothes. The information I found said the porters entirely set up each camp, cooked all the meals, and broke the camp down each morning. If true, I could get used to this kind of service on any mountain!

I hired an outfit called Tusker Trails, which boasted years of experience on Kilimanjaro and had a reputation for how well they treated their guides and porters. Like my usual choices based on quality and reputation, they turned out to be a little more expensive than most of the other guiding companies, but more meaningful to me, I knew the climb would occur with a leader in eradicating unfair treatment of laborers on the mountain. Also, I had used Tusker for my climb of Aconcagua, so I knew they would do a great job for me on Kilimanjaro.

The next decision became which route to take. There are five main routes that all start in the jungle, then meander up through five distinct microclimates. The five paths then narrow into three distinct ascent routes to the summit. Two of the routes offered a more leisurely pace up the mountain with greater acclimatization. I decided on the Lemosho Route, as it is the less crowded of those two.

Booking a five-day wildlife safari at the end of the trip felt even more awesome. This would take me to three of Tanzania's national parks. I cannot explain the excitement I felt.

Before I knew it, the big day arrived. At the end of August, I boarded a plane in Phoenix and flew to Amsterdam. From there, I flew straight to the Kilimanjaro Airport in Tanzania. A representative from Tusker picked me up, and we walked to the company van. As I stepped out into the warm, dry, African sun, I experienced an energy in the atmosphere that I had never experienced anywhere else. Raw, natural, *real* vibrancy. Africa at last!

We took the van to a hotel in the Tanzanian city of Moshi, where I settled in for two nights, sleeping in mosquito netting, even in the hotel room (malaria is a concern). I learned that most of the people in Moshi belonged to the Chagga tribe—one of the first African tribes to convert to Christianity, and also one of the most relatively wealthy. The next day at breakfast, I met the six other climbers in my group; our head guide, Kobi; and his junior guide, Bolu. Kobi, unlike most of the other Tanzanians, did not smile much. He maintained a stern, focused demeanor, which I would later realize was because he took his responsibilities seriously. For that, I would become grateful.

Kobi and Bolu spent the morning doing a gear check with us. Bolu, unlike Kobi, had a constant smile on his face. The contrast between the two amused me, and

I instantly liked them both. While most of the people in Moshi were of the Chagga tribe, I learned that both Kobi and Bolu were of the Sukuma people, a northern tribe and also the largest ethnic group in Tanzania. Sukuma means "people of the north." I met many of the porters as well, who were from various tribes such as the famed Maasai, Sukuma, Chagga, and a Cushitic people called the Iraqw. All spoke heavily accented English with differing dialectic lilts.

After the gear check, we all drove into Moshi to have lunch and do some shopping. Moshi seemed typical of most small cities in developing countries: indisputably poor but beginning to develop. Some roads in Moshi were paved and some were dirt, a telling sign of the city's financial status. I noticed most of the people smiled and greeted me far more than in many European countries or America.

The next day, we were ready to get started on our adventure. We headed out on a two-hour drive to the park's Londorossi Gate and registered with the authorities before driving another eight miles to our starting point. This side of Kilimanjaro is still wild. We hoped we might spot some wildlife, but to our disappointment, we saw nothing remarkable.

We had lunch at the trailhead, then started a short trek up to the first camp, Mti Mkubwa Camp, at 9,000 feet of elevation. True to Tusker's word, the porters carried everything for us and traveled ahead at a faster pace, despite hauling all the gear. I even noticed one guide, named Denmo, carried a heavy oxygen cylinder in case of an emergency. I had to wonder if he would carry it all the way to the summit because that would be something to see. Denmo, like most other Tanzanians, smiled constantly, even while lugging this huge oxygen tank up one of the seven summits.

The usual language barrier existed, but I tried to show my gratitude and awe at the feats of the porters ferrying such heavy stuff up the mountain. Unless you've been there, you wouldn't know this, but most African people display tremendous humility and camaraderie. It's what Central and Southern Africans call *Ubuntu*. This is a term meaning "I am because we are," which aptly captures the African virtues of compassion and humanity. Most Africans are gentle people, smiling constantly. The Kilimanjaro porters portrayed the epitome of this hardworking yet happy group effort toward a goal. They reminded me of another time my company acquired a smaller semiconductor organization.

The first acquisition I ever participated in was when we purchased a small semiconductor company in Rhode Island. A family-owned company, in business for thirty years without ever having had any significant layoffs, and with a true family atmosphere, they nevertheless would have gone out of business because of the aforementioned semiconductor crash in 2001 if we hadn't bought them.

The other reality is that the company I worked for itched to do an acquisition. They had spun off from Motorola three years prior and wanted to stretch their wings and grow. So they did. But instead of treating the acquisition as more of a partnership, we went in heavy-handed and treated those poor people as if they knew nothing at all useful to us. We had the attitude that "we are the acquirer who is *not* in financial trouble, so we know what's best and we are here to save you from yourselves."

Sadly, I have seen some climbers treat their porters and their Sherpas the same way, and it makes me furious. Good climbers appreciate their porters and Sherpas, knowing they could be the ones to save your life in the event of a catastrophe. Good corporate leaders, in much the same way, spend quality time with all levels of the organization. They walk the floor, get to know the people, and take an interest in their team at every level. If you want to be energized as a leader, spend more time with those lower-level team members and treat them with the utmost dignity and respect. You'll find they have wisdom, experience, excellent ideas, and can teach you many things.

The porters on Kilimanjaro were incredible, and I didn't take them for granted. They brought joy, comfort, and safety to all the members of the climbing group. With pleasure, I watched the pride and effort they put into making sure they helped create as memorable an experience as possible for us. The level of customer service from the porters astounded me.

I wish I could say the company I worked for appreciated the Rhode Island people the same way. Their culture seemed similar to that of the joyful African porters. The reality was, we made a mess of the acquisition, and within a couple of years, we ended up having to shut the manufacturing plant down. This experience is something I still think of with sadness, but it provided a strong lesson that became engrained early in my career.

On Kilimanjaro, when we arrived at the Mti Mkubwa Camp, to my astonishment, everything was fully set up and ready for us. The porters had even put up a dining tent with tables and chairs! My tent had been prepared with my sleeping bag neatly rolled out. *Man, Africa is first class all the way! I can sure get spoiled by all this.* I smiled to myself. The porters then cooked a delicious dinner of fried chicken and French fries! I halfway expected a traditional Tanzanian meal, but the porters had even carried a deep fryer up the mountain, smiling all the while!

For dessert, the porters served us avocado. I had never had avocado for dessert in my life before, but I loved it. In fact, I rarely eat any kind of dessert as I'm allergic to sugar, so avocado meant a treat for me. Yes, I'm allergic to sugar in even the tiniest amounts. Sugar makes me intensely nauseous, and I feel deathly sick if I eat much of it. As you can imagine, this has serious implications on my climbs as almost everything has added sugar. I have to be extremely careful about what I eat. Often, entire meals are ruled out. This can be a serious issue on difficult climbs that expend great amounts of energy, but it would be more problematic to be horribly ill atop a mountain. Basically, I eat lean most of the time and eat extra foods I can tolerate. But that's not always possible because of team rations. Frequently, I'll simply skip meals.

Another unique thing about me is I don't take a drug called Diamox, which aids with acclimatization. Most climbers use Diamox, and on Kilimanjaro, all the climbers in my group took it. I have never once taken Diamox on any climb, as I seem to do extremely well at high altitudes. Diamox also has "interesting" side effects that do not sound pleasant, so I vehemently avoid it. Soon, however, I learned Diamox was an unofficial requirement on Kilimanjaro.

Kobi and the other guides were not happy to hear I planned to forego this acclimatization aide. Understandably, they worried that without the drug, I would not effectively acclimatize, which could be a problem for me and the group higher on the mountain. I assured them this would not be the case and explained on every high mountain I had climbed, I had never used Diamox. But I could tell by their expressions this frustrated them, and they did not believe a word I said. Regardless, nothing official demanded I had to take the drug, so I did not take it.

After dinner, we relaxed for a few minutes, talking and getting to know one another better. The first camp nestled in the middle of a tropical rain forest, so as soon as the sun set, we could hear birds, insects, and even monkeys. At first, I'll admit the wildlife felt a little unnerving, but once inside my sleeping bag, being at a higher altitude and tired from the day's trek, I quickly fell asleep.

The next morning, a porter named Talo (I think) woke me, handing me a hot cup of tea, and saying with the warm, signature Tanzanian smile, "Time to wake up! I bring you hot tea!" I smiled back and gratefully took the tea. "Breakfast will be ready in fifteen minutes, Mr. Mark! Then we leave." Talo grinned.

"Okay, thank you, my friend!" I said, rubbing my eyes. *What a way to wake up*, I thought happily. I didn't know this would be the routine for the entire trip. It really brought a whole new meaning to "service with a smile." Breakfast consisted of local fruit, scrambled eggs, bread, and juice, all of which our porters had carried up the mountain. I devoured the eggs and got ready to head out.

On the second day of our journey, we had a hike of about ten miles, which would take us roughly seven hours. A lunch break was scheduled for the four-hour mark. As we hiked, we transitioned from the wet rainforest microclimate to a low alpine zone. This meant the lush jungle fell away after two hours and we found ourselves in an area of low scrub brush, strange trees, and exotic flowers. Still, the trail remained smooth, with only a few spots that required scrambling over boulders, but nothing technical presented itself at all.

We ate lunch at a place called Shira Camp 1 at around 10,000 feet and continued up the mountain to Shira Camp 2, where we would spend the night at around 12,300 feet. The camp spanned a large area in a natural clearing, sparsely surrounded by trees. Over a hundred guides, porters, and climbers bustled about because this camp merged with the Machame Route. This reminded us that as beautiful and exotic as Kilimanjaro is, it isn't just a walk but an actual climb up a mountain. One of my teammates began to struggle with the altitude. I could not see any way he would make it all the way to 19,000 feet. Kobi tested my oxygen saturation level as well and appeared somewhat surprised to find it perfectly fine. I knew he would keep testing my oxygen saturation level, both morning and night, which didn't bother me. His competency instead assured me.

From this camp, the view became one of the most beautiful I'd ever seen. We had a perfectly clear line of sight to Kilimanjaro's summit, while a glowing, red sunset spread across its backdrop. As I took in the sunset, Bolu came and sat next to me to enjoy the breathtaking view and moment that few in the world experience. I asked him about his life, and he told me he had been an accountant in a city called Dar es Salaam but had been miserable in his job. His family had wanted him to be an accountant, but the adventurer blood flowed powerfully in him. Finally, he decided he couldn't take it anymore, and he pursued his dream of becoming a guide on Kilimanjaro, embracing this extraordinary life. He explained that he started out as a porter, then worked his way up to his present position as a junior guide. He hoped to be a lead guide within two years.

I'd encountered this familiar story on several mountains, so I asked Bolu if his career decision made him happy. I was fairly sure of the answer, as it had never varied before.

"Mark," he said, stretching his arms out wide, "look out at this view. This is my office." Bolu looked at me until I realized he was making a profound statement. "How many people in the world get to work in an office like this?" I nodded thoughtfully. Message received. *Someday,* I vowed, *I will have an "office" similar to Bolu's. I just need to figure out how to make that happen.*

I have never forgotten Bolu's words, and I will admit they haunt me to this day.

Day three took us east from the Shira Plateau, passing through a fascinating area called the "Garden of the Senecios," which had a strange, otherworldly plant called the giant lobelia. This plant, tall and cylindrical with some leaves around the middle, looked somewhat like a desert yucca, but the leaves on top formed a giant honeycomb. This top part was at least three-feet tall and over a foot in diameter. Encountering things like this that look like they could be from another planet is part of what makes climbing all around the world so fascinating.

That day, the trail took us from 12,300 feet up to 15,000 feet, then back down to 12,500 feet, consistent with the climber's axiom of "climb high and sleep low." On the way, the smooth trail led us to a feature called Lava Tower at the top of the day's route. Lava Tower is a huge formation of volcanic rock jutting out of the Earth's surface, also known as a volcanic plug. A volcanic plug is somewhat like a champagne cork, suppressing the dormant volcanoes' vents and gasses, although there was next to no risk of it "popping" out.

After pausing to admire the lava rock, we then descended on a steep and rocky trail through a landscape so barren and strange, we could have been walking on the moon. Grateful that, so far, the weather had been perfect, I hoped it would continue. This wasn't a spot I'd want to be in if the weather turned.

We arrived at Barranco Camp just before sunset and got our first view of Barranco Wall. Scaling this wall would be our "breakfast" climb the following day since it's the first thing we'd do after breakfast. The Barranco Wall is a 600-foot tall, stepped, but almost vertical rock wall that allows you to quickly get to the top of the Karanga Valley. We had a good dinner and I slept well, waking up before Talo brought me my morning tea, eager to get going on the scramble up the wall. We hiked for a half hour to get to the wall and soon arrived at its base. It is a Class 3 climb, which basically means we had to use all four limbs to move our bodies higher on the rock. The guides were there to assist, and with the rock being dry, everyone in my group did well and had fun with this part of the journey.

At the top of the Barranco Wall, the microclimate switched to a high alpine zone, which means there are no trees, little vegetation, and cold began to seep in. We followed a path that wound through many inclines, declines, and then inclines again. After about eight hours, we arrived at the Barafu Camp at 15,300 feet. Each morning and night, Kobi dutifully took readings of our oxygen saturation levels. To Kobi's waning surprise that night, like each night before, my oxygen level registered perfectly fine, even without the Diamox. The climber who'd had a tough time with the altitude at lower camps, however, began to struggle at over 15,000 feet. The test revealed this gentleman's oxygen saturation level dipped too low for him to continue on the journey. The guides, concerned about some form of edema setting in, decided to send one of them down the mountain with the man to get him to a lower and safer altitude. The guy appeared to be disappointed, but I had a feeling that deep down he felt relieved.

It's a little-known fact that Kilimanjaro is comprised of three volcanoes: Mawenzi, Shira, and Kibo. Mawenzi and Shira are extinct, but Kibo, the highest volcano and the one we would summit, is dormant but could potentially erupt again. In fact, there has been activity in the last two-hundred years. So far, we had seen Shira and Kibo's summits for much of the ascent, but at the Barafu Camp, we could see Mawenzi for the first time. Its ragged crater rim again looked like something from another planet! I couldn't remember seeing such a varied landscape on any climb. From this vantage point, we could also see our route to Kibo's summit. *How cool*, I thought. We ate a big lunch at Barafu, then retired to our tents. Our wake-up call would be around midnight, so we tried to get to bed early. The next day would involve twelve to sixteen hours of trekking and climbing, so it was imperative to get some rest.

I got a few hours of sleep and woke at about 11:00 p.m. to dress and get ready. Up to this point, I had been wearing hiking clothes—shorts or hiking pants with layers—but that morning I put on my high-altitude gear: long underwear, Gore-Tex pants, heavy underlayers, a Gore-Tex jacket, and a hat and gloves. We had a quick breakfast of biscuits and hot tea, then began the summit push. With our headlamps turned on, we started the slow journey up the scree slope, a steep incline with loose rocks amassed typically at the base of a near-vertical climb. The temperatures were mild—maybe thirty-five degrees—but because of the scree slope, we slowly plodded along. We figured it would take about eight hours to make the summit.

The night's temperature felt perfect to me, though, and because we were in no hurry, I could soak in the moment. As is my way, I thanked God for the opportunity to live my dreams in this glorious place. The more wonderful the moment, the more I always feel His presence a little stronger. At this point, many other climbers surrounded us, pushing for the summit, so a familiar trail of headlamps snaked up the mountain. As we continued, we began passing climbers sitting on rocks with their heads between their legs. Some of them looked totally spent, even though their teammates were trying to give them encouragement. The altitude had stepped up its claim of victims.

We climbed for several hours, then slowly, the sky began to lighten. Once we passed 17,500 feet, our team's pace slowed even more due to the extremely thin air. Our guides offered us hot chocolate, but I still felt great, so water alone satisfied me. As I assessed my condition, all I can say is maybe because Africa completely enamored me—or maybe because fulfilling one of my lifelong dreams energized me—I felt totally alive and totally at one with the moment. As dawn broke over the Tanzanian plains thousands of feet below, I felt God's majestic presence in a powerful, tangible way.

Suddenly, we came upon Stella Point, the crater rim at 18,800 feet. This presented a decision for our group. Kobi explained that over sixty percent of climbers stop at Stella Point and do not make it to the true summit. After a quick show of hands, everyone in our group made it clear we wanted to continue to the true summit, so we kept going. The trail follows the crater rim, and I found myself surprised to see only dirt and no snow. In fact, I realized, we had not hiked through snow once during the entire journey. I did, however, stop to get some pictures of me standing next to the glaciers that Kilimanjaro is so famous for which flow from the top of the mountain. Sadly, these glaciers are rapidly disappearing, and I feel blessed that I had the opportunity to experience them before they disappear. I read somewhere this will happen by 2022. As I pondered this, I marveled with joy and melancholy at their beauty and majesty.

From Stella Point, feeling energetic, I pushed ahead of the team as the trail gradually gained elevation. After only about twenty minutes, I arrived at the true summit. There, the famous sign says, "Congratulations! You are now at Uhuru Peak, Africa's highest point and the world's tallest free-standing mountain." I again thanked God for enabling me to experience this incredible journey. I stood in awe of His majesty atop one of His great mountains. Moments like this are once in a lifetime, yet I wish every person on Earth could experience them.

The rest of my team joined me about twenty minutes later, and we took the obligatory photos of group and individual celebratory pictures. One person on our team struggled to breathe, and with gratitude (and amazement) I saw Denmo had, indeed, hauled that oxygen tank all the way to the summit. Without it, this lady might not have made it down. That's no exaggeration. Kobi and Bolu quickly took our oxygen-saturation readings, and my oxygen level turned out to be higher than Kobi's, which I think surprised him. He admitted that had never happened before. I just explained the truth, which is that I have been genetically blessed to do well at high altitudes. I smiled and reminded him that's why I did not need the Diamox. For the first time, Kobi cracked a wide, warm smile. "Yes." He grinned. "You proved me wrong, and I am proud of you!" I grinned back.

We hung out on the summit for about an hour, as the temperature was around twenty degrees Fahrenheit with no wind. We then headed back to Stella Point and began back down the mountain. The descent back to Barafu Camp is essentially sliding down a scree slope and reminded me of going down certain 14,000-foot peaks in Colorado, like Mount Bross. The descent from Stella Point should have only taken about two hours, but one lady in our group really struggled to make it down the scree. Too afraid to let herself slide on the loose rock, the guides had to help her down, step by step. I'll admit this frustrated the rest of us, as we were eager to get off the scree and back into Barafu Camp for a break and some lunch. Regardless, though, we were a team, so I just took a slow slide down the slope and tried to enjoy myself. Finally, after three hours, we made it into the camp.

We quickly ate lunch, then packed up our gear. We all wanted to hike another four hours down to Mweka Camp at about 9,500 feet. Although tired and not looking forward to more hiking, I reasoned since it was all downhill, it wouldn't be too bad. As we traveled down the trail to Mweka, I noticed some interesting contraptions alongside the trail. They looked like stretchers of sorts—basically, metal frames balanced on a fat bicycle tire. The guides explained these were used to transport injured climbers down the mountain, which made me glad I did not have to experience that unique ride.

Finally, we arrived at Mweka Camp back in the rainforest. After being in the alpine temperatures of higher elevations, Mweka felt humid and extremely hot. I slept well, though, and the next morning we received a wonderful, unexpected treat. All the guides and porters put on a mini show, singing and dancing to show us some of their African culture. We were all charmed and moved by this incredible gesture—the proverbial cherry on the top of a perfect expedition. I quietly thanked God again for this incredible experience.

The hike down through the rainforest took about three and a half hours, and while we saw plenty of birds, to our disappointment, we still saw no other wildlife.

Maybe we were too noisy. Usually, I am happy to be at the end of a climb, but a bit of sadness came over me when we reached our endpoint, the Mweka Gate at 5,000 feet of elevation. We signed out with the park authorities and received our certificates for reaching the summit of Kilimanjaro. We then headed back to our hotel in Moshi for a much-needed hot shower and night's rest.

The prior few days had been some of the best and most memorable of my life, but I wouldn't allow even a little sadness at the climb's conclusion. Another journey awaited me, and it promised another extraordinary adventure.

The next morning, a different guide from Tusker picked me up to spend the next five days on a wildlife safari through three of Tanzania's national parks.

CHAPTER 11

The Cradle of Life

I COULD HARDLY BELIEVE HOW BLESSED I WAS. I HAD just summited the iconic Kilimanjaro, one of my dream climbs, and was about to fulfill the second half of that dream: an African wildlife safari! The first stop on my safari schedule was Lake Manyara National Park, a small national park adjacent to . . . Lake Manyara! This is a soda lake, which means it is high in alkalinity and rich mineral compounds, like bicarbonate of soda. The lake fills with water during the rainy season but often gets little or no water inflow during the dry season. September, unfortunately, is the lake's dry season, and I would say it was only a quarter full. Still, Lake Manyara is surrounded by a rich diversity of wildlife, including many species of birds like yellow-billed storks, white-necked cormorants, pelicans, and Egyptian geese, which you do not see in parks that aren't adjacent to water.

I checked into the Kirurumu Manyara Tented Lodge, which was a new concept to me. The lodge sets on a high ridge with luxury canvas tents overlooking the entire park. There are twenty-seven of these tented rooms, and while they are actual tents, they are as luxurious as any fine hotel in which I have stayed. My room had a soft, comfortable, king-size bed—with the requisite mosquito netting—and a lush bathroom with double sinks, a toilet, and a spacious shower. You would never know you are in a "tent" once you are inside, but there remains a certain wild, adventurous feel to the entire experience.

After checking in and having lunch, the time had finally arrived for my first wildlife safari. My guide explained the "Big Five" animals of Africa to me. These five animals are the largest and most regal animals on a continent full of majestic, exotic wildlife. Our goal for the following five days would be to see at least one of each of the Big Five: elephant, Cape buffalo, rhinoceros, leopard and the king of the savannah, the mighty lion. My guide said we would almost definitely see elephants, Cape buffalo, and lions, but leopards are shy and elusive, and sadly, rhinos have been poached almost to extinction. (Poaching is a *huge* problem in Africa, and I highly recommend reading up on the issues and getting involved in helping to fight it.) I said a quick, silent prayer to God that if it was His will, He would grant me the privilege of seeing all of the Big Five.

Off we went in a raised safari truck, with our guide carrying an obligatory .30-06 bolt-action rifle, capable of pulling down literally any size of animal. This is a necessary precaution and a firm reminder I was on the wild African plain. Almost immediately, we came upon a herd of about twenty elephants in the jungle by the lake. I was utterly awestruck and instantly transported back to a time in childhood when my parents took me on the Jungle Cruise ride at Disneyland. I remember being enthralled at how lifelike the animatronic animals were. But I could now see how much more splendid real elephants were, up close and personal. For the umpteenth time, I quickly thanked God for this life-changing blessing He was bestowing on me.

We took many pictures, admiring the size and wild beauty of the animals. Eventually, the elephants wandered off. We continued driving and were blessed to see many other kinds of wildlife that afternoon, including scores of monkeys and baboons, zebras, plenty of gorgeous birds, and more elephants. I sighed with joy. A magnificent tone had been set for the next few days. That night, in the dining hall, I had a delicious dinner that included wild game, then retired to my comfortable tent and slept like a Mopani log.

The next day, we headed out to Ngorongoro Crater National Park, which is also a World Heritage Site. This awe-inspiring crater is a 110-square-mile volcanic caldera, which collapsed over two-million years ago and is completely encircled by 2,000-foot sheer walls. The crater floor is now a verdant paradise with over 30,000 head of wild game, stalked by lions, jackals, hyenas, cheetahs, and leopards. Ngorongoro is one of the few places on Earth where you can still see the rare black rhino in their natural habitat.

On our way to Ngorongoro, we stopped at a Maasai village. The Maasai people are one of the more famous African tribes who still live as they have for centuries. Their huts are made of buffalo dung (it's apparently quite durable), and they're always close to a water source so the women can fetch water in huge pots they expertly balance on their heads. They do this at dawn and dusk every day, while the men tend their cattle herds, always keeping a vigilant eye out for lion attacks. These people mesmerized me. They allowed us to go into the village. There, the males of the tribe performed a uniquely Maasai dance where they leap as high as they can off the ground—which is ridiculously high. I genuinely don't believe any NBA players can leap higher than some of these Maasai, as their vertical clearance must have been thirty-six to forty-eight inches.

They invited me to join in with them, which I did, and I quickly embarrassed myself with a pathetic six- to eight-inch vertical leap. The Maasai are renowned for their colorful clothing, which is mostly red. These Maasai were also adorned with all sorts of beautiful, intricate jewelry. I had the chance to go into one of their dung huts, and it surprised me that it did not smell at all. There were no windows, only a hole in the roof to let wood-fire smoke out, so little light entered, which made it quite dark. Eight- to ten-foot sticks about four inches apart surrounded the entire camp, with a gate at the entrance made out of sticks roped together. At night, they bring the cattle inside the gate, then it is closed to protect them from marauding lions.

I came upon some Maasai selling some of their arts and crafts in the village. That excited me because it gave me a chance to browse through their various wares while chatting and laughing with all the vendors. Then I saw it—an intricately beaded Maasai war club that I knew I wanted. I bought it immediately and admired my new ornamental weapon as the young Maasai men around gave approving nods for my choice. I still treasure that club. As I thanked the vendor and prepared to make my way back to the group, one of the grandmothers of the village came up and gave me a beautiful bracelet she had made out of tiny beads, solely as a gesture of goodwill. Moved by her kindness, I immediately tried to insist she take some money for it. She firmly refused. I wore that bracelet for three years as a remembrance of that great day. Sadly, the wire on it finally broke.

I said my goodbyes grudgingly, feeling like these people were already part of my heart, in some deeper way. We then headed up to our lodge at the top of the crater and checked in. This lodge was a regular hotel. I found it fascinating that there were warning signs all around the grounds to not walk at night because elephants and Cape buffalo tended to wander onto the hotel property. I knew I did not want to startle a group of either of these animals at night. I had another scrumptious lunch, then we headed out to journey down into the crater.

Driving on a winding road that, at times, had sheer, vertical drop-offs, it took us about forty-five minutes to get from the top of the crater to the bottom. The ride both unnerved and exhilarated me at the same time! When we arrived at the bottom, I realized how huge the crater when I looked at the dirt roads that crisscrossed it. One of the most amazing experiences of my life followed. If climbing the Matterhorn was the greatest day of my life, being at the bottom of the Ngorongoro Crater was the second greatest day. Immediately, we came up to a pond full of hippopotamuses. There had to have been twenty to thirty of them. Completely enthralled, I asked my guide if I could go near the pond; he nodded but warned sternly, "Not too close." I cautiously made my way up to the water and got within twenty feet from the edge of the pond. If I had known at the time that hippo run faster than any man and are responsible for the most human deaths by animals *by far*, I probably wouldn't have been so brave. But I'm glad I was!

We then traveled on and saw vast herds of zebra, elephant, wildebeest, and many other hooved mammals, far too many to describe or count. The array of glorious color and beauty astounded me. We saw two Cape buffalo, so that made two of the Big Five. They were huge—way bigger than they look on *National Geographic!* They grazed and chewed as they cast me their disinterested looks. I couldn't stop smiling and fervently hoped I might see all of the Big Five.

Continuing our drive, we suddenly came upon a young male lion casually snoozing within four feet of the road. We stopped, and from the protection of our Land Rover I snapped pictures literally four feet away from a wild, adult male lion who didn't seem to have a care in the world. He didn't even move, except for swishing his tail once in a while in a futile effort to deter the flies buzzing around him. One can't explain moments like this. I can say I was in awe and could only marvel at how magnificent God's creation was, but it is really something one must experience. Words simply fail the moment. I had seen three of the Big Five. As we kept driving, we saw countless animals, including another male lion surrounded by three huge lionesses. I was in *heaven*!

Suddenly, the guide stopped. With his experience, he knew exactly what to look for and would spy completely hidden or camouflaged wildlife. His eyesight was *incredible*. He pointed and told me to look quietly to my left. I turned and there, about a hundred yards away, stood a magnificent black rhino. For several minutes, I stared at the great beast, hypnotized by his size, prehistoric "armor", and giant horns, all juxtaposed against his seemingly docile nature. A deep sadness fell upon me as I thought of how these exquisite creatures were being hunted to extinction because of their horns. I prayed God would protect this big guy and all his buddies and females, then thanked the Lord again for this rare and thrilling experience.

I'd crossed off four of the Big Five from my checklist and confidently believed the next three days would hold plenty of time to see a leopard.

After seeing literally thousands of magnificent animals, we drove back to the top of the crater. Eating dinner at an outside restaurant, I witnessed the sun as it set over the crater. As the huge, African evening sun slowly dropped on the horizon, it cast its warm glow over the landscape, down 2,000 feet into the floor of the crater, as if giving a smiling salute to the memory of all the gorgeous, happy animals I had seen down there that day. As darkness slowly crept across the crater from one side of the floor to the other, I could not shake my smile. Superlatives cannot begin to describe the moment.

But I hadn't had enough. After a restful night filled with dreams of stunning rhinos, lions, and hippos, I awoke, smiling again, and got up and got ready. My guide and I ventured back down into the crater for more of the incredible wildlife. A cheetah sprinting in the distance provided the highlight of the day. The area felt like Disney World times ten, except it truly was as if God orchestrated the show, giving me a look at His glorious creations.

I saw my first hyenas, which appeared to be curious, if somewhat mangy, animals. Native Africans are often superstitious about hyenas; some believe they are the animal companions of witches. Even those Africans who do not believe these outlandish tales regard the hyena as a repulsive animal. I was just happy to see one slinking around. I saw a few more lions, including two regal young males walking next to a streambed together. I did not see another rhino, which made it more special that I had seen one the day before. And still no leopard.

As I look back at this day, I can't think of a time when I was happier or felt freer. I kept thinking back to Bolu's words on Kilimanjaro, "Mark, look at this view. This is my office. . ." At that moment, I truly embraced the challenge of living an extraordinary life. *And it felt like I was walking hand-in-hand with God.* People are different in terms of where they feel closest to God. For some, it is at church, or at a Bible study, or maybe a church camp. For others, it might be in their bedrooms or on their knees in prayer. For me, it is when I am out in the middle of His creations, immersed in everything that carries His gorgeous, divinely creative, unmistakable signature. And to me, there is no more divine place in creation than the Ngorongoro Crater.

We spent the day in the crater, roaming around, searching for new animals to enjoy. When it was finally time to go up to the top for the night, I couldn't bear to leave. I honestly believe I would be content to spend months, even years, exploring this crater. Grudgingly, I returned to the lodge and had another spectacularly delicious dinner, then retired to my room for the night.

The next day, we headed to my final park, Tarangire National Park. Tarangire is a grassland park, similar to the more famous Serengeti. According to my guide, it is a better place to view wildlife in the dry season than the Serengeti, which is better in the wet season. This park is renowned for its large population of elephants and iconic baobab trees, which are easily recognizable from any show or movie about Africa. Africans often call the baobab the "upside-down tree" because they appear to be planted "upside-down" with what looks like roots sticking out in the air (they're actually the tree's branches). The park is also famous for the giant termite mounds that dot the landscape.

Tarangire did not disappoint. During our safari, we saw hundreds of elephants, some as close as ten feet away from our vehicle. This is nothing to underestimate, as an agitated male elephant can easily charge and tip over a Land Rover if he feels like it. We gazed upon herds of zebra, wildebeest, and Cape buffalo numbering in the thousands. Dozens of giraffe and other hooved mammals like the tiny dik-dik, bouncy impala, and ginormous eland, as well as many gazelles who graced us with their presence. Various kinds of monkeys, mongoose, and baboons engaging in all kinds of activities from sleeping to playing to eating. One of the most venomous and aggressive snakes in the world—the infamous black mamba—slithered right in front of our vehicle as it quickly crossed the road. Our guide reacted with displeasure. I learned that most Africans *hate* snakes, holding some of the same superstitions that cause them to revile hyena, but also because snakebites are tough to deal with out in the wild. Later on, a pregnant cheetah walked right in front of our vehicle, then plonked down on the ground and casually observed us from about thirty feet away. What a thrill to see her!

I am not doing the park's birds justice. There are over 550 species of birds there, so it is truly a bird lover's paradise. I am normally not that into birds, but they were of such indescribably beautiful colors, that soon my camera filled with picture after picture of some of these astonishing creatures. In contrast to the myriad birds with stunning color and beauty, we also saw huge, black vultures hanging out in the baobab trees. Almost thirty vultures perched in one tree, silhouetted against the sun, either waiting for an animal to die or searching the plain for a carcass. This was as iconic a picture of Africa as you could get.

The biggest thrill of the day occurred on the drive out to a lone baobab tree. I don't know how our guide spotted them, but a pride of over twenty lions lay at the base of the tree. Most were adult females with their male and female cubs. The sight of them rendered me speechless. *Thank you, God! Thank you so much for allowing me to see this!*

Still no leopard, though.

Another amazing tent camp became that night's residence, except this one had a twist! They warned us not to go outside in the dark because of *the lions*! What a place! The guides assured everyone the lions would not bother with our tents, but that's like telling a person to not think of a lion. That night, once again, I prayed that I might see a leopard, no matter how elusive they are. That was the last thing I remember before falling happily asleep.

We headed out to enjoy the last day. Once more, I prayed God might grant me the privilege of seeing a leopard. I had seen four of the Big Five. I couldn't leave without gazing upon a beautiful leopard! We drove around, and I got to witness a special sight of a different kind. Three female lions were feeding on a freshly killed zebra while a hyena circled them, trying to get at their prey. I almost had to pinch myself to make sure I had not fallen asleep on my couch during a *National Geographic* special. The hyena kept getting closer and closer, then, like lightning, one of the female lions would charge at him, sending him scurrying, but never far. He knew his range precisely and kept circling and circling. After a while, the lions simply ignored him. Sensing his moment, he dashed in, grabbed a chunk of raw meat, and dashed out. One of the lionesses chased him for about a hundred feet, but he safely escaped with his prize.

With only about an hour left on my final day in this miraculous place, I began to wonder why God hadn't given me the opportunity to see a leopard and became a bit disappointed, perhaps even somewhat downcast. More than anything, I didn't want to leave, but I really wished I had seen a leopard. Then I realized I was being silly and ungrateful. I had seen four of the most majestic animals in the world and had experienced the trip of my dreams. Africa had revealed herself to me in all her mysterious and magical splendor.

Suddenly my guide stomped his foot on the brakes, jerking me out of my thoughts. He grabbed his binoculars. Excited, he handed the binoculars to me, pointing out a tree in the distance. "Focus on the limb sticking out horizontally, about fifteen feet high." I nearly shouted for joy. Sure enough, sprawled over the thick limb l saw a sleek, gorgeous leopard. Transfixed, I watched as the leopard lifted his head, glanced around, then chilled back on his branch. He stayed like that for several minutes, then stretched lazily, stood up, and effortlessly climbed down the tree and vanished into the tall grass. What an incredible sight! I wanted to run around and shout, but I just smiled and silently thanked God for giving me the desires of my heart, yet again and in full. I had seen every one of the Big Five! *What a way to finish my trip!*

I praised the guide for having such keen eyesight. When he dropped me off at a hotel in the city of Arusha a couple of hours later, I gave him an extra big tip.

I waited for a few hours at the hotel before heading out to catch my flight out of Kilimanjaro Airport to Amsterdam and then home. While I waited, I genuinely wished I could stay in Africa for much, much longer. I reflected on my trip. Three weeks in Africa fundamentally impacted my thinking in terms of what is important in life. Something about the natural, wild freedom of Africa—the warm, innocent, hospitable love of the people—made me determined to live my life differently, be more willing to taking risks, and trust more in God. He had made Himself so real to me during this trip. I became even more committed to embracing the challenge of living an extraordinary life. At the same moment, I also knew I had to embrace life wherever I was and practice gratitude every day for the blessings God provides.

CHAPTER 12

The Silent Climb

ONE OF THE MOST IMPRESSIVE MOUNTAIN MASSIFS in Colorado is in the southern high deserts of the state, just north of the small town of Alamosa. (The term "massif" means a compact geological group of mountains which are connected together.) There are three 14,000-foot peaks (fourteeners) in this massif: Little Bear (one of the most difficult Colorado fourteeners to climb), Ellingwood Point, and the mighty Mount Blanca, which is the high point of the massif at 14,351 feet.

In 1993, my friend Todd lived in Dallas, while I lived in Phoenix. We hadn't hung out since college, so we decided to meet in Southern Colorado to climb Blanca. By this time, Todd and I had surpassed the level of experience we'd had in the Longs Peak days, but wisdom gained told us not to underestimate Blanca.

Weather can be an issue, and loose and falling rock and ice can be present higher up on the mountain. Every so often, Blanca reminds enthusiasts it is not to be trifled with when it claims an unwitting victim.

In July, Todd and I made our respective long drives and met in Alamosa. We figured we would grab a motel room, eat dinner, then go to bed early for a 5:00 a.m. start. When we arrived in town, we were dismayed to discover motel rooms within a fifty-mile radius of Alamosa were booked. A huge summer festival meant everything had filled for the weekend. If not planning ahead wasn't mistake enough, we then made the foolish decision to drive up to the trailhead and sleep in Todd's truck.

What an utterly miserable night. Even in the high desert, mosquitoes plagued us. The insane heat, way too hot to have the windows of the truck closed, meant the second we opened them, mosquitoes ravaged us. It was a no-win situation, which meant neither of us got any sleep. Perhaps we should have heeded that night as an omen.

At 3:00 a.m., we called it quits and started hiking up the road. We had begun our ascent of Mount Blanca.

High on the Blanca Massif lies a gorgeous freshwater lake called Lake Como, at about 11,750 feet of elevation. The road to Lake Como is one of the most infamous four-wheel-drive roads in Colorado. If you don't have a high-clearance, four-wheel-drive vehicle, you have to park in the high desert and do an eighteen-mile, round-trip hike to climb Blanca. If you do have a good four-wheel-drive vehicle, you can drive about three miles farther before you have to stop. Only ATVs and specially modified short-wheel-drive Jeeps can potentially make it all the way to the lake. Unfortunately, having only Todd's two-wheel-drive truck meant we'd have to do the full eighteen miles.

Despite the extra trek, we reached Lake Como around sunrise. The lake is idyllically situated beneath the three 14,000-foot summits and is one-hundred percent postcard material. The view is inspiring. After taking in the scenery, we continued up to Ellingwood Point. Now, smart people hike to the lake the first day, then spend the night, and climb whatever summits they are chasing the next day. They might hang out at the lake or head down on the third day. Unfortunately, Todd and I didn't fit into the smart-people category on that trip. We planned to do it all in a day . . . on no sleep.

The climb up Ellingwood is straightforward and looks much harder than it actually is, but on so little sleep I already struggled. This can make climbing dangerous. There isn't one trail you must follow to the summit; you can choose from a variety of routes, and they all end up on a big ridge just before the summit. Around 8:00 a.m., we made it to Ellingwood Point's summit and rested for a while. I did not want to admit I had already lost all enthusiasm to summit Blanca. Because Todd didn't say anything, we kept going, heading down to the saddle between Ellingwood and Blanca.

At this point, Todd and I stopped, looked at each other and, without saying a word, knew we were not going to summit Blanca that day. We were too spent from lack of sleep. Slowly, defeated, we headed back down to the lake, knowing we had to slog an additional seven miles down that horrid road to get to the truck.

By the time we reached the lower portion of the road, the temperature had risen to the sweltering nineties, which caused the unpleasant sensation of being baked alive. I could see the truck in the distance, but it seemed like we would never reach it.

The Blanca Massif had kicked our butts. Todd and I share a hatred of defeat, so we vowed to return.

The following summer, Mark, Todd, Bill (Todd's older brother), and I decided to meet in Colorado to do a fourteener trip, one of which would be Todd's and my revenge climb on Blanca. Todd and Bill drove up from Texas again, while I picked up Mark from a conference he attended in Santa Fe. Since Todd and I had failed on Blanca the year before, we were eager to give it another go. I knew his determination to conquer this peak matched mine.

This time, we made sure to secure motel reservations in Alamosa long in advance. We planned to do Blanca, then drive up to a town in Central Colorado called Salida and do a few fourteeners in the Sawatch Range. We would then do Pikes Peak, catch a Colorado Rockies game in Denver, and end our trip with Longs Peak. We foresaw a fun but grueling week.

We all met in Alamosa, had a great dinner full of laughs, and retired to our respective hotel rooms for a 2:30 a.m. wake-up call, as we wanted to be at the trailhead by 4:00. Once again, we had to park at the bottom of the mountain as we didn't have four-wheel drive, which meant a long, eighteen-mile day ahead.

Our first surprise came at the trailhead where we encountered a search and rescue team preparing to go up the mountain. When we inquired what they were looking for, they told us a climber had been missing for three days and was assumed to still be on the mountain. They told us he was a federal judge from Grand Junction, Colorado and an experienced climber who had summited fifty of the fifty-four 14,000-foot peaks in the state. We were all grimly silent. We knew three days missing on Blanca didn't sound good. They asked if we could be on the lookout for him as we went up, and we nodded soberly.

Beginning our hike in the dark with only our headlamps lighting the way, thinking about potentially finding a dead person somewhere on the climb, felt a little eerie. I hoped the guy might still be alive and just too injured to make his way down, but I knew that was a long shot. The sad and frightening reality is, it has long been trendy to "peak bag" Colorado's fourteeners, which lends itself to a unique sort of summit fever that can sometimes have fatal consequences. Colorado's fourteeners attract all kinds of hikers and climbers, some of whom are not experienced and make rookie mistakes (like Todd and I did on Longs). Some are not as fortunate as Todd and I were, and they pay dearly for their mistake. But even for those with experience, when you climb fifty-four peaks, the odds are that something will eventually go wrong at some point. So, while being prepared is always crucial, the reality is you can't prepare for every eventuality. All you can do is pray God protects you when your "eventuality" comes around. I suppose this is the rush of risking your life to do what you love.

We made the arduous trek up the seemingly never-ending Lake Como road, finally reaching the lake just after dawn. We rested for a while, then headed above Lake Como to continue hiking until we reached the timberline at 12,000 feet. We pushed up to a group of smaller lakes, finally gaining a series of ledges at 13,000 feet. Then we heard the whomp-whomping of the search helicopter overhead. The atmosphere instantly became tense.

It made sense for the helicopter to search in this area because traversing the ledges is one of the trickiest and most dangerous parts of the climb. The drop-off from either side of the rocky crags is between twenty-five feet to eighty feet—a near-certain fatal fall in any scenario. With Todd on point, we kept pushing up, thankful for the good weather, our steps extra careful with the audible reminder from the helicopter of the dangers of the terrain.

Suddenly, Todd stopped dead in his tracks.

We all stopped behind him, wondering why he had frozen. Todd turned back to us, his face a ghostly white. "I found him," he whispered. I followed his gaze to the rocks about thirty feet below, where I saw the man lying at an awkward angle, eyes still open, staring straight up at nothing. I knew he was dead.

What a strange feeling to see him. He could have been any of us on any of our climbing trips. We all just stared in a mix of shock and horror. I noticed he had on rain gear, so the first logical thought that broke through was, *I wonder if he slipped on some slick rock and fell?* I also remembered the search-and-rescue team had told us he had been climbing solo. Going solo in extreme weather without anyone to help or bounce decisions off is a bad combination. Although warned we might find him, the discovery still stunned us.

Bill snapped out of the trance first and started waving and yelling at the rescue helicopter. This jolted us all back to reality, and we began wildly waving our arms to get the helicopter's attention. Well, all of us except Todd. He kept staring at the dead climber.

The helicopter crew did not see us for a good while. It took some time, but after about ten or fifteen minutes, the helicopter turned in the right direction and flew close enough to see us waving. It immediately soared toward us, and we pointed to where the body lay. The chopper wiggled to acknowledge us, then quickly descended to land next to Lake Como. The team eventually made it up to where we'd stopped. Not sure what to do, we asked if we could do anything to help. They simply said "no."

We watched in silence as the team prepared a fixed-line to rappel down to the body. Two of them rappelled down and managed to load and secure the fallen climber onto a gurney. They then lifted the gurney up to the ledge and the team carried him to the helicopter to take him off the mountain.

The experience felt unexplainably surreal. I had known of people who died on mountains I had climbed, but at that point, I had never seen a body on a mountain before—especially a person so recently deceased, so close, and on the same trail. Maybe this climber being a fellow Coloradan and it being a mountain so near to my home made the whole experience even more unnerving.

After the search and rescue team left, we remained somber for a few pensive moments, not quite sure what to say or do. Eventually, we knew we had to keep going to successfully summit and get back down the mountain in good time. Mark, Bill, and I prepared to keep going up the mountain, but as we started back up the ledges, we saw that Todd couldn't move. He seemed glued in place.

Finding the dead climber's body had spooked Todd so badly, he couldn't go up or down. Like a child on a high building or those people who freeze on a glass bridge after looking straight down into the canyon, he couldn't move. Each of us, in turn, tried to convince Todd he would be fine and told him we were all together, looking out for danger, and reminded him the weather was great. But he wouldn't budge. I could understand his dilemma; the terrible reality of death had gripped us all. Maybe because Todd had found the climber first the grim fear of his own mortality had seized him and wouldn't let go.

I wondered if Todd and Bill losing their parents at such a young age had created some residual fear. Since Todd's older brother, Bill, had taken care of him when their parents died, Todd trusted him more than anyone in the world. So eventually, Bill convinced Todd to turn around and head back down the mountain.

As Todd relented and began back down the ledge with his older brother guiding him, Bill looked back and told us he and Todd would head down to Lake Como and wait for us there. This surreal moment added to the grave experience.

Mark and I exchanged a glance that said, *What a day!* We briefly wondered if we should just call it quits. We were concerned for our buddy, but there wasn't really a lot we could do to help him feel better. Plus, we knew he was in good hands. Because of the perfect weather, Mark and I decided to continue to the summit.

We traversed the ledges, then gained Blanca's northwest ridge at 13,750 feet. We scrambled up the ridge and did some bouldering to reach the summit. Neither one of us said a word during the entire climb up to the summit, both of us lost in our own thoughts about what we had just witnessed.

The view from the top made us feel better. As expected, the scene was spectacular, as Blanca is the highest point in that part of the state. I took a long moment to savor the view. For me, views like this are the reward for climbing. That day, it sank in a little deeper it was also a reward for risking my life to scale mountains. The thought did not taint the view . . . it enhanced it. I became extra grateful for what I had been given. I thought back to when Todd and I were only eighteen and had embarked on our foolish venture up Longs

Peak in sneakers and thin sweaters. It could so easily have cost us our lives, but yet again, God had protected us, and we escaped unscathed.

I began to deeply ponder the day. The climber who died on Blanca had been experienced, successfully summiting much more technical and dangerous mountains, but for some reason, he had died on Blanca. He was only four summits short of his goal of climbing all of Colorado's fourteeners. In a moment like that, all kinds of questions race through a climber's mind. It would be foolish not to ask yourself if *you* were prone to the same errors. *Why had this happened? What mistake had he made? Why was he climbing solo? Did he get too confident? Too sure of himself? Was he overcome with summit fever, maybe getting caught in a storm when he should have turned around? Did he die instantly, or did he suffer up here all alone on this mountain?* These questions whirled through my mind as we sat on the summit, gazing out at the breathtaking view.

Our rest on the summit had somehow broken the spell of silence, so as we started back down, Mark and I began to discuss these things, futilely trying to make sense of why the tragedy occurred. One thing we were fairly sure of: the man died doing what he loved. At least we hoped so. I somehow knew he had a love of the mountains as strong as my own, that the reason he'd set out to climb all the fourteeners in Colorado wasn't just to accomplish a noble goal, that doing so was his passion. His love. His burning desire, deep within his heart. I hoped he felt the same peace, serenity, and inner contentment that I do whenever I am in the mountains. Maybe, just maybe, he felt the same closeness to God I experience when I am on one of my beloved mountains.

Yet again, I had to consider that a solo journey is a risky journey. This federal judge may not have died if he had not been climbing alone, but no one can know for sure. Still, the more I thought about it, the main takeaway was that a life worth living can sometimes involve risk. Even though this man ended up dying, he took the risks to do what he loved, and I know, without a doubt, he loved it. He was out in nature, trying to conquer all the fourteeners in Colorado, and sure, unfortunately, it didn't work out and he paid the ultimate price, but I'll bet anything that if you asked him, "Was it worth it?" he would answer with an emphatic "yes." This is why I believe so strongly in pursuing your extraordinary life; you never know when your number will be called, but when it is, at least you can look back and say, "I loved what I was doing, and that gave my life meaning."

As we made our descent, the culmination of the day's thoughts struck me: we are all mortal, and we all have a limited time on this Earth. Yes, there is a risk to everything we do, but in the end, it is appointed unto every single man and woman to die—not even the Son of God escaped death. Since we have no idea when that moment will come, wouldn't you rather spend your precious time doing something you love?

Wouldn't you rather embrace a life that is extraordinary?

Ask yourself if the regret of losing everything in

pursuit of your deepest desire would be worse than the regret of never trying.

What are you passionate about? What in your life is worth dying for? Could it be God has placed a desire deep in your heart as part of His calling to you? A desire that's part of *who* He has made you to be? Could it even be a way to somehow serve Him?

Are you willing to risk alleged comfort and security to embrace the challenge of pursuing an extraordinary life?

CHAPTER 13

The Frozen Moment

AT 14,505 FEET, MOUNT WHITNEY, LOCATED IN THE Sierra Nevada Mountains in Eastern California, is the highest mountain in the lower forty-eight states (below Alaska). It looms just west of a little town called Lone Pine and in recent years has become a popular summit among American climbers. In fact, so many people want to hike or climb Mount Whitney, California found it necessary to implement a permit system to restrict the number of people on the mountain at any given time.

The Hiker's Route up Mount Whitney is an extremely long, but fairly straightforward hike once the snow has melted (which may take until late July, depending on the snowpack). To complete this hike in one day is quite an accomplishment, as it is an almost twenty-three-mile round-trip, with over 6,000 feet of elevation gain. I have attempted this day-hike four times, only three of which I have successfully completed. Besides my hikes in the Grand Canyon, those were some of the longest and toughest day-hikes I have ever done. And the Hiker's Route is Whitney's easy path.

I'd long ago set the goal of attempting a winter ascent of Mount Whitney up the Mountaineer's Route (M.R.). This route is not a challenge to be taken lightly, and a winter ascent becomes about as technical a climb as on any of the seven summits. The M.R. is shorter than the hiker's trail, which means it's much steeper. The grave fact of the matter is that there have been many more climbers killed on the M.R. than the trail, even though it has far less activity.

A winter ascent of the M.R. is something to be undertaken only by highly experienced mountaineers skilled in technical, winter mountaineering. The climber must have extensive, real-world practice with crampons and an ice ax, he or she must understand avalanche danger, and the climber needs significant experience with snow and ice rope work. Experience, maturity, and situational awareness, knowing when to back off if the conditions so warrant, are all crucial, too. The underlying key to any technical climb, however, is *preparedness*.

I knew I had to research this climb, study what equipment would be needed, and be sure I prepared for any eventuality. As I researched, solemn reminders of the people who had died on my various climbs came to mind. I quietly thought back to finding the climber on

Mount Blanca twenty years ago. I'll never know what caused him to fall, but one certainty endured: I could never become so confident that I'd believe I could not make the same mistakes, especially on a mountain like Whitney. To underestimate the M.R.'s winter ascent is an almost sure guarantee of fatality. Unfortunately, far too many climbers have made that error.

My climbing experiences in Nepal and Alaska gave me the confidence to climb in winter conditions. I also had the technical skills to attempt this challenge. Even so, I needed at least two other climbers with the same kind of experience. Around the middle of 2016, I started contacting my climbing buddies. I soon discovered that finding two guys who wanted to climb this mountain in the winter, and on Christmas Day, no less, wouldn't be an easy task. Around fall, I finally convinced two of my friends to do the climb. I'd scheduled the climb for Christmas Day because that was the only time I could be sure we'd all be off work and that nothing in our busy schedules would crop up while we were thousands of feet up on an icy mountain. At least, that was my hope.

I'd met both of these guys while enrolled in the MBA program at the University of Arizona. We all shared a love of hiking, climbing, and simply spending time in the mountains. I had also done a good deal of camping with them and knew I could trust these guys, both as friends and as skillful, experienced climbers.

Carl grew up in a small Nebraska town and graduated from the University of Nebraska, which guaranteed he would be a huge Nebraska Cornhuskers football fan.

Carl is one of the nicest, most down-to-earth guys you could ever meet. He is exactly what you would expect from someone born and raised in a wholesome little town in Middle America. He has spent his entire career in marketing for a large Japanese car company.

John was raised in Tucson and is a University of Arizona grad. Once a highly competitive swimmer, he has remained extremely fit. John is also one of the smartest people I have ever met in my life.

I couldn't have asked for two better climbing companions for Whitney's infamous M.R.

Carl and John flew into Vegas, where I picked them up, then we drove back to Ridgecrest, California, where I lived at the time. We hung out and caught up for a day, then drove to Lone Pine that afternoon and up to Whitney Portal, where we camped on Christmas Eve. The mountain's roads were clear enough that we could drive all the way through to the trailhead at Whitney Portal, which is at 8,000 feet. Starting at Whitney Portal makes the approach significantly shorter, for which we were grateful. During much of the winter, if the snows are heavy, you cannot get close to the portal, which adds miles to the climb.

At 5:30 a.m., before leaving the vehicle, we double-checked our gear, ensuring we had our ropes, crampons, ice axes, and climbing helmets (which, incidentally, I rarely wear). Using our snowshoes and headlamps, we trekked up to Iceberg Lake in about four hours, which felt like pretty good time. Calculating from that rate, we reasoned we could do the climb in a day, so we made that our goal. Since most of the approach is through avalanche terrain, however, we weren't going to be fanatical about this goal.

The climb got tougher and colder as we continued upward. We finally reached a point where we had to trade our snowshoes for crampons and ice axes. This is the point at which the climb gets "real." By the time the sun rose over the Inyo Mountains to the east, bitter cold had crept in, but once it did, the weather became perfect. The sky remained cloudless and, thankfully, the sun warmed us as we climbed. As the sun rose on the horizon to warm us, the risk of an avalanche increased. We didn't worry, though, as we believed we had made good time before the sun could melt too much of the ice and snow.

When we reached the last (and steepest) 500 feet of the climb, we decided to rope up, as a vertical, icy chute rose ahead. This becomes as technical a climb as one on any major mountain. I took the lead and used my ice ax and crampons to gain purchase and slowly climb the ice wall to the summit. We had been climbing a short while when, without warning, a piece of ice (or ice-encrusted rock) weighing about thirty pounds suddenly broke off high up on the mountain and tumbled through the air toward me.

People talk about how things happen so fast in desperate moments, but until you experience that moment when your life depends on you reacting swiftly, you really have no idea how fast things can happen. Plus, you tend to freeze.

I saw the rock but could do nothing. It hit me square on the head. I have no memory of what happened, but John and Carl tell me I was instantly struck unconscious, dropping my ice ax as I fell off the chute. Thankfully, John was belaying me, and his technique and equipment were perfectly sound, so I only fell about ten feet before the line jerked me to a stop, after which I swung limp along the side of the ice wall.

I have climbed several of the highest and most technical mountains in the world, but it wasn't even the highest mountain on the North American mainland that almost claimed my life. As I said previously, I rarely wear a climbing helmet. For some reason, on Mount Whitney, I did. I have *zero* doubt that helmet saved my life. Preparedness had saved me.

After about five minutes, I slowly regained consciousness. Despite my friends screaming at the top of their lungs to see if I was okay, for a minute or so I had no idea where I was. As the confusion gradually cleared, I realized I was hanging from a rope on an icy chute. I still had no clue where I was, or why I was hanging off the side of a mountain, but my instincts kicked in and I dug my crampons into the ice. I realized I had no ice ax, so I cautiously punched my fists into the ice to gain purchase. Then, sluggishly moving sideways across the chute face in what felt like an eternity, I moved about fifteen feet to reach a shelf where I could rest and reduce the severe exposure. My head pounded like a sledgehammer had hit me, and the sunlight pierced my eyes like daggers.

I managed to dig into my pack and pop four Ibuprofen, hoping they would at least take the edge off the pain. No doubt I had a severe concussion because I felt extremely groggy, nauseous, and somewhat disoriented. Carl and John climbed to the shelf and sat beside me, both failing to hide their panic. They explained what had happened. I dozily shook my head, thanking God for protecting my life.

After resting for a good while, we discussed what to do next. I insisted I could make the descent back to Whitney Portal. But I don't think Carl and John believed me. They wanted me to activate my satellite transponder to alert the authorities for an emergency response. I assured them we should only do that as a last option because I was in good enough shape to make the descent. The sight of that boulder hitting their friend in the head must have been traumatic because they weren't sure, even though they knew I could handle a lot. I knew I could do it, though, and eventually convinced them we should start down cautiously, promising if I reached a point where I could not physically go on, we could then activate the transponder.

As we began back down the ice chute, I prayed to God to give me the strength to make it down. I also thanked Him profusely for protecting me on the mountain and, without me even being aware, leading me to climb with a helmet. My friends are not religious, so I prayed to myself, feeling, without a shadow of a doubt, God's presence. I had just survived a direct hit from a thirty-pound falling rock, so I didn't question that He would get the three of us down safely.

I know I continued to pray and give thanks to God the entire way down, but to be honest, I don't remember much of the descent. I remember moving slowly and being grateful for the patience, encouragement, and, at times, physical assistance I received from my friends. I know it took us many hours to descend. When we eventually made it down to the car, we were all exhausted.

Then we faced a new challenge.

We had driven my Nissan Xterra on this trip, which has a manual transmission. No way could I drive back to Ridgecrest, but I urgently needed to get to a hospital, so Carl or John had to drive. Carl had never driven a vehicle with a manual transmission before, and John hadn't touched a manual transmission since Drivers' Ed decades before. Still, he was the most qualified at the moment, so working with what we had, we decided John would drive home.

Predictably, he popped the clutch several times and killed the engine while trying to leave Whitney Portal. I tried not to become stressed, as I worried about how we would make it back. My body screamed that I had to get to the ER quickly. After a few more tries, he jerkily got the vehicle into second gear, and from there, it wasn't too bad to get it into third through fifth gears. I lay back on the seat, finally able to rest a little. As I did, I desperately fought drowsiness because I'd heard of the danger of falling into a coma if you fell asleep after a head injury. But for the literal life of me, I could not stay awake. I fell into a deep sleep, only vaguely remembering my friend popping the clutch again at a stoplight in Lone Pine.

As I knew He would, God covered us with His protection and we eventually made it back to Ridgecrest. My friends drove me straight to the emergency room, where the doctor diagnosed me with whiplash and a grade three concussion (the most severe). I had extreme light sensitivity for over a month, and I did not feel totally normal for about two months after that. Yet, I still marvel at God's providence and protection on that mountain. My experience made me that much more sure that if you trust Him, God will not let you go, even when catastrophe strikes. He is always there, and He will protect you. He is a loving Father, and He cares about His children, looking out for us even when we don't realize it. And He wants every man, woman, and child to be His. When you come that close to death, it makes you aware of what is important in life. Although it was a close call, it could have easily been fatal. I will be forever grateful to God, and to my two friends, for successfully getting me off the mountain that day.

You may have already figured out the leadership lesson in this chapter. The fact that I wore a climbing helmet on Mount Whitney saved my life. *Why* I wore a helmet on that climb, I'm not sure (although I claim God's background providence). I *hate* wearing climbing helmets, and there have been many times where I should have worn one and didn't. But thank God, I wore one that day on Whitney, making me adequately prepared when it mattered most.

Your career is probably the most time-consuming

part of your life, but do you take the time to minimize risk? Are you well prepared for any eventuality? Do you know what the risks are to embrace a truly extraordinary life? Make no mistake, this will not happen by accident, and there are many pitfalls along the way. But you can still achieve whatever you want to.

The truth is, whether in climbing or in business, risk exists. You can never eliminate all risk, but you can minimize it by being prepared and having the right equipment. In business, proper due diligence is the equivalent of wearing a climbing helmet. It is guaranteed to minimize the risk.

Often in business, I have seen people use the (non) strategy of "Ready, fire, aim," instead of taking the time to prepare, do their due diligence, *prepare some more*, and then "fire away accurately." Always take the time to ensure your strategy is "Ready, aim, fire!"

Why do leaders make this mistake? Well, I'll talk about it in depth later, but I believe "deal fever" is analogous to "summit fever." In a previous chapter, I mentioned the Rhode Island acquisition. Truth be told, we probably should have never made that acquisition, but our company had deal fever, so despite being hasty and ill-prepared, we went ahead with it. We were simply not mature enough as leaders to make the acquisition intelligently and our lack of preparedness affected many people.

If you do your best to wisely prepare, when the unexpected happens, you'll survive and go on to thrive.

CHAPTER 14

The Greatest Day of My Life

FIRST WENT TO DISNEYLAND AT AGE TWO, AND although I have seen old home movies of that trip, I don't remember any of it. I do remember my next vacation to Disneyland at age seven. On that visit, the Matterhorn Bobsled Ride interested me, but the Disneyland version of the Matterhorn itself captivated me. I'd become a mountain fanatic at a young age. By the age of seven I had started to memorize all the Colorado mountains, and anytime my family took a drive into the ranges, I would tell them I felt like a kid in a candy store (except I am allergic to sugar!).

I had never heard of the Matterhorn until we went to Disneyland, so when I discovered the ride replicated a real mountain in a magical, faraway land called

Switzerland, I became mesmerized. Even more exciting, Disneyland had cast members undertake "expeditions," climbing the Matterhorn during the day. More than wanting to go on any rides, I wanted to sit and watch them climb all day.

On that day I made two promises to myself: I would someday work at Disneyland and be one of those climbers, and I would travel to Switzerland to climb the real Matterhorn. In 1988, I kept my second promise.

I traveled to Italy to study International Business at a school in Milan through a University of Arizona MBA graduate exchange program. The Italian school was called the IPSOA Graduate School of Business. As a young adult, engaging in this new chapter of adventures thrilled me and I felt like a real jetsetter as I traveled to northern Italy for the summer. I would live in an idyllic town called Cernobbio, which rested sleepily on the shores of Lake Como in the foothills of the Italian Alps. The entire experience felt like being inside a dream or playing a lead role in a foreign movie.

I lived with several other U of A students, and each day we took a train from Cernobbio into Milan to study. We had every Friday off, so on Thursday afternoons we could catch a train to travel somewhere in Europe for the long weekend, then return on Sunday. With this in mind, I knew I would take one weekend to travel to the town of Zermatt, Switzerland at the base of the Matterhorn. In August 1988, I did just that to attempt a climb of the iconic mountain.

The train took only a few hours to reach Zermatt

that evening (European public transport is awesome). Arriving in the evening allowed me to experience the wonder of the sun setting over the full 14,692 feet of the looming Matterhorn. To this day, seeing the golden-orange sun slowly bidding all a warm, peaceful night as the glowing red-and-gold backdrop faded behind the shimmering, icy-blue white of the majestic mountain remains the most spectacular sight of my entire life. That stunning contrast is something I wish every man, woman, and child could witness.

Once the sun had mostly descended, still on a natural high from the view, I checked into a little hotel. Looking over some sightseeing brochures while a bit of light remained, I decided to visit the local cemetery in the center of town. This may seem like a macabre choice, but the graveyard was filled with climbers who had lost their lives pursuing their passion. Perhaps as a reminder of my mortality and to honor their memory, I felt drawn to visit the site.

The atmosphere in the graveyard seemed both serene and eerie. It didn't take me long to find climbers' graves. Each headstone bore the name of the mountain on which the climber had perished. Some graves even had little ice-ax reliefs engraved on them. I may have been imagining it, but it seemed like every other headstone exhibited an etched name and an indication the deceased had died climbing the Matterhorn. I will freely admit, in that moment, as I saw the number of dead climbers filling that cemetery, I freaked out. I began to consider changing my plans to hiking around the Matterhorn instead of climbing it. The reality of potentially paying the ultimate price to risk the extraordinary life I had chosen hit me like an avalanche.

Somewhat shaken, I retired to my hotel room, obsessing over the various graves, picturing in my mind's eye what the climbers might have experienced before they died. I knew it didn't take much—just an unfortunate "perfect storm" of events. Discouraged, I decided to pray and decide in the morning.

After a good night of rest, I awoke and remembered where I was. I pulled open the quaint curtains and sunshine flooded the room. What a spectacularly sunny Friday in this gorgeous, little mountain town. I looked out the window and the sight of outdoor adventurers of all kinds milling about the Alpine, cottage-like buildings, complete with colorful flower boxes and log accents, filled me with joy and enthusiasm. I grinned widely, thanking God again for the opportunity to fulfill so many of my heart's longings. My desire to attempt a climb of the Matterhorn instantly renewed.

The town of Zermatt is touristy, but without losing that signature, it has an old-world charm. Despite the volume of tourists, I think Zermatt is one of the best places on Earth. This is because there are no cars in the town, it's filled with picturesque inns, lovely little restaurants, and the general atmosphere sort of feels like Christmas all year round. A stream even babbles through the town, and you can sometimes hear cowbells clonking in the distance as fat, happy, Swiss cows graze on lush, green meadows. I wouldn't have been at all surprised to meet a delightful little girl named Heidi, skipping around in the meadows, picking wildflowers with her friend Peter. And, of course, the Matterhorn stands guard over the village. Honestly, I felt like constantly pinching myself.

I had contracted with a local company to hire a guide, so I checked in with them first thing that morning. It would cost over $500, but I wouldn't have dreamed of attempting such a climb without a guide. The weather concerned me. Friday's weather seemed perfect, but when I heard weather predictions for it to be just as good the entire weekend, my spirits soared. As with most mountains, the fear of inclement weather is ever present because it's the cause of many deaths, the Matterhorn being no exception. In fact, after visiting the cemetery, I vowed not to attempt the climb if the weather forecast looked sketchy.

But it appeared some of the best climbing weather of the summer would provide the chance to take a shot at my dream.

I walked over to the guide company's office and met my guide, Andreas. A Swiss native, born in Lugano, he'd moved to Zermatt to guide on the Matterhorn. Close in age to me and affable, Andreas and I got along instantly. He spoke excellent English. Remember, I had only been on one international climb before, namely Chimborazo, so I had little experience with guides.

I didn't ask, but Andreas assured me he had successfully guided experienced and not-so-experienced climbers to the summit numerous times. After we met, we headed to my room to do the obligatory gear check. Confident that everything looked good, we made plans to meet later that day to begin the adventure.

The route we planned to take is called the Hörnligrat (Hörnli for short), which traverses a ridge that is the most common climbing path on the Swiss side of the mountain. It has a climbing distance of about 5,500 feet with a vertical rise of about 4,000 feet. It normally takes between nine to twelve hours to successfully ascend and descend. The Hörnli is a straightforward climb under good weather conditions, but in poor conditions it rapidly becomes difficult and a scarily dangerous proposition. Each year, many a climber, whose ability is not entirely up to the task, underestimates the length and difficulty of this route. Numerous rescues, unplanned bivouacs (hunkering down on the mountain to wait out a storm), and deaths result. The sobering fact is, over five hundred people have died on the Matterhorn.

When first climbed on July 14, 1865, the ascent heralded one of the most impressive mountaineering feats of the era. Four Englishmen, Edward Whymper, Charles Hudson, Douglas Hadow, and Francis Douglas, along with their three guides, Michel Auguste Croz, Peter Taugwalder, Jr., and Peter Taugwalder, Sr., comprised the first party to successfully make it to the summit. On the way down, however, Hadow slipped and fell, dragging Douglas, Hudson, and Croz with him. They fell 3,000 feet down the Matterhorn's sheer north face to their deaths. Whymper and the Taugwalders survived because the rope attached to Francis broke. The story is a grim reminder of how much more dangerous the descent is. These days, about 3,000 people climb the Matterhorn each year. On average, about a dozen die.

I was determined not to be one of 1988's dozen.

At about 2:00 p.m. on Friday, I met Andreas to head up to the ski lifts above Zermatt. Most climbers on the Hörnli Route take the lifts to a place called Schwarzsee, then follow a well-maintained trail up to the "Hörnli Hut." The Hörnli Hut is a refuge/hotel that can sleep dozens of people and is the unofficial starting point for the Swiss side of the Matterhorn's climb.

We reached the hut around five that afternoon and checked in. We stayed in a large room that had four bunk beds and slept eight people. We enjoyed a hearty, classically Swiss dinner and settled in to get some sleep before a predawn start.

I didn't know it then, but as would become my frequent affliction on climbs, I lay awake from a mixture of excitement, anticipation, anxiety and from the great amount of snoring going on from my roommates. I finally fell asleep around midnight, and in what seemed like minutes, Andreas woke me at 4:15 a.m. We wolfed down a cold breakfast of raw oatmeal, milk, and nuts and prepared to start up the mountain.

As we headed out in the brisk morning air, the line of headlamps flickering up the mountain mesmerized me. A joyous thrill bubbled up in my heart—the same thrill I experienced in my childhood when I imagined what it would be like to climb this mountain. *Except, I'm actually doing it!* I laughed to myself. I shook my head in amazement as we began to climb.

We ascended a series of rocky stretches first while the sky gradually brightened in the East. By the time the orange sun broke gloriously over the horizon, we had reached the Bohr Löcher—a perch above 12,000 feet that overlooks the magnificent Furgg Glacier. We took a moment to savor the sunrise. Andreas and I communicated without words our mutual appreciation for the splendor of the view.

After passing the Bohr Löcher, we began to navigate a steepening stretch of rock called the Lower Moseley Slab, which involves Class 3 climbing. Class 3 climbing means using one's hands and feet, with plenty of exposure.

We made it past the Lower Moseley Slab without incident and reached a small refuge called the Solvay Hut at 13,100 feet. At the Solvay Hut, we took a well-needed break. Physically, I still felt strong, but mentally, I fatigue from dealing with the extreme exposure set in.

Exposure, in climbing terms, simply means falling would be a very bad thing. The Matterhorn is not a technical mountain to climb in good weather, but it requires fitness, determination, and surefootedness. Surefootedness is the ability to be agile and secure when scrambling on rock, snow, and ice. Because of the exposure the Matterhorn presents, surefootedness is crucial, as losing your footing is potentially (and likely) fatal. This means the climb is mentally stressful because you're focusing intently on every single step, leap, foothold, and handhold.

I have never been a clumsy climber, but Andreas showed astonishing balance. He could hop from boulder to boulder like a mountain goat, lithe and surefooted, making every move look ridiculously easy and graceful. He never charged ahead, though, and patiently talked me through the highly exposed parts. I was thankful for this, but the mental endurance had been exceptionally taxing, and the break felt welcome. And, as usually happens, the view rewarded me.

Sitting on the steps of the hut, looking down over the route we had just ascended, I have truly never felt more alive. I was experiencing the culmination of a dream in real time. In fact, I encourage you to look up a picture of the Solvay Hut on the Internet. You'll see it is a lone little hut, obstinately anchored onto a sharply exposed ridge just over halfway up the Matterhorn. On one edge of the hut, there is a small rock outcropping where you can stand over a sheer drop-off. From here, the views are unexplainably exhilarating. You're literally above the clouds on most days and can see the Alps in the distance, with valleys peppered with small towns lying far below. Looming over the hut is the Matterhorn's iconic summit, beckoning you to an even more spectacular view.

I have had many experiences since then, but I have never since felt the *vividness of life* flowing through my veins as strongly as I did at that moment at the Solvay Hut. For at least five minutes, I thanked God for allowing me to experience this view of His creation. *If a mere mountain in God's creation is so majestic and awe-inspiring,*

I reasoned, *how majestic and awe-inspiring is our great God?* I meditated on this thought with deep reverence. I then prayed He would keep me and Andreas safe for the rest of the climb so I could share what I had experienced with others.

I truly have never felt closer to God than I did at that moment. It was a deeply spiritual experience.

Energized, I looked up at the remaining 1,000 vertical feet above me. Part of me wanted to stay at the Solvay Hut and continue to soak in the wonder, but in a mountaineer's blood flows something that always pulls you to a higher point. I got up, smiling involuntarily, and we navigated left to climb the Upper Moseley Slab, which isn't technically difficult but shouldn't be underestimated, either. At the Upper Moseley Slab, a little bottleneck formed where more experienced climbers struggled to arrest their impatience while some people "played" with simple belaying techniques.

After traversing the Upper Moseley Slab, we set our sights on the top of an encampment called the Shoulder. At this point, I needed to put on my crampons. We had about a dozen fixed ropes to climb on the final push to the summit. As I put on my crampons, visions of the cemetery intruded. It became apparent why there are so many Matterhorn graves. Mentally fatigued already, the extreme exposure could only get worse when we pushed up the near-vertical last stretch. Anxiety fought for control as I pondered the danger, but then I was transported back to the moment at the Solvay Hut. I smiled warmly again, feeling God's presence around me. I pushed the fear out of my mind, promising myself I would just concentrate on the next step, and the next step after that, carefully placing each foot where I knew it needed to go, feeling confident I could do that while allowing God to "order my steps."

I stepped up and began to pull myself up the first fixed rope. Although my legs were beginning to feel some fatigue, I dug my crampons firmly into the wall of sheer rock and ice and hoisted myself higher and higher up the incline. Within minutes, I'd reached the top of the first roped section. *Only eleven more ropes to go,* I tried to assure myself. Doing what I promised myself and God, I put one foot in front of (or above) the other and kept climbing, higher and higher, slowly conquering one rope pitch after another.

After about an hour, I plopped down on the Roof— the homestretch on the summit ridge. It felt so good to have made it up the ropes, but I now rested atop a 600-foot fin of snow and rock. I stood up after a brief rest and looked around. The sensation of standing on a giant, iconic mountain on what feels like the top of Europe, with such extreme exposure, is a ridiculously intense rush. But this is the rush that keeps you climbing higher and higher, despite the pain in your legs, hands, arms, feet, and joints.

As we steadily made our way up the fin, we passed a statue of Saint Bernard, the patron saint of mountain climbers and the namesake of the powerful but loveable breed of giant Swiss mountain dog. I knew from my research this landmark meant we were almost to the summit.

After just over five hours of some of the most mentally draining climbing I have done, I stood atop the summit of the Matterhorn.

Andreas and I immediately gave each other a high five and a hug. Even though Andreas had done this climb many times before, we were both enthralled. I sat down to stare out over Italy to the south and Switzerland to the north, trying to figure out where Cernobbio might be, but I couldn't make it out. As I took it all in, I felt much of the same exultation I experienced at the Solvay Hut.

I soaked in pure ecstasy for several moments, but slowly a mild dread crept back. I recalled the plight of the first team to stand where I stood and knew, with the exposure being the same, going down presented far more danger than going up. The climbing is just as, if not more, technical, but the body is fatigued, concentration is more difficult, and one is more likely to make a mistake . . . as Whymper and his team found out over a century ago.

But something in my heart—a small, still voice— reminded me the weather remained magnificent, and I had an excellent guide. I again thanked God for both, as they were crucial things I did not have to worry about. I whispered another prayer for His protection over Andreas and me on the way down and prayed for all the climbers on the mountain that day. After lingering a bit more, and feebly trying to put the view into words, we got ready to start our descent.

Going down was indeed much, much harder than

going up. In fact, I lost my balance a couple of times and almost slipped, making my heart feel like it would leap out of my chest. But I kept repeating my mantra of one step at a time, one foot in front of the other, as I tried my best to focus carefully on each spot to place my cramponed boot.

After some grueling down-climbing, we reached the Shoulder. Then, after a bit more down-climbing, we made it to the Solvay Hut, where I felt strong enough to skip the rest break. We navigated down past the Upper and Lower Moseley Slabs, then suddenly the Hörnli Hut came into view. We had done it. I had summited the great Matterhorn!

Andreas and I enjoyed a well-deserved celebratory lunch and drink and relaxed, talking about the mind-blowing views from the top and how much of a rush climbing the Matterhorn gave us. He told me the climb never got old, no matter how many times he scaled the peak. I didn't doubt him for a moment.

We then hiked down to the lift, and by six that evening, we arrived back in Zermatt. Andreas congratulated me again and bid me farewell. I treated myself to a brilliant dinner outside a little café fit for a postcard. I made sure my table faced the mountain, so I could gaze up at the majestic Matterhorn in the day's last light, reliving various moments of the climb. I found it hard to fathom that just hours before, I stood on the summit of the incredible peak. I decided the Matterhorn was the most aesthetically breathtaking mountain on the planet. I maintain that to this day.

As I enjoyed my dinner under the shadow of the mighty Matterhorn in the fairy tale Alpine town, I felt not only joy and immense relief but also the most humbling gratitude to God I have ever experienced. I finished my meal and prepared to head to my hotel for some well-deserved rest. I even thanked Walt Disney for having the vision to create the theme park ride that had inspired me to have the greatest day of my life.

Climbing the Matterhorn felt the same to me as what I imagine it feels like to a child who dreams about playing in the World Series or at Wimbledon, then becomes a professional athlete and finds himself or herself fulfilling that dream by pitching in the World Series or playing on Centre Court at Wimbledon. There are just no words to explain the joy.

I hope I have imparted the wonder of fulfilling your lifelong desire. The lesson from this chapter is for you to find a way—*any way*—to live your dream. That one thing you have always wanted to do. Go out and find the way to do it. You *can* make it happen.

And I encourage you to ask God for His help. It makes it so much easier. He really can make dreams come true if you make time for Him. He wants you to embrace the challenge of living an extraordinary life. He put that desire in your heart! Share it with Him. Ask Him to help you manifest your dream and glorify Him with it when you achieve the dream.

Climbing the Matterhorn in 1988 was—and still is—the greatest day of my life. When are you going to experience the greatest day of your life?

CHAPTER 15

Mother's Necklace

WHEN I CLIMBED EVEREST IN 2000, ONE OF THE thrills of trekking to base camp was seeing, up close and personal, a 22,494-foot mountain called Ama Dablam. In the Sherpa language, Ama Dablam means "Mother's Necklace." This moniker stems from a giant, hanging glacier that drapes around the mountain's "neck," while the long ridges on each side also resemble the arms of a mother (ama) protecting her child. This gorgeous peak is known as the "Matterhorn of the Khumbu" because of its magnificence and striking profile. I highly recommend looking it up, as Ama Dablam is one of the most beautiful mountains in the world.

When I walked by this remarkable mountain in 2000, I never dreamed that in only six years I would fly back to Nepal to climb it. To be honest, it had never been a mountain I had any desire to climb. Ama Dablam is too technical for me and does not align with my focus of climbing the seven summits and all fifty-four of Colorado's 14,000-foot peaks. In July 2006, however, I received a call from Greg Bishop, a climbing buddy of mine. In October 2005, he and a friend had booked a trip to climb Ama Dablam, but his friend had been injured and had to pull out.

I met Greg when he posted on a Colorado fourteeners' website looking for a climbing partner to climb Crestone Needle. We met up and did "The Needle" and got along well, so we started doing some other fourteener trips together. Greg is a software engineer who lives right outside of Boulder. He often brought his dogs along when we did a few fourteeners, which always added to the fun. Greg has a sarcastic sense of humor, which I personally appreciate. That humor is somewhat revealed by his favorite TV show, *Impractical Jokers*.

The guiding company Greg and his friend selected offered me a substantial discount to take the vacant place. After some initial hesitation, I let Greg talk me into going—especially when he agreed to pay half of the discounted price. So, I made reservations for the thirty-hour flight to Nepal. When I flew to Everest, I had layovers in Los Angeles and Bangkok, but it is actually cheaper to fly in the opposite direction. On this trip, on my way to Kathmandu, I flew through New York City and Abu Dhabi.

The long flight gave me plenty of time to reflect on what going back to Nepal meant after my failed Everest attempt. Logically I knew I had made a wise decision to turn back, but it still haunted me that I'd gotten so close (300 vertical feet) without making the summit. I tried to push the thoughts out of my head, even though Ama Dablam posed a more technical climb with arguably more exposure than Everest.

When we landed in Kathmandu, it disappointed me to find that not much had changed in six years. It was just as noisy, chaotic, and polluted as ever. Perhaps God chastised me for my disappointment because Greg and I ended up spending four nights in Kathmandu. Our flight to Lukla was grounded twice due to weather. *Not a good start to the trip*, I thought more than once.

While we waited, we got to know our Sherpas and guides. The lead guide, a strong Norwegian named Leif, had grown up climbing the mountains and cliffs around the fjords of Norway. He came from a family of physicians who were all thoroughly disappointed Leif lived the itinerant life of a climbing guide. I could tell his family's disappointment bothered him—you could see sadness in his eyes.

Thankfully, Leif spoke excellent English, which is quite important to me since effective communication is crucial on challenging mountains. He had spent a year as an exchange student at a high school in St. Louis, Missouri, living with an American family with whom he was still close. As a result, Leif was a huge St. Louis sports fan, loving the Cardinals, Rams, and Blues. He really fell in love with Cardinals baseball, as the family he lived with took him to a number of games. This immediately resulted in us having a bit to talk about.

On our fifth day, boredom and champing at the bit started to get to me. We finally boarded a Twin Osprey for the forty-minute flight to Lukla Airport. Lukla, also known as Tenzing-Hillary Airport, is a tiny strip of runway about 9,000 feet up the mountain range. It is the natural starting point for climbing some of the Himalayan mountains, including Everest and Ama Dablam. As hair-raising as the flight can be, it is an easy choice between a five-day hike (in addition to whatever peak you're climbing) and a forty-minute flight. But having landed at Lukla six years before, I secretly dreaded the flight.

Picture a plateau, no wider than a few thousand feet, nestled among gargantuan mountains. Cutting through the village, a narrow runway, just over 1,200 feet long, begins at a stone wall against the mountain and ends with a sheer 600-foot drop. The combination of the tiny runway, sometimes rough weather, and soaring altitude makes this a technically dangerous and ridiculously nerve-racking flight. And yes, there have been fatal crashes at Lukla, one of which is on YouTube, if you have the stomach to view it.

Everyone in the plane held their breath as we made our approach. The small plane veered and bobbed as wind and turbulence bounced us around. All eyes were glued on the strip ahead, ignoring the dazzling green carpet covering the valleys and crests around us. The pilots zeroed in and steadied the plane, calculating all sorts of factors and accommodating for the direction of the wind. I gripped the seat handles tightly as the plane made its descent to the runway; one miscalculation and we'd slam into the side of a cliff thousands of feet up.

Suddenly, the cliff's edge swooped below the plane's belly, and we rapidly descended onto the runway. The tires bounced and screeched a little, then bounced again as the pilots hit the brakes and flaps hard to slow us in time to avoid slamming into the mountainside, only a few hundred feet away. Soon enough, though, the plane reduced speed and everyone cheered for the pilots as we taxied to a stop. The first critical danger lay behind us.

From Lukla, we began our trek, following the same route I'd taken for Everest's base camp. It took a few days to trek in, and we stayed at teahouses every night, taking a couple of rest days to help acclimatize. Just like in 2000, the warmth, optimism, and resilience of the Nepali people touched me the most. They truly are remarkable and special folk.

Finally, we reached Ama Dablam's base camp, set in an idyllic, grassy field at the base of a creeping glacier—a bonus because we didn't have to worry about melting snow for water because water seeps out from the base of the glacier. The air was crystal clear. I will never forget the view of the mountain; the iconic peak loomed tall and proud, glistening white with snow against the backdrop of a rich, blue sky. At eye level, the contrast of the meadow's opulent green grass filled me with delight. Like so many times before, yet fresh every time, I felt humbled and blessed to witness the spectacle.

Still, a view so awe-inspiring is a hair's breadth from

being just as fear-inciting.

As I gazed up at this mountain, I suddenly questioned why I'd agree to this. The mountain looked unclimbable, even though I knew it had first been summited in 1961, and many climbers conquered it each year. My stomach churned as I wondered if I had the ability needed for this ascent. At that moment, I had an overwhelming urge to simply hang out in the meadow while Greg and the others attempted to climb the daunting peak. But I couldn't let Greg and the others down. Plus, it would be a little embarrassing to fly all the way to Nepal without even attempting to climb the mountain. I prayed about it, as is my custom, but I did not have peace in my heart about the climb.

That night, I shared my apprehension with Greg as we lay in our tent. I knew the climb would begin in earnest the next day. Greg encouraged me to keep praying, then wisely suggested I go only as high as I felt comfortable. With this sage advice, I resolved to climb at least as high as I could.

I turned in for the night, determined to get some sleep. But as can be the case, base camps can often be noisy. Sometimes people are up and about in the meal tents, laughing and, as was the case on Everest, even partying. If the wind is blowing, it can be scary. There have been a couple times on climbs when the wind became so strong I truly worried about my tent blowing off the mountain (with me in it). Sometimes it feels like the tent could just be shredded and flung into the night.

In the middle of that particular night, I'm not sure

whether my mind decided to play tricks on me or if the legends could be true, but I swear I heard a large bipedal animal walking around my tent. My mind began to imagine a Yeti circling my tent, as heavy, dual footsteps crunched around the tent to the point I began to freak out. You might wave this off as laughable imaginations, but the Nepali people–especially those on the mountains— definitely believe in the Yeti. In fact, some of my Sherpas and guides claim to have seen footprints. Fortunately, nothing came of the unexplained nighttime visitor, and to this day I still don't know what might have lurked outside my tent. But the event seriously spooked me.

Our climb began with fervor the next day, the goal being to simply make it to Camp 1. The climb took about three hours and turned out to be more of an uphill hike than a technical climb until we needed to do some bouldering at the end. *Not too bad*, I thought, even though most of the trail edged a steep, exposed perch. I felt good, and even though we camped at 18,500 feet, my oxygen saturation level registered high and I had zero issues with the altitude. But I also knew this area represented, by far, the easiest part of the climb. That evening we cooked, hung out briefly, then I fell sound asleep.

The next morning, we prepared to haul a load of gear partly up the route to the base of Camp 2. This day would be a lot tougher. I knew the most treacherous part of the climb lay between Camp 1 and Camp 2, as right before Camp 2, stood an infamous, huge wall of mixed rock and ice known as the Tower. As we reached this intimidating landmark, I stared up at almost forty vertical feet of rock and ice, with old and new fixed ropes dangling and swaying in the wind. Looking up at the sheer rock wall, I felt dismayed. The wall looked well beyond my capabilities. Immediately, my thoughts plunged back into every dark recess of my mind, as fear and doubt gripped me. I stood there for some time and must have been visibly fretting because Leif came up to me, patted my shoulder, and in his Nordic lilt, smiled and said, "Come on. It does no use staring up at it. It's another day's challenge." I appreciated his encouragement, but I wasn't convinced. We dumped our gear at the base of the Tower and turned back to climb down to Camp 1. This is where we spent another night before returning to base camp to rest for a few days, following the climber's mantra of "Climb high and sleep low."

Ama Dablam's base camp looked like a miniature version of other base camps I had been to. When we got back, a few other expeditions had arrived. The camp had two dining tents, a latrine tent, and a cooking tent set up, but didn't have anywhere near the scope and scale of Everest's base camp. I knew the waiting that came next would not be good.

The next three days of rest and acclimatization caused a cauldron of emotions to bubble up inside me. Still wounded by my failure to summit Everest, part of me desperately wanted to succeed on this climb. But no matter how I reasoned with myself, fear still reigned. The horribly daunting Tower presented a challenge even for experienced climbers, and I had no desire whatsoever to even attempt it. As I mulled these things over, weighing the pros and cons, a nearly overwhelming feeling descended over me, urging me to just leave and get out of Nepal.

I spoke to Greg again about my reservations and desire to leave Nepal. I imagine my distraught appeared evident to the rest of the group, too. Then, on our third rest day, the weather turned bad, so we just hung out in our tents as the wind and snow buffeted us for hours. That day, Leif braved the conditions and came over to ask if he could talk to me for a minute. He obviously knew my serious apprehension about continuing and he asked if he could at least discuss it with me. "Sure," I said, unconcerned about Greg listening because I had been honest with him the whole time.

Leif asked me one of the most profound questions I have ever heard. In his mild-but-pointed Nordic way, he asked, "Is it difficult, or is it impossible?" I laughed when he said it because one of my favorite climbing bloggers is a guy named Alan Arnette. This phrase is one of his mottos: "Is it hard, or is it impossible?" I explained this to Leif, who smiled and nodded at the confirmation. He then said, "Yes, the Tower is difficult, as are other parts of this climb . . . but ask yourself if it is *impossible*." I mulled over his words as he continued. "Many other climbers, some with skill levels no better than yours—some who, unlike you, have never been to 28,800 feet on Everest—have successfully made this climb." That's all he said. It was maybe a five-minute conversation, then he left.

Throughout the night, I wrestled with his words. I thought about other things in life that may seem impossible but, in reality, are just difficult. So many things, like getting into medical school, or getting an athletic scholarship, or completing a marathon or triathlon . . . are undoubtedly difficult, but not impossible. Many people accomplish these things every day. I thought of a good friend who competes in Ironman triathlons and wondered if he had the same self-doubts and worries the night before one of his events. I doubted it, but you never know.

I thought back to when I first read Alan Arnette's same words. This led me to consider my career experience. I pondered and analyzed all the ideas associated with this concept of "Is it hard or is it impossible?" First, I knew I had to assess and manage the logistics. Did I have the energy and skills to climb the Tower? Well, at the least, I trusted Leif's climbing skills and leadership, and he assured me he would guide me up, slowly and steadily. I knew from experience, slow and steady is always better than fast and erratic, especially in new territory. Next, I had always claimed that fear can be a valuable tool. Complacency can do you in, but you have to identify the source of the complacency. Most often, it is fear or doubt (trepidation is usually fear in disguise). The key, once again, is self-awareness. *Do I have the energy and skills to climb a rock-and-ice wall if I had a huge air pillow beneath me?* I had to admit I did. Therefore, fear was hindering me. But fear can lead to hesitation, and hesitation can lead to a misstep. A misstep during extreme exposure is likely fatal.

Finally, I had to decide if Leif was an effective leader. My life literally depended on this. Was he pushing me beyond my limits, and if so, what was his motivation? The worst possible event for a climbing guide is to lose a climber, so the next question would be, *Is Leif reckless?* No, I'd seen him be methodical and unhurried on a path on which he was an expert. I couldn't detect any hubris in the man, so I had to conclude Leif objectively saw beyond my fear and truly believed I could summit Ama Dablam. This is an example of the process a leader should step through when making crucial decisions.

Still, logic stretches only so far when facing one's deepest fear in the middle of a grueling, lonely climb you really had no desire to do in the first place. This lack of desire, while nonetheless finding myself committed, proved the most difficult part. I found it interesting how my predicament reflected many situations I'd experienced in life. The core of the decision I faced was certainly a common one. I continued to pray about it until I finally fell asleep.

CHAPTER 16

Matthew 19:26

THE NEXT MORNING, THE STORM HAD BLOWN OUT and the day dawned bright and sunny. Yet again, it seemed like God provided these sun-filled, brilliant days whenever doubts assailed me. The weather, forecasted to hold for the next few days and then turn really nasty, predicted a clear weather window to go for the summit. I woke up feeling strangely at peace, seemingly reconciling my questions and thoughts on a subconscious if not spiritual level while I slept.

I prayed for safety, then decided to go as far as my skills and nerve would allow. With stouter resolution, I joined Greg and the rest of the group as we climbed back up to Camp 1, ready to make our summit bid.

We climbed back to the base of the Tower and prepared to make our ascent. I tried not to look up at the rock wall, as I did not want to feed any fear. *One step at a time*, I reminded myself. I knew I could take the next step, and when I reached that step, I would make the decision for the following one. Our strong Sherpas had already checked the fixed-lines and I could see them hauling our packs up the Tower. I went right behind Leif so I could follow his route and moves exactly. He gave me a confident smile, then dug his crampons and ice pitons into the ice and began his ascent.

I kept repeating the mantra, "Is it hard, or is it impossible? *It's just hard!*" I also interspersed the words of Philippians 4:13, "I can do all things through Christ who strengthens me." I followed Leif's path up the vertical ice and rock, careful to keep three points of contact at all times. Slowly, we moved upward. Since most of the Tower is rock with only small amounts of ice, it is actually less desirable than a sheet of ice since it is more difficult to gain purchase with the crampons. Now and then, Leif would look down to check on me, but before long, my legs, arms, and knees ached to the point I hated the sound of the crampons scraping the rock. I refused to look down, as the tremendous exposure meant that in case of a fall, the ropes would have to hold or there would not be a sliver of a chance of survival.

What makes mountain climbing so difficult is it's really an exercise in suffering. To be a climber, you have to be able to push through what I call the "pain cave." While climbing, you may suffer from jet lag; stomach issues from food you're not used to; altitude sickness; loneliness from missing your home, friends, and family; headaches; boredom; loss of appetite; severe cold; the inability to sleep; waiting for days on end in cramped tents; and not to mention the constant aching of your joints and muscles. You are miserable, yet never more alive. And for many climbers, never happier. *That is the part I have to focus on.* I appreciated waking up to the most incredible views in the entire world and experiencing cultures radically different from my own. But I also know I must push myself beyond exhaustion to achieve goals.

When I am suffering during a climb, every time I vow I will never climb again. In the most challenging moments of a world-class mountain, a climber genuinely considers if they are insane. *I could die out here* is the terrifying reality you have to face if you unwisely push yourself too hard. Many have done so. Yet, as soon as I am down, I can't wait to start planning the next climb. The best way to describe the addiction is the word ALIVE. You are always in the moment. Your senses are heightened, and you have never been more one with the wild, raw, free, beautiful creation. I, for one, am always incredibly grateful to God for allowing me to be there, despite having to become comfortable with being uncomfortable.

But fear is ever-lurking, waiting for unanticipated moments to pounce. To this day, I sometimes have a frantic fear of heights, and I have never become completely comfortable with exposure. Every time I face exposure, I have to mentally push myself through intense, near-debilitating fear to keep going forward or up, reaching out for the next grip on a cold, unforgiving rock, pulling my leg up to find the next impersonal foothold. Each time, I seek a way to use the fear to sharpen my focus, instead of allowing it to cause panic.

But the exhilaration threaded through all that suffering is indescribable. You are a million miles away from your boss, deadlines, earnings reports, meetings, budgets . . . that entire corporate world seems so trivial, insignificant, and meaningless in the face of a behemoth of rock and ice that intimidates, as much as it lures with its raw magnitude and splendor. No, that corporate world is not what living is about. Being on the mountain is truly living.

We pulled ourselves higher and higher, the butterflies in my stomach never quite leaving but somehow "falling into formation." I, too, fell into a rhythm of sorts and knew, from gauging the distance to the top, we'd made good progress. I may have been terrified and somewhat out of my element from a technical standpoint, but I considered the positives—my fitness level and my ability to handle altitude so well. Although as winded as anyone else, I still felt fairly strong, even on the face of the Tower. Then my foot slipped.

My heart leapt into my throat, and I scrambled to recover as Leif's head swung around to check on me. Somehow, I managed to keep three points of contact on the wall and steadied myself as I tried to keep my breathing under control.

"You good?" Leif called with a questioning thumbs-up.

I responded with a thumbs-up and started climbing

again. I focused intensely on each foothold, each handgrip on every rock, each pull up to a higher vantage point. Then I slipped again. It appeared my hands and legs had become more tired than I realized and were sabotaging my efforts. I recovered quickly again and took a moment to focus. I chanted my mantra, "This is not impossible. This is not impossible." Leif stared down at me, trying to assess how much I was struggling. I gave him another thumbs-up, but we continued a little slower. I forced myself into a tunnel of focus, meticulously following Leif's every move as I pushed higher and harder, approaching the top of the Tower.

Finally, Leif crested the top of the Tower, then turned to pull me up with a broad, proud grin. I breathed a huge sigh of relief and collapsed to the ground several feet from the edge, thanking God. I had made it. The Tower was *not* impossible. Scaling it *felt* impossible and ridiculously frightening, but I had proven to myself I could push through fear.

After helping the others up over the ledge, I looked around at Camp 2. Little more than a tiny, stepped ledge atop this huge pillar of rock, with room for only a handful of tents and lacking any running water, the camp had been dubbed "Camp Poo." To my eye, it met its notorious reputation for being utterly filthy. Our Sherpas warned us not to touch anything we hadn't personally set up and to take as little rock space as possible. I heeded their advice. With all the other challenges of Ama Dablam, I didn't need to add gastro issues.

The crazy exposure of the camp stunned me. I looked out at tents anchored down on nothing more than jagged rocks, literally on the edge of a cliff, thousands of feet up a mountain. I didn't even want to think about the winds that would surely whip the tent while I slept.

That evening, we ate a simple meal of noodles, then hunkered down into our bags. With nights in the Himalayas being so exceedingly cold, it's good to make bedtime early. I lay awake as the wind howled and tugged my tent around. I tried not to think of the drop if the ropes came loose and my tent flew like a kite and tumbled down the sheer drop-off of the Tower. Eventually, I resigned to telling myself, "There is nothing I can do if the wind rips this tent off the mountain. If it's my time to go, it's my time." Mercifully, sleep ultimately took over after a long, intense day of climbing.

The next day brought another challenging climb up to Camp 3. It would involve climbing up a couloir with a steep sixty- to seventy-degree slope, and once again, a highly exposed area. Yet somehow, after the previous day, the exposure did not bother me as much. Securely clipped onto the fixed-lines and focusing on each move, I placed my crampons carefully as we inched up the mountain.

I cannot say I enjoyed it, but Greg said he had a blast climbing this slope. He does much better with exposure than I do, so he smiled, seeming full of energy as we made our ascent. Having such good weather in the couloir made it perfect for climbing. This surprised me a bit because the previous night, after the sun went down, the temperature fell way below zero. Once we reached the top of the couloir, we still had to traverse a few ridges to get to Camp 3, but we finally made it. Only then did I realize the mental drain. Two days of extreme exposure had worn me down to a mental nub.

I sat down to rest and examined Camp 3. Little more than a flat ridge of snow, the camp sat right below "the Dablam"—the huge, glacial protrusion of ice that took its name from the mountain. The wind whistled in my ears as I admired the great, white snowcaps of the surrounding range, which appeared to be roughly at the same height as our camp. I marveled at the contrast of the pure, bright-white caps slowly turning into the dark, sooty gray of the lower halves of the mountains.

I couldn't have foreseen that just a few weeks later in this very spot, three climbers and three Sherpas would die as an avalanche would roar down from the Dablam, completely burying them. Clueless to the fact that snow built up as we camped and anything could have set off the avalanche at any time, I thought only of the day ahead. Had I had the faintest idea this avalanche was forming, I would never have even taken the call from Greg to climb the mountain. I guess sometimes it's good we don't know everything.

We crawled into our bags early that night, mentally preparing for the summit push in the morning. Although colder than the night before, I slept decently, despite the howling, whipping wind and subzero temperatures. We woke around 5:30 a.m. Part of me wanted to stay snuggled in my warm sleeping bag, but my desire to get the climb over with drove me out of the warmth and into the frigid Himalayan morning.

The altitude made for icy-thin air, but the upside of this meant the climbing would not be nearly as technically difficult as the prior two days. We packed our gear, then followed the fixed-lines to the summit. As the sun broke over the horizon, the day again turned brilliantly sunny, but although we climbed over 22,000 feet, it remained viciously cold in the open air of the exposed peak. I had to measure my breathing carefully in the thin air at that altitude, and my legs and arms ached from exertion. Thankfully, there wasn't the added burden of this area being a technical stretch.

After five hours of near-silent, thoughtful climbing, we reached the summit. I plonked down on the ground and looked around. Time for my reward. Everest and Lhotse are only about ten miles away, which gave the illusion I could almost reach out and touch them. After recovering for a minute, I suddenly felt a deep sense of pride at having pushed past my fears to reach the summit. *You made it.* I smiled happily, basking in this joy, relishing the view for as long as possible. The Himalayas truly have a regal yet mystical air about them.

Then the ever-familiar concern about a safe down-climb crept into my mind. We were all exhausted, and no one could afford to lose focus on Ama Dablam.

I prayed quietly for our safe descent, at least one more day of good weather, and a safe flight back to Kathmandu from Lukla. Despite the sun shining brightly as we celebrated on the summit, bitterly cold wind whipped at us. We lingered only long enough to get the requisite pictures, drink, and eat some nourishment, then we prepared to head back down. As I had done before, I chuckled over the craziness of going through more than a full day of travel just to reach Nepal, enduring days of tough trekking, and facing my paralyzing fear of heights, coupled with the extreme technical aspects of the climb, just to spend a scant thirty minutes on Ama Dablam's summit. *No wonder normal people think we climbers are crazy!*

We descended to Camp 3 that evening, again having no idea of the avalanche that could be triggered. It took us less than four hours to climb down, yet, if we had done this climb just a few weeks later, we would have been buried beneath thousands of tons of snow. The next day, God again blessed us with good weather as we made our start back to Camp 2. We then rappelled down major sections of the Tower, which, to my surprise, I found enjoyable. From there, we descended past Camp 1 and finally all the way to base camp. Descent is much faster, which also makes it more dangerous. All the while, I stayed determined to remain focused.

Only when we reached base camp did I truly feel I had survived Ama Dablam. Leif intuitively gave me a high five, perceiving my thoughts. I nodded my thanks, appreciating his words of wisdom. God had once again given me an exhilarating experience and kept me safe the entire way. Philippians 4:13 came to mind once more. Through Christ, God had given me the strength to accomplish something remarkable.

I spent that late afternoon outside my tent, sprawled on the beautiful, grassy meadow, staring up at Ama Dablam. It astounded me that just twenty-four hours earlier I had been standing on the summit of this gigantic peak, which now towered over me. It just didn't seem possible. Yet, on this climb, I had learned a thing or two about what is and isn't possible. I thought about how our God is an awesome God, both in creating this incredible mountain—one of the most spectacular in the world—and for letting me experience it in a way most people never will. I lay there thinking about the responsibilities of work that awaited me when I returned and how they paled in the majesty and grace of the mighty "Mother's Necklace." I prayed I would always remember my experience and never forget when confronted with something in life that seems impossible, to remember it is most likely just difficult. Like climbing Ama Dablam, most things can be conquered if I push through my fears and negativity. Of course, I have no doubt that God's help makes all the difference.

We trekked back to Lukla and again boarded the little twin-engine plane for the white-knuckle flight from Lukla to Kathmandu. I watched out the window as we accelerated down the steep incline of the runway, praying furiously. We lifted off before the ridiculously short runway ended and the plane dropped a little into the gaping gorge. But our pilots maneuvered the plane back into a steady ascent while we all exhaled a huge sigh of relief.

Soon we were back in the teeming chaos of

Kathmandu Airport, and it seemed strange that I had already climbed the mountain. Not long after that, I lifted off for my long journey back to the States. I didn't know if I would ever return to Nepal. What I did know is that the people and mountains of that spectacular country have forever touched my soul. I have relived my experiences in Nepal and the lessons I learned there, over and over again, and hopefully I can continue to teach those lessons to a people I encounter throughout my life.

CHAPTER 17

Hubris at 15,774 Feet

PARIS IS ONE OF THE MOST CULTURED AND ROMANTIC cities in the world—maybe even my favorite city— but perhaps surprisingly, not my favorite spot in France. That honor goes to Chamonix, a breathtaking ski and mountaineering village on the French/Italian/ Swiss border. Chamonix bustles at the base of the great Mont Blanc.

My first visit to Chamonix took place during the summer of 1990. I had just finished a year of studying in Italy and decided to visit this iconic, French resort town before heading home. I just had to see Mont Blanc—the undisputed Alpine heavyweight and what I thought was the highest mountain in all of Europe. Mont Blanc had captured my heart as a boy.

I traveled from Milan by train to the Italian mountain town of Aosta, and from there took a bus over the border past Mont Blanc to Chamonix. While not as spectacular as the Matterhorn, Mont Blanc presented itself as advertised: a glaciated giant, the broad and bold granddaddy of the Alps. I instantly fell in love with the town of Chamonix, an idyllic mountain paradise set in a sharp-cut valley with soaring spires on both sides. Perhaps one paid for the charm, for the prices there were ridiculously expensive.

As a poor graduate student, a humble youth hostel fit my budget. The hostel, little more than one giant room with twelve bunk beds, slept twenty-four people. I took a bottom bunk, and when I introduced myself to an old German man, he glared at me. I turned away awkwardly and chuckled over Europe's cultural differences. During the night, though, this German guy got down from his bunk and started pacing the floor and circling my bunk. His weird behavior kind of creeped me out. I turned my body to face him, in case I had to defend myself, and waited until he got back into bed. I only had to spend two nights at the hostel, thank goodness. Fortunately, he didn't show up the second night, and no one slept in the bunk above me.

I spent my two days hiking the lower mountains on the opposite side of the valley to the Alpine peaks, which included Mont Blanc. Although I had recently climbed the Matterhorn and the weather looked perfect, I did not feel up to tackling Mont Blanc, as it is a long and grueling day-climb. The views across the valley, however, were breathtaking beyond words, but I'll try: carpets of lush, green meadows sat at the base of snowcapped peaks against a sky so royally blue, it appeared to have been photoshopped. I relished every moment of the fresh, crisp mountain air, taking in the splendor that only the wealthy are typically able to view.

I saw a chamois on one of my hikes. The chamois is a species of goat-antelope native to the Alps. A stout, hundred-pound male with antlers of deep brown and a bright, white-and-brown face stared back at me. After my hikes, I returned to the village to have a modest lunch while feeling like a king. The entire trip kept me spellbound. I vowed to return to climb Mont Blanc.

That opportunity came in 1997 when the company for which I worked acquired a plant in Toulouse, a gorgeous city in southwestern France. Toulouse is an industrial hub, best known for being the corporate home of Airbus. I decided to tack on an extra week when the company required me to make a trip. I planned to take a train to Chamonix to attempt a climb of the famed Mont Blanc.

As always, I contracted with a guide service, and while I usually go with U.S.-based companies, this time I decided to use a local company in Chamonix. This would prove to be a huge mistake.

I boarded the train in Toulouse at 8:30 a.m. and traveled all day, arriving in pouring rain at a little village called St. Gervais Le Fayet around 3:30 p.m. Twenty minutes later, I caught the Mont Blanc Express for the final fifteen miles of the trip to Chamonix. I disembarked, walked to my quaint hotel (this time, thankfully, I could afford a hotel), dried off, and feasted on cheese fondue at the hotel's charming little restaurant.

I planned to spend the next day hiking in the hills like I had done seven years before, but it rained on and off all day, so besides checking in with the guide company, I napped and read in my room most of the day. By early evening, the rain cleared, so I strolled around town, soaking in the scenery and the atmosphere in the postcard-worthy village.

The next day, I met my guide, Jean, for lunch, along with an older Italian gentleman named Alberto, who would also be climbing with us. Alberto spoke little English, and while Jean had a better grasp of English, I knew within five minutes that this trip would be a challenge.

At lunch, he could barely remain focused on our conversation, flirting with every moderately attractive woman who walked by. Admittedly, his good looks appealed to all the women, but all the guy could talk about was living to party and sleep with women. In fact, he confessed the only reason he guided up Mont Blanc in the summer was to afford to ski in the winter, party, and hook up with as many women as possible.

I found this distasteful and disrespectful, purely because it is so unprofessional. Jean hadn't bothered to build rapport with Alberto or me, yet he had no regard for flaunting his crass hedonism within minutes of meeting us. Plus, he proved to be abrupt, condescending, and rude when I asked a few technical questions about the mountain. His attitude gave me the impression he thought we should take his word as gospel and I should do what he told me, when he told me. Annoyed, I groaned internally.

Perhaps because of his broken English, I would describe my climbing mate, Alberto, as reticent. He'd grown up in the Dolomites and had spent his life hiking and climbing those mountains. Alberto stood about five-feet eight-inches and weighed around 180 pounds, and while he had a muscular frame, he had a bit of a gut. I couldn't imagine he'd have the energy to do the climb. This concerned me because I knew Mont Blanc's reputation for being a long, tough day-climb, and we had a strutting peacock of a guide to contend with as well.

Alberto didn't have the stereotypically loud or emotional demeanor of some Italians. He had a pretty laid-back personality. He did not seem as affected by Jean, maybe because he regularly dealt with the French—or rather Parisians. At least that wouldn't be an issue, as I preferred not to have to deal with major drama.

After lunch, we took a bus to a village called Les Houches, halfway back to Saint Gervais, where we caught a cable car up the mountain. We exited at a point called the Nid d'Aigle at almost 8,000 feet and began our hike up the mountain. The trail, marked with regular blotches of red paint, started out with many twists and turns. As we began hiking, I began to wonder how I would survive my time with Jean. I have been on adventures with guides all over the world, and ninety-nine percent have been entirely courteous and professional. Most have been patient, nurturing, and team-focused, as any leader on a grueling, life-risking climb should be.

Jean exhibited none of these characteristics. Without a woman in sight who he could preen for, his selfish, arrogant, rude, demanding, and impatient behavior came through. He barked orders to Alberto and me and showed apathy and disinterest the rest of the time, preferring instead to scout for female climbers in other groups. It shocked me that someone with his personality had been able to make a career in mountain guiding. Only in France, I guess.

While we hiked, we heard from other climbers that a high-pressure system was moving in. This meant the weather would be clear and sunny for the next several days, which translated into a green light to begin our climb the next morning. While I should have been excited, Mont Blanc loomed over me both physically and in my thoughts. The mountain is actually a massif composed of many peaks and spires, each with their own routes and climbing lore. The true summit had been reached in 1786 by Jacques Balmat and Michel Paccard, and again in 1808 by a remarkable lady named Marie Paradis.

I knew the climb was doable in good weather, and I felt eager to begin. Still, I hated to face what I knew would be an extremely irritating time on a harsh mountain. I prayed the combination of these things would not become dangerous, since Mont Blanc should not be underestimated.

We continued hiking until we reached a little emergency hut called the Baraque Forestiere des Rognes, a spot only used when the weather turns nasty. From there, the trail became progressively steeper, and parts of it were scarily exposed. This is because it zigzagged up the ridge of a peak that is part of the massif, called the Aiguille du Goûter. Interestingly, the ridge separates two glaciers that are rapidly disappearing: the Griaz and the Tête Rousse.

By nightfall, mentally spent, I finally sighted a shelter called the Tête Rousse Hut. Jean's attitude and demeanor had not improved. I slowly began to dread spending a stressful summit day under his leadership. I'm not sure how Alberto felt about Jean since we couldn't really communicate much, but he couldn't have been thrilled with the brusque, rude treatment, especially since he appeared to need more rest stops than I did. I sorely regretted picking that guiding company. Heavy with thought, I entered the Tête Rousse Hut and picked out my bunk.

We could have spent the night three hours closer to the summit at the Goûter Hut, but this would have involved crossing a feature called the Grand Couloir. This couloir is a narrow gully cut into the mountain, with an intensely steep grade. Most concerning, however, is any time spent climbing this couloir is incredibly dangerous because of the high rate of rockfall. Many people are struck and seriously injured or killed each year.

Since there is no other path, it's essential to cross the Grand Couloir to summit. The most dangerous time of the day, as I'm sure you know by now, is late afternoon when the temperatures are warmest. This is because melting ice and snow are most likely to cause rocks to break away and fall. By staying at the Tête Rousse Hut, we planned to make our initial couloir crossing in the middle of the night when temperatures are freezing and the threat of rockfall is greatly reduced. We would, however, have to cross the Grand Couloir in late afternoon on the way back.

Another advantage of the Tête Rousse Hut is it is less popular than the Goûter Hut and thus much quieter, making for a better few hours of sleep. You need reservations to stay at the Tête Rousse Hut, but it accommodates up to seventy-two people. When we arrived, though, it pleased me to see only about fifty people there. We ate a simple dinner, and I went to bed early since I had no desire to spend a minute more with Jean than I had to. We also planned to leave around 2:00 a.m. to begin our summit bid, so an early night made sense.

My internal alarm clock woke me up at 1:15 a.m., fifteen minutes before Jean's watch alarm went off. I put on my cold-weather gear, down jacket, Gore-Tex pants, boots, climbing harness, and helmet. I then wolfed down some cold cereal and bread and drank some hot tea. Ahead of us lay the infamous Grand Couloir. I prayed quietly before Jean began to bark orders for dealing with the couloir. "This early, the couloir will not be busy," he began in his disaffected Parisian lilt, "but it will be on our descent. Find a safe spot under an overhang and wait until I tell you it is safe to cross. Do you understand?"

It took everything I had to merely nod in agreement.

"We need to move quickly across the couloir, minimizing our time of exposure to the rockfall," he continued. "There is a wire hanging across the couloir. Quickly clip your carabineer to it, then move across. We will be roped together but maintain plenty of slack in the rope as you move across. Carry the slack in your hands so you do not trip like a fool over it. I say again"—he paused until we acknowledged he was the boss—"move as quickly as possible!"

Despite how much Jean's attitude grated me, I knew I needed to heed his advice. It is unwise to ignore the advice of an expert in his particular field simply because he lacks character. Still, I had spent good money to hire Jean as a guide. It irked me his motivation revolved solely around having a glamorous job that helped him pick up women and live in Chamonix. It is difficult, sometimes, having a forensic psychology background because you hate to auto-analyze everyone, but sometimes you don't even have to; they practically scream their disorders at you. Jean presented a textbook case of narcissistic personality disorder. He didn't want to grow up. He wanted zero responsibility, and like any narcissist, everyone and everything that happened needed to be manipulated to suit his ambitions. He had no genuine interest in other people, with vulgar arrogance as a gaping by-product.

The most glaring of Jean's offenses, in my opinion,

showed up through the violation of foundational leadership principles by putting his needs and emotions ahead of his team's. My epitome of leadership is one who is a servant-leader; Jean portrayed the antithesis of this. A good guide should make you feel you are his or her one-and-only priority, and that your safety, emotional well-being, and overall positive experience on the mountain completely supersedes their own. Jean exhibited the exact opposite attitude. With every question or area of exposure on the mountain where I had degrees of challenge, he made me feel like I was a burden. I got the sense I bothered him and that I could barely count on him—he'd merely go through the motions—to get us up and down the mountain without incident. In a nutshell, Jean's priority was Jean, and despite our considerable payment to him as a guide, we were merely excess baggage.

Even with our early start, the bobbing headlamps above us said we were not first to the couloir that morning. Jean clipped onto the wire, and without as much as a backward glance, he started moving across. Alberto did the same, and I brought up the rear. The Grand Couloir was about a hundred feet wide with a forty-degree slope. Despite the subconscious temptation to sort of shrug one's shoulders and lower one's head (as if that would help to reduce the impact of a giant piece of falling rock), I moved quickly across the couloir without even a pebble falling. Jean had warned us, however, that even when we were past the couloir, the next 150 vertical feet held the threat of a rockfall, so as soon as we unclipped, we kept moving at a fast pace. The incline and altitude left us completely out of breath by the time we reached the top of the 150-foot pitch. But we had made it; we were relatively safe from rockfall. Jean graciously let us rest for about two minutes.

I looked up in awe and wonder. The crisp, clear night showcased billions of stars that twinkled against the black of space like so many angels winking encouragement. The view instantly transcended the cons of the climb, as once again, I experienced God's presence descending upon me. Enraptured with this moment of rare beauty, I felt utterly alive . . . and bitterly cold with the temperature hovering at about a brisk ten degrees Fahrenheit. Not even close to having my fill of the experience, Jean stood up and started moving again. Since Alberto was roped to Jean, and I was roped to Alberto, we had no choice but to continue. My awe and wonder turned into bubbling anger.

I tried to focus on the climb and use my anger as motivation. The first pastels of dawn began to show in the East, which definitely helped. With the new light and the glow of my headlamp, I could tell we were following a vague path, since I could see occasional red paint, indicating the route. We had to do some rock scrambling, which is not that easy in the dark, before reaching a point where wire cables had been installed as handrails. We followed those up to an old, abandoned hut. We then climbed a snow slope to the top of the Aiguille du Goûter.

From there, we traveled about a hundred yards

south, then finally reached the Goûter Hut. We had been climbing for three hours up difficult and steep terrain, so Jean begrudgingly allowed us a ten-minute break. We then joined a long queue of climbers heading up the northwest face of the Dôme du Goûter—another peak that makes up the Mont Blanc Massif. Jean warned us of crevasses, so I kept alert, but in general, this part of the climb consisted of gentle switchbacks with little to worry about.

At 14,121 feet, we passed just under the summit of the Dôme du Goûter, then continued on to the Vallot Hut. We stopped outside this hut to grab a quick snack and some water. Although still brutally cold, I refrained from going into the hut as I had heard disgusting stories of human waste and trash piled up inside. Most people only use it in case of a dire weather emergency.

We continued past the hut to a stunningly exposed snow ridge called Bosses Ridge. On the east side of this ridge is a terrifying, sheer drop-off of thousands of feet. Thankfully, there is a fixed-line going up Bosses Ridge, but the assurance of the line was almost moot since many climbers were already coming down as we made our way up. This meant we had to clip and unclip to pass anyone going the other way. If you pass on the same side, you almost hug each other to get around. At times I ducked underneath to the other side of the fixed-line, holding on to it with my hands and digging my feet into the snow at an angle to avoid falling down the slope to my death. This allowed the climber going the opposite way to pass me without the "hugging", and it just felt safer. It wasn't always feasible, though.

Passing other climbers at Bosses Ridge became tricky and insanely nerve-racking, as one wrong jostle could mean slipping off the ridge. Many climbers were courteous, but to add to the craziness, others were downright rude, dangerously shoving past me, insisting they be let by. I tried to keep calm and not allow the anger surging in my chest to cause me to make a fatal mistake.

The silver lining is that anger is extremely motivating for me. I can deal with a lot, but my friends will tell you I perform best when I am angry, pressured, or my back is against the wall. There is a line past which I refuse to be pushed, so despite my acrophobia and mounting fatigue, Jean's condescending attitude, and the reckless selfishness of some climbers on the Bosses Ridge, my anger served as rocket fuel. I admit I was seething at the insane negligence of these people as they pushed past a first-time climber of the peak. It is downright disrespectful and outrageously dangerous to behave like that, and I had rarely experienced anything like it on any of my climbs. There is a climber's code, and these people were breaking every part of it.

The Bosses Ridge leads right up to Mont Blanc's summit, and thanks to my boiling ire, I felt strong up the final push. Adrenaline surged through my body, giving me more energy than I knew I had, so despite the arduously long prior ascent of about eight hours, I had no issues in the final stretch.

Eventually, I crested the slope and stood victorious

on the summit. I felt jubilant, looking around in joy, taking in the splendor of the Alps. Then my adrenaline instantly dissipated, and fatigue fell on me like a wall of bricks. I staggered to take a seat and tried to gather myself, but my legs became rubbery as the last of my energy drained from my body. I grew concerned.

I tried my best to focus and enjoy the moment, to soak it in, but now thoughts of the descent had me feeling leery. I realized my anger had blown most of my adrenaline resources early, and Jean wouldn't be a forgiving so-called leader. The greater danger of falls on the descent loomed tall and terrifying. We had to cross Bosses Ridge and the feared Grand Couloir again and multiple areas with a significant amount of exposure.

We remained on the summit for only ten minutes, as the wind continued to blow icily bitter; with the wind chill, the temperature dipped well below zero. Jean got up and, following his pattern, began walking to make his descent without checking to see if we were ready to go.

Physically beat, I could not believe I had to hike back down this mountain, let alone under the guidance of Jean. It would take every ounce of self-will I had. Fortunately, Alberto appeared to be pretty fatigued as well, and Jean, despite his prima donna persona, couldn't very well leave us behind. So, we began our descent as fast as we could, focusing intently on our footing. I did not want to become a statistic on this mountain.

After a couple of hours, we reached the dreaded Bosses Ridge. Fortunately, fewer climbers came up later in the day, so our ascent, while not as crazy, was still busy. I noticed my hands shaking a little as I unclipped and re-clipped to the fixed-line, going around other climbers. This is with thousands of feet of exposure yawning below if you screw up on the line.

Eventually, we made it across Bosses Ridge without incident, and I realized with my eyebrows crashing together, my eyes wide open in crazy, desperate focus, I probably looked like people with the thousand-yard stare who have just survived a firefight or traumatic event. We continued on.

When we reached the section that overlooked the Grand Couloir, Jean instructed us to shout "*CAILLOU!*" (pronounced *ky-oo*—French for rock or stone) if we saw a falling rock to warn the climbers crossing the couloir below. When we got to the crossing, Jean reiterated the same warnings he had given hours earlier. The danger of rockfall had increased in the afternoon sun. We clipped to the line and began our dash across. I prayed continually and moved as fast as my rubbery legs would take me. I alternated between looking down to where I placed my cramponed boots and looking up for falling rocks. When we were halfway across, I heard the distinct clatter of bouncing rock.

I cringed and looked up to notice rocks tumbling down the mountain. They finally rolled to a standstill a few yards in front of us as Jean looked back as if to say, "Oui! I told you so! Let's move faster!" My thousand-yard stare felt permanently etched onto my face. I kept praying, and my body somehow found some small, untapped reserves of adrenaline.

Finally, we made it across without incident and unclipped. I collapsed to the ground, not caring if Jean had to drag me to keep going. Alberto and I both heaved a sigh of relief, and I offered some not-so-silent thanks to God for our safe crossing.

After a few minutes, I made myself get up, but as we continued, hiking felt like pushing through water or mud. The last three hours of the descent seemed more like nine due to my complete physical and mental exhaustion. But I had no choice except to keep fighting through. This served as a solemn reminder that every climb is unique. You never know what situation you'll find yourself in and how you'll have to adapt. When I booked the trip, I hadn't expected I'd need to face a narcissist leader and French maniacs pushing past me on a narrow ridge in the sky. I could not control my adrenaline surge on the ascent, and therefore could not control the subsequent adrenaline drain. I simply had to fight to hustle through the rockfall Death Zone and make it back down in one piece. Although an experienced climber by that time, I'd never encountered a situation as maddening as this one.

After what felt like a lifetime, we reached the Nid d'Aigle for the cable car ride down to Les Houches and then back to Chamonix. I had just completed a fifteen-hour day of intense climbing in mercilessly cold weather under mentally stressful conditions involving significant exposure and the threat of a rockfall. And all this under a poor leader who pushed us to the max of *his* abilities, not ours.

I always try to take responsibility and hate making excuses, but I believe it is undeniable that Jean made the climb far more difficult. Joy and camaraderie are powerful, energizing forces. Arrogance is unnecessary, and joy and goodwill are like the glue that fills in the cracks of disparate parts of a team.

My thoughts returned to the acquisition we made in Rhode Island. I regret to admit our leadership went into that merger acting like Jean on Mont Blanc. We felt we knew what was best, with a "We are from the big corporate world, and we are here to fix your failing little company." We knew everything and didn't need to listen to anything they told us, and frankly, we treated them like country bumpkins and saw ourselves as sophisticated professionals.

I am horrified when I think about how badly we botched that acquisition through our arrogance. Thank God, the silver lining came in the lesson learned. From then on, we looked at an acquisition as "We are Company A and you are Company B, and together we will partner to form a better Company C that takes the best from both companies."

We can learn from everyone, and hubris is a common but highly fatal flaw with some leaders. Be warned. Take an introspective look frequently and check your hubris barometer. Business is stressful—at times it is easy to feel "entitled" to a little arrogance. That is a trap. Believe me, an employee or team who feels how I did about my guide under high duress on Mont Blanc will not make the situation good for you long term.

Mont Blanc offered challenges yet, as always, God stayed with me. I lavished immense praise and thanks on Him for keeping the three of us safe on our tough, but successful summit bid of Mont Blanc.

To this day, I retain extreme respect for this massive mountain. It had beaten me up. Climbing it once was enough.

CHAPTER 18

Servant Leadership on a Stratovolcano

A FTER CLIMBING MONT BLANC IN 1997, I FELT A little jaded from the guide experience with Jean, but I also had a real itch to climb another big peak. The closest mountain of significance offered both a challenge and stunning beauty. At 14,111 feet, Mount Rainier is the highest of the picturesque Cascade Range of the Pacific Northwest. It is also an active stratovolcano. Although located fifty-four miles southeast of Seattle, Rainier utterly dominates the city's skyline, which makes sense since it is the most topographically prominent mountain in the contiguous United States (only Denali in Alaska has a higher prominence). In fact, the imposing view of this gigantic mountain from the seventy-third floor Sky View Observatory of the Columbia Center is surreally beautiful, dwarfing the city. Looking down at

Seattle from the observatory is something I recommend to anyone traveling anywhere near Seattle.

Like Mont Blanc, Rainier is a *beast* of a mountain, with the greatest danger being bad weather. Because Rainier is so close to the ocean, it can suddenly be battered with tempestuous Pacific fronts. In fact, the town of Paradise, Washington, which sets on the slope of Rainier, averages 120 inches of rain a year and claims to be the snowiest place on Earth. Mount Rainier is quite a unique mountain in that it has three summits, with a summit crater over 1,000 feet wide. There are also twenty-six major glaciers on Rainier, with the largest being the Emmons Glacier. Rainier is considered one of the most dangerous volcanoes in the world, even though its last eruption occurred in 1894. The downside of Rainier boasting over thirty-five square miles of glacial ice and snow is any eruption on Rainier could produce massive mud and debris flows that would threaten the entire Puyallup River Valley and pose a severe threat to sections of Seattle.

Despite these risks, over 1.8 million people a year visit Mount Rainier National Park. This includes over 10,000 climbers, one of which—in September 1997—would be me.

I chose RMI, or Rainier Mountain Incorporated, as the guide service I'd use. They were the best known, had a good reputation, and had been guiding there since 1969. I hoped I would have a better experience than I did on Mont Blanc. Back-to-back negative experiences would not be good. I drove from Phoenix up to Nevada, then through Death Valley to Lone Pine, California, the home of Mount Whitney. The thermometer hit a brutal 125 degrees in Death Valley. To my amazement, the view in Death Valley included Telescope Peak, rising to 11,000 feet of elevation out of the lowest part of the desert, which is below sea level. Telescope Peak is quite a mountain, and the view made a big impact on me. I stopped for the night in the little town of Lone Pine so I could also see the beautiful Mount Whitney, which rises to 14,500 feet above the town. It surprised me to see a good deal of snow still hanging around in the High Sierras.

The next day, I continued north and visited the idyllic mountain town of June Lake, just north of Mammoth and south of Yosemite. Rumors of June Lake being one of the loveliest mountain towns in America proved true, and it did not disappoint in the least. I then traveled over Yosemite to the coast of California and drove up the world-renowned, pine-forest coast of Oregon, being sure to stay one night in Cannon Beach. This stunning beach is another one of my favorite spots in the country (it's the town with the huge "Haystack Rock" where *The Goonies'* closing scene was filmed). I figured even if the climb on Rainier turned out to be as negative as Mont Blanc, I had already experienced so much energizing beauty, I could walk away from the trip feeling content. Finally, I arrived in Ashford, Washington, a tiny tourist town just west of the main entrance to Mount Rainier National Park. I would spend the next three nights there.

Day one began with an orientation at Rainier Base

Camp in Ashford. Here, we met our guides and fellow team members. *Wow*, I thought immediately, *what a difference from Jean on Mont Blanc.* From the time we were introduced, the RMI guides appeared to be pleasant, professional, helpful, and most of all, they inspired confidence. My attitude soared, and suddenly I became really pumped about the climb. We did a gear and safety check, then just talked "mountain shop" and hung out.

Mountaineering Day School the next day included practicing crampon, rope travel, and self-arrest techniques. What fun! Our group included people with an array of experience from beginners to more advanced climbers. I leaned in to listen in fascination as the guides showed us how we'd travel on snow using a technique called the "rest step," with pressure breathing. The rest step is a deliberate gait used to climb steep, often snowy, slopes. A human's normal walking gait maintains a slightly bent knee at all times, which, on a steep slope, never allows the quads or glutes to rest. Since these are two of the largest muscles in the human body, it's easy to see how quickly one can become fatigued on a serious mountain. As you step up an incline, the rest step straightens the downhill (rear) leg, locking the knee so the leg is vertical and fully extended. All weight is placed on the rear leg as the climber's skeleton (straight, locked knee) carries the body's weight. This is so the rear leg's quads and glutes can rest, as well as resting the bent front leg. I looked forward to seeing how much the rest step would add to my endurance. This "day school" time also gave us a preview of how slowly and methodically the guides would climb and of how patient and accommodating they would be.

We met around 8:00 a.m. the next day and took a shuttle to the Paradise Ranger Station at 5,400 feet, where we began the hike to Camp Muir at 10,600 feet. The hike is only 4.5 miles, but with the slow pace the guides set and the significant elevation gain, it took almost the entire day. Since most people do this route as a day-hike, we found ourselves on a crowded trail. By late afternoon, however, we reached the hut and stowed our gear on our bunk beds, then had a team meeting where the guides detailed the specifics of the upcoming climb. This included the route, conditions, food, equipment, and what clothing to wear. The guides were meticulous in their explanations and took time to answer any questions. After a quick dinner, we headed off to the bunks to attempt to get a few hours of sleep before the exciting beginning of the climb.

Summit Day began before midnight, as the guides roused us, and we began donning our cold-weather gear, ropes, crampons, helmets, and our trusty ice axes. By 12:30 a.m., it was go-time. The guides, sensitive to both the excitement and fear in the group, were awesome about putting our fears to rest. Unlike Jean in Chamonix, never once did they belittle anyone, and they showed total respect, especially to the least experienced people in the party. I'd climbed Mt. Blanc and Rainier back-to-back within just a few months, so the contrast between Jean's arrogance and the patience, humility, and professionalism of the RMI guides stood in stark contrast. More than once, I wished I could teleport Jean to Mount Rainier just so he could see how a guide should treat clients. In a nutshell, Jean treated me like an interloper on his precious mountain, while the RMI guides treated us like honored guests.

The brisk early morning air felt good. I started walking to get my blood flowing. The climb began with a slow-rising traverse of the Cowlitz Glacier, then continued up several switchbacks to what is called Cathedral Gap. Right away, I could tell I stood on a volcano because of the heavy pumice on this part of the route. As we marched in a steady rhythm using the rest-step technique we had learned, we slowly but steadily gained altitude until we reached the Ingraham Glacier. We circled around this glacier and came to a large, rocky ridge to the north called Disappointment Cleaver. Since this section is steep and icy, it contains fixed ropes necessary for crossing the precarious crevasses. Our guides had emphatically prepared us for this part. We slowly and nervously climbed the fixed ropes, each of us making small but measured progress. Even though we climbed slowly, some less experienced people showed visible stress.

Eventually, the last of our climbers arrived at the top of the ridge, thankfully without incident. Here, the ropes ended, and the climbing eased. We all breathed a huge sigh of relief, grateful to have made it through the treacherous area. We then took a well-deserved break and got some nourishment. In 1997, this was still early in my climbing career, and I realized my time on Mont Blanc had made me strong. With the slow, steady pace the guides set, coupled with the rest step, I felt like I could go all day. The crevasses and the dangers of climbing on ice and snow confirmed I'd made a good decision to use a guide service.

It hit home on this critical part of the climb what a tremendous difference a good guide made.

I got the sense the RMI guides were there to make this "bucket list" experience of climbing Rainier as safe, enjoyable, and "doable" as possible. I wish I could remember their names, but for the life of me, I can't. These guides smiled, had great senses of humor, and bantered back and forth with each other, much to our team's amusement. They also took the time to get to know each of us on a personal level. I noticed this served a dual purpose, as it enabled them to be firm when needed, but never in an arrogant or condescending manner. The RMI guides were almost like good psychologists, helping some of our party push through their fears since Rainier was their first time on ice with exposure. Furthermore, these guides seemed compassionate about the physical challenges but motivated us to push through our exhaustion and pain.

Put it this way: if Yelp existed in 1997, Jean would have received one star (because minus five stars isn't an option) and these people a glowing five stars. The guides on Rainier were young, vibrant, humorous, accomplished, but, most of all, humble, in that they seemed to be grateful to have what they considered the best job in the world. At the time, I had to agree. They just loved serving people to accomplish the momentous goal of summiting their beloved mountain.

After our break, we kept climbing and soon hit the well-beaten path on the ridge above Disappointment Cleaver. Thankfully, the guides knew exactly which route would avoid the many crevasses and the frightening ice. After navigating this hairy section, we then scrambled onto the enormous Emmons Glacier to make our final push up the steep summit slope. Despite the route being clearly marked with wands, which is encouraging and helps mentally, some in our party really struggled on this section. Admittedly, for some unknown reason, being above 13,000 feet here felt different than 13,000 feet-plus in Colorado. The air seemed thinner and breathing became harder than what I usually experienced on a fourteener in my home state. Furthermore, I noticed clouds starting to build and swirl below us around the lower slopes. Trying to put this potential danger on our descent out of my mind, I moved forward with my team. As we climbed, however, I began to get frustrated with the teammate behind me who I was roped to. He somehow kept getting tangled in the rope. I couldn't see what he was doing, but it happened three times, which is a bit much. The problem is, when he got tangled, it pulled me back and we had to wait for him to untangle himself. After the third time, along with having to face the increasingly strenuous climb, my patience rapidly drained.

Suddenly, my irritation and aching muscles fled as

I became distracted by the terrain instantly changing from snow to rock and ash. My spirits lifted, as I knew we had arrived at the crater's famous summit rim. Years later, when I reached the summit rim of Kilimanjaro, that summit reminded me of this climb. With both volcanoes, you reach this apex, but to attain the true summit, you must go left for about twenty minutes along the rim. On Rainier, the true summit is called Columbia Crest.

We dropped all our ropes and gear and headed for the true summit, as we didn't have to worry about crevasses on this part of the mountain. As on Kilimanjaro, I noticed some teams inexplicably turned around when they hit the summit rim. For the life of me, I could not understand that. They were only twenty minutes away from the true summit! They had come this far, why not push through the exhaustion and have no regrets after the descent? I shook my head and kept hiking.

Finally, we reached the top—before the swirling clouds below rose and really rolled in. I stood at Colombia Crest, tired but triumphant, drinking in the spectacular panoramic view. To the west, I could see the mirror-like Pacific Ocean, sprawling Seattle to the north, and the eastern edges of the Cascades; looking south, I saw a row of other white-capped volcanoes: Mount Adams, Mount Saint Helens, Mount Hood, and Mount Jefferson. It felt like I was standing on top of the world, with pure beauty stretching out in every direction!

The view, however, is almost as disconcerting as it

is gorgeous, since at the summit it is evident Rainier is still an active volcano. The guides pointed out steam emitting from several vents below, and I had noticed certain areas on the crater rim were warm to the touch.

Still, I prayed silently, thanking God for the opportunity to experience His majestic and magnificent creation, as would become my long-standing custom. I also thanked Him profusely for leading me to RMI, who had displayed the epitome of what I call "Christ-like servant leadership."

We hung out on the summit for about a half-hour, then began our long descent. While it took us about eight hours to make the summit, it only took us about four-and-a-half hours to make it back down. The down-climb occurred without incident under the excellent leadership of the RMI guides. When we reached Paradise Ranger Station, we collapsed inside the shuttle bus, which carted us back to Ashford. That night, we celebrated heartily as a team, then crawled into our beds, and I, for one, slept like a rock. I had summited another major mountain and had my faith in guides restored. I had also learned a lot about servant leadership.

In the same spirit as the RMI guides, the person who comes to mind most prominently when I think about an exemplary leader is a man named Laurie Skreslet, the first Canadian to climb Everest. I have never seen such powerful leadership, before or since, in business or on any mountain.

Watching how Laurie led his team, the humility he exhibited (despite being a climbing legend), his ridiculous skill (I couldn't believe how fast he could go down a rocky couloir—probably three times faster than me, even though he was in his sixties), and the way he served his team, never asking them to do a single thing he wouldn't do. *That* is a leader. The lesson here again is humility over self-confidence, service over domination, and refining your skill to a fine edge.

The next morning, I bid my team adieu and left for the long drive home. I made sure to stop and view the legendary Crater Lake on the way back, then headed south on a different route through Utah. I stopped for a while to admire Bryce and Zion National Parks, then stopped outside Kanab in Southern Utah to visit the most heartrending place. At the time, it was called Best Friends Animal Sanctuary. I took a guided tour of this surprisingly joyful, no-kill animal rescue sanctuary set on fifty acres in the beautiful Red Rock Canyon. That night when I got a hotel room in Kanab, I enjoyed a huge treat when one of the Best Friends' rescue dogs slept over. What an extraordinary way to conclude my trip and give something small back for the amazing blessings I had received. Finally, I headed south to the North Rim of the Grand Canyon and then home to Phoenix through Page and Flagstaff.

That trip cemented my love of adventure. I had hit seven national parks, three national monuments, summited Mount Rainier, met some wonderful people, some exemplary guides, and got to tour the most adorable animal sanctuary in the world. It really doesn't get much better than that.

I joyfully worshipped God for allowing me to experience such a trip, for keeping me safe on the journey and on Mount Rainier, for no breakdowns with my car, and most of all, for allowing me to marvel in the incredible majesty that is His creation. He had allowed me to see some of the most beautiful scenery in the entire country. Then, and to this day, I am so grateful to Him.

CHAPTER 19

The Cost of the Summit, Part I

ENALI, ALASKA, AT 20,310-feet, IS THE HIGHEST and most unforgiving mountain in North America, a requirement of the seven summits. I had seen Denali once through a jet's window when traveling to Japan. I vividly remember the size and scope of the mountain. What a sight! Denali is the peak's native name—formerly Mount McKinley—and it has some of the largest vertical relief (or gain) on Earth, with over 13,000 vertical feet from the base to the summit. This is even greater than Everest (at just over 10,500 feet) and second only to a mountain in Pakistan called Nanga Parbat. Denali stands tall, proud, and foreboding, only 300 miles from the Arctic Circle.

In early 2003, I had the time and resources to consider undertaking the nearest of the seven summits. I knew the biggest challenge on Denali would be the weather, as storms can keep you socked in for days or weeks. After college, one of my friends had traveled to Alaska, and he camped out at Denali National Park for almost two weeks before the clouds cleared, revealing the majestic mountain. Even so, he could only see it for about three hours before the clouds converged, and once again, hid the peak. In fact, only forty to fifty percent of all climbers successfully summit Denali, mainly because of lousy weather. Everyone knows it is plain suicide to ignore weather warnings on Denali. Many climbing teams never get a clear weather window to make a summit attempt.

My strategy? Prayer. I prayed for safety on this mountain most of all, but I also prayed God might grant me clear weather to make a summit attempt. Nothing more. Oh, and I believed in my heart that He heard me.

I had never flown on Alaska Airlines before my trip from Phoenix to Seattle, then finally Anchorage, and I must admit the airline impressed me. From the cleanliness of the planes, to the prompt travel schedule, to the friendliness of the staff, I thought to myself more than once, *What a great airline!* On a cool, misty day in late May 2003, I landed in Anchorage and was met by the Seattle-based guiding service I'd hired for the trip. They are one of only a handful of companies the Denali National Park Service permits to conduct guided expeditions on the mountain. All members of the expedition met at an Alaska Airlines carousel, and, once gathered, the guide company loaded us onto a shuttle bus to begin our three-hour journey to the little Alaskan town of Talkeetna.

I'll always remember our lead guide's name: Arlo. He had been named after Arlo Guthrie, the American folk singer and songwriter. Arlo grew up in Oregon, hiking and climbing the huge, picturesque Cascade Range. He had summited the mighty Mount Rainier over twenty times, and this was his third year guiding on Denali. An outgoing man, he immediately struck me as competent and he had a fantastic sense of humor to boot. I would come to learn he also liked to tease, but only in an appropriate way. He quickly united our group of six climbers into a team, an obvious sign of a good leader.

Since I had never been to Alaska, the scenery kept me utterly enthralled. On the way to Talkeetna, besides the giant mountains on the horizon at every turn, we also saw all kinds of wildlife, like deer, moose, fox, and other small animals, and two bald eagles soaring over a lake. A fat grizzly bear lumbered close to the road, likely on his way to find some salmon. *What a phenomenal place!* Contented, I soaked in the wild sense of freedom.

We stopped in a town called Wasilla to buy last-minute groceries and finally arrived in Talkeetna around nine that evening. We checked into a small hotel called Latitude 62, where I shared a room with one of the climbers named Charles. I had to chuckle: our expedition had nearly filled the entire hotel. We had dinner at the hotel's restaurant and prepared for the first of our last two nights of sleep in a bed.

As we got to know each other, I began to really enjoy

my group. None of them were world-class climbers, which triggered a small concern because Denali is not really an amateur's mountain, but four of the six were pursuing the seven summits, so I had to believe they were ready for the challenge. Also, Denali is a tough mountain, not because there are many highly technical features, but because of the altitude, weather, bitter cold, and grueling stretches of long climbing. The other two climbers had done Rainier and wanted to do something more challenging. They also expressed interest in Aconcagua and Kilimanjaro, and maybe Vinson, but they said right away that they had zero desire to do Everest. Everyone seemed friendly and supportive, and not one person showed any arrogance. I gave thanks for the collegial and friendly environment, for I thought I knew what lay ahead.

The next day began with a breakfast meeting at a local restaurant and an orientation session by the National Park Service. This covered the various aspects of the mountain's routes and special preservation considerations about Denali National Park. We then did our obligatory gear check with Arlo and the guides inspecting everything. That night, we had our final meal before the expedition began. I ate a three-quarter-pound cheeseburger in honor of the upcoming climb, and I say in all sincerity, it was one of the best burgers I have ever eaten. I don't know if the beef in Alaska is better, or if I knew I wouldn't see a burger for three weeks, but I enjoyed every delicious melt-in-your-mouth bite. I decided, on the spot, to have the same burger in about three weeks when I returned safely back down the mountain after, hopefully, bagging the summit.

After breakfast the following morning, we received news the weather would not allow us to fly. Denali's weather had smacked us down on the very first day, causing us to be stuck in Talkeetna. Although weather has delayed many of my climbs, I always find myself slightly frustrated. It's like a horse getting into the starting gates at the Kentucky Derby, then being led back to the stable. You're all mentally pumped and ready to rock, only to become deflated. I spent the day mainly napping in my room, then had another three-quarter-pound cheeseburger that night in honor of the upcoming climb. I figured with all the calories I would burn on the mountain my waistline could easily afford it.

Thank God, the next day the weather forecast looked good, so we shuttled to a place called K2 Aviation to prepare for our bush flight to the Kahiltna Glacier. Once more, I got to experience a *spectacular* view of the incredible Alaska Range. With my face glued to the porthole, I watched as jagged, snow-blanketed mountain after mountain rose gloriously above a sea of fluffy, white clouds, making the view a climber's pure delight. I firmly believe it is impossible to avoid the sense of ultra-remote wild that Alaska immediately thrusts on you. This untamed allure of the region is reflected in the rugged charm and natural intelligence of the people who enviably call the last frontier their home.

We landed on the southeast fork of the Kahiltna Glacier at 7,300 feet of elevation. This is where our base camp would be, twenty miles of climbing and 13,000 feet below Denali's summit.

We immediately began setting up camp, digging a cache in the snow for our gear. We then used a handsaw to cut out square blocks of ice to build snow walls around each tent, protecting them from the harsh and violent Alaska wind. This would be our routine for the next several weeks. Once we'd constructed our camp, we spent the rest of the day on the second most important task—rigging sleds to pull our gear behind us on the mountain. We also reviewed our crampon and ice ax skills, which included practicing what to do if a teammate fell into a crevasse. Since we would be roped together at many sections of the climb, in the very real possibility someone dropped into a crevasse, without a second's hesitation we would have to fall on our ice ax, jamming it into the ice as fast and hard as we could to both save our teammate's life and avoid the entire group being pulled into the gaping void.

When night fell and bedtime arrived, I found sleeping on the ice with insulated mattress pads under our bags kept the cold from permeating upward. I appreciated this because we would not experience an ice-free environment for three weeks. Also, my bag is rated to thirty below zero—perfect for that climate. On the flip side, however, Alaska is a strange beast because at the high latitude the sun never really sets, making the days quite hot in the tent when the sun is shining.

The next morning, we started at 3:00 a.m. by packing our gear and preparing to move up to the next camp. We planned to travel at night when the air is coldest and the snow most firm. This makes climbing easier and less risky. The guides cooked all our meals for us, so after a good breakfast, we left Kahiltna Base and proceeded to *descend* 400 feet down Heartbreak Hill. This slope is named this way because when you return, it breaks your heart to have to climb one last uphill segment.

As we hiked off the main Kahiltna Glacier, we turned toward Denali, traveling 5.5 miles up the gently rising glacial rolls. Pulling the sled took some getting used to. It took me a couple of days to figure out the optimal distribution between the sled and my backpack, as each of us carried group gear, plus our own personal gear. I discovered optimal distribution to be about forty pounds on the sled and sixty in my pack. After an "acclimatizing day" of climbing upward, we arrived at Ski Hill at 7,800 feet and prepared our camp, building the requisite snow walls and setting up our tents.

Over the next few days, we fell into a routine of "climb high and sleep low." As is typical of major climbs, we would move some gear up to the next camp, cache it, then return to sleep at the lower camp. The following day, we would move all our gear up to the higher camp, build snow walls, and set up our tents.

We'd camp next at 9,600 feet, just below the Kahiltna Pass. From there, the glacier turns to the east, so our camp after that followed the glacial valley and lay at 11,200 feet, the base of which is called Motorcycle Hill. We spent a full day at this camp just resting and acclimatizing. The following morning brought terrible weather, so we stayed an extra day at 11,200 feet, praying the storm would pass.

Thankfully, the weather cleared, and we climbed to our next camp, rounding Windy Corner at 13,300 feet and stopping at 13,500 feet. We dug a cache, dumped the gear, and headed back down. What a gorgeous climbing day. We had stunning views of great landmarks on Denali, including the Fathers and Sons Wall and Peters Glacier. The Fathers and Sons Wall is an incredibly steep, icy, 6,000-foot feature on Denali. It consists of rock, snow, and blue icefall, and only the most experienced and boldest (perhaps craziest?) climbers attempt to scale this feature. Peters Glacier is a long, beautiful glacier that snakes through the Alaska Range and makes for amazing views. We headed back down, spent the night, then after breakfast broke down the camp to get ready to head to 14,000 feet.

At that point in my life, I had climbed to over 14,000 feet many times, but 14,000 feet on Denali does not feel like 14,000 feet at other latitudes. Somehow, it feels more like 16,000 feet. The air seemed thinner, the oxygen less abundant, and my body reacted as though at higher altitudes. I'm not sure why this happens at more extreme latitudes, but I found the same thing to be true near the South Pole when I climbed Mount Vinson. On this day, we hiked past our cache at 13,500 feet, moving on to our camp at 14,200 feet. I began to get winded more easily, and my muscles burned a little more. It was weird and surprised me a little. Interestingly, there were National Park Rangers stationed at that camp. I figured they had to be in great shape, or they were accustomed to the altitude/latitude combination. When my head hit my sleeping bag that night, I was out for the count. After a decent night's sleep, we hiked back down the next day and retrieved our cache. Thankfully, we spent the next couple of days at this 14,200-foot camp to acclimate and recover.

Next came the challenge of caching a load below the high camp at 17,000 feet. I knew the day would be tough since this climb involves a significant amount of travel across the deeply crevassed glacier and somewhat technical snow and ice climbing on a slope of up to forty degrees. By midday, everyone felt the pain. Despite the two days of acclimatization and my body's typical good altitude response, this challenged even a seasoned climber like myself. Still, after pushing hard through some tough ice climbing, we eventually ascended out of the north side of the Genet Basin. For the first time on the expedition, at around 15,000 feet, we used fixed-lines where the slope became steep. The fixed-lines, however, top out at the ridgeline called the West Buttress at 16,200 feet. After our long, treacherous climb, some on our team really felt the effects of the altitude. So, after some discussion, we decided to play it safe, drop our cache, and head back down. The climb had just gotten "real."

I had become firm friends with most of the people on our team, but when our physical strengths began to show some disparity, I pondered the full scope of leadership, as I do on many climbs. I always try to remind myself I cannot lead (or vote) by my area of strength alone, but must accommodate, when necessary, the weakest person on the team. Sure, everyone has to give their best, but you can severely harm your entire team by trying to push everyone to your strengths. Despite undoubtedly feeling the effects of the altitude and days of climbing, since I am competitive even with myself, I would have pushed to 17,000 feet without a second thought and could have voted to do the same within the group. Had I done this, not only could it have badly injured someone on the team, if someone had to abandon the climb it would have slowed us all down since we would have to disperse more group gear to pull on our sleds. This is the kind of wisdom that isn't always readily apparent in a business environment. Sometimes you have to recognize and remind yourself of this. Whether in climbing or business, you truly are only as strong as the weakest member of your team.

Strong can flip to weak dizzyingly quick, so that should be kept in mind.

This is still painful to recall, but years ago I quit my corporate job because I decided to follow a deep desire to own my own business. Owning a franchise seemed like the smart way to go. I researched various franchises and settled on something close to my heart that also seemed profitable for a number of reasons: a doggie daycare.

The first reason it seemed profitable was because of the rising "dink" phenomenon (dual income no kids); the pet market is exploding; and people in the U.S. are spending more and more on their pets every year, which shows no signs of stopping. The second reason is I am an animal lover, and I'm fulfilled and happy around dogs and other animal lovers. Third, I saw owning this kind of business as an opportunity to save some shelter dogs, as I planned to keep a couple of my overnight bays always open for shelters to place their dogs in. Fourth, I hoped it would provide a path to quit the corporate world, which I had grown to find unfulfilling, so I could do something that would bring me more joy while hopefully being profitable enough that I could maintain my lifestyle.

I decided to buy an existing business instead of building one from scratch because I believed it would be a quicker entry into the market, with more potential for the income I needed. Again, I made the fatal mistake of getting so caught up in doing the deal that I ignored any warning signs (and advice) and did not do proper due diligence. Worse, the owners I bought it from were not truthful about a number of things that ended up being crucial.

Due to an onerous lease arrangement and other factors, I began to lose significant money every month. It got worse and worse and worse. To make a long story short, I eventually had to sell the business at a $300,000 loss. The whole experience devastated me.

I had to go back into the corporate world and a new reality slapped me in the face—I couldn't land a job. I kept making it as a finalist for "VP of HR" positions but would invariably come in second. This had never happened before, which struck another blow to my assaulted mental state. My financial situation grew tighter and tighter, and I became more and more depressed.

Finally, I ended up taking a VP position with a credit union in Eastern California. I had to leave my friends, my family, and the dream house I had built in 2006 and move to a little community called Ridgecrest in the middle of the Mojave Desert. I lived in a tiny apartment, making $100,000 less than I previously had, and I was 1.5 hours away from any significant city. To be honest, the job bored me, and I felt lonely and miserable.

This is what I now call being "in the middle of a pain cave", but worse than suffering on a mountain—this misery consumed twenty-four hours a day and involved every aspect of my life. I had lost all that money and my career had subsequently spiraled downward.

Thankfully, I held on to my house in Arizona by renting it out, but the idea that other people lived in my dream home, while I lived in an old, somewhat rundown apartment built in the 1950s (it was all I could find that would take dogs), just gutted me.

I would often read the book of Job as a source of inspiration because if anyone went through a "life pain cave," it was Job. I kept applying for other VP of HR jobs to get me out of Ridgecrest, but nothing ever came through. Then I went through a four-month interview process for a great VP of HR job with a large company in Texas. The CEO called me on a Thursday and told me they'd be making me an offer. She said they were working out the details and paperwork, and

I would get a call from the recruiter with the offer the next morning. I rejoiced. Finally, I could get out of Ridgecrest and back into a meaningful role in a large city. That same Thursday night, the Board of Directors fired the CEO. My opportunity became dead in the water. I felt like someone had punched me in the gut. Proverbs 13:12 says, "Hope deferred makes the heart sick . . .", which I experienced firsthand. It almost seemed like a supernatural blockage kept me from finding something new.

Still, I persevered, kept reading Job, and even though my faith was tested, and at times waned, it never left me. I kept pushing through.

Back on Denali, we took another acclimatization day the next day because of lousy weather. I had planned to take a short walk to a point called "The Edge of the World," where one could look 7,000 feet down to the Kahiltna Glacier, but with the weather too poor to see anything, I opted not to go.

The next day, the weather improved, so we broke camp to take on what we knew would be the hardest day to that point—pushing up to 17,200 feet. We slowly climbed back up the fixed-lines to 16,000 feet, took what we thought we needed from our cache, and moved up to the high camp. The day stretched out, long and grueling, and when we reached the high camp, we all felt the ruthless effects of the altitude. Joints ached, muscles burned, and our breathing was ragged . . . and we still had to cut ice and build snow walls. By dinnertime, completely spent, we all had to rest for several hours before we could feel any strength seep back into our bodies.

We received news that we would have a perfectly clear weather window the next day, but that might be it for the next few days. To make our summit bid, it would have to be the next day, or not at all. This is a climber's dilemma: often, the stretch before your summit bid is the toughest, yet despite your exhaustion, you know this might be your only chance at good weather. You have to suck up the pain and face an even tougher day with a smile. This is why climbing is not for the weak-willed.

We all agreed to make a go of it. Privately, I had concerns about some people on our team.

CHAPTER 20

The Cost of the Summit, Part II

DESPITE SOME WIND NOISE, I SLEPT LIKE A LOG. Still, our wake-up call came way too soon. Reluctantly, I slid out of my toasty sleeping bag into the sharp, cold, early morning air. We had at least a sixteen-hour weather window for our summit attempt. We had to make the time count. I donned my serious gear: double-insulated plastic boots, thermal underwear, down pants, down jacket, balaclava, down hood over a heavy-knit cap, ski goggles, and heavy mitten liners covered by Gore-Tex mittens. After a quick breakfast and hot tea, I said a quick personal prayer, and we were ready to go.

Our climb began with a long traverse up a flat section of the glacier leading to Denali Pass. This section is called "The Autobahn" after a team of German climbers who lost their footing on the ice and slid to their deaths.

The park rangers had grimly warned us The Autobahn carried a reputation for more fatalities than any other section of the mountain. When we reached this feature, however, I almost wondered why. At first glance, the climb looked inconsequential, but I knew better. Despite the ever-present danger of an avalanche, the snow density on The Autobahn can range from soft and deep to rock-hard. This sudden disparity in density can easily cause a climber to slip and lose their footing. One climber, who had to chase a dropped backpack that slid downward, stepped onto hard snow, and immediately lost his footing. He slipped and slid onto hard ice down The Autobahn, ultimately plummeting to his death.

Hard snow and ice are not the only dangers. With hard snow comes the ominous risk of concealed crevasses. I knew we had to heed the rangers' warning and measure every step on The Autobahn purposefully. Painstakingly, we climbed ever upward, but despite the dangers I stopped several times on this section to enjoy the magnificent view of Mount Foraker (the second highest mountain in Alaska) while also looking back at High Camp to see how far we had traveled. Who says you can't have fun while suffering?

By the time we reached Denali Pass at 18,200 feet, our progress became painstakingly slow. The bitter cold and altitude began exacting their merciless toll. One member of our team couldn't go a step farther and had to turn back. He felt the all-too-common dizziness and nausea and wisely decided to go down to a lower camp before more serious altitude sickness set in.

After some warm wishes, the rest of us continued up a ridgeline, past a couple of beautiful and famous features called the Zebra Rocks and Archdeacons Tower. Standing at a spot higher than all the surrounding peaks, the view felt awe-inspiring. We gazed at the jagged, craggy rocks of Denali, offset by its brilliant-white snow ridges, while the background of the hazy Alaska Range mountaintops peeped through an ocean of cottony-white clouds, giving us a view more than words could begin to describe. The view offers a unique sense of liberation that I wish could be bottled and kept for frequent future experiences. Despite the burning fatigue, I smiled when I felt the all-too-familiar, powerful presence of God descend upon me. *This is why I climb. This is what it's all about.*

At a little over 19,000 feet, we crossed another long, flat section aptly titled the Football Field, after which we were ready to ascend the final slope called "Pig Hill." I still have no idea why this hill carries its unusual name, but by the time we hit Pig Hill, my energy had fizzled. Denali is unlike any other mountain I'd climbed. I won't say I underestimated the challenge, but I hadn't expected the exaggerated fatigue and more dramatic effect of the altitude/latitude. Every muscle in my body screamed, and my breaths became measured, focused gasps. On the final push, I kept repeating to myself, "Just one more step. Breathe. Breathe. One more step, Mark! One more step." I fell into a kind of trance as I mechanically climbed one slow step at a time, caught my breath, then ritually took another step.

Eventually, we reached the summit ridge. This ridge didn't have any surrounding mountain to shield us from the sudden, whipping winds. I desperately did not want to slip this close to success, but my legs had begun to tremble involuntarily. If I misstepped and didn't slide to my doom, I didn't know if I'd have the energy to re-climb the ground I'd lose. I pushed on carefully but with determination. It took every last ounce of focus and grit I had left.

Finally, we crested onto the summit.

Neither the highest nor the most technical mountain I'd climbed, it's the raw, wild nature of Alaska that makes Denali special. It challenges you in ways like no other place on Earth does. Yet this great mountain, in this wild, unforgiving and spectacular range, is relatively in my backyard. That is why summiting Denali provided a tremendous sense of accomplishment and elation—not to mention my total gratitude to God. Less than fifty percent of climbers who attempt Denali get to stand where I stood. I smiled as I gave God all the glory for making it happen. Even though we'd had a tough day's push, He provided the weather window for us to summit. It is that rare quality of faith that allows one to go farther and harder than ever thought possible. With all my heart, I believe God's Spirit gave me extra endurance because I asked for it.

Our team joyfully congratulated each other, took a celebratory team photo, and then collapsed on the snow to rest and get some nourishment. The bright orb of the sun shone in the dark, rich blue sky. Stretched below us lay a 360-degree sea of clouds, with only the highest summits of the Alaska Range poking through. Denali dwarfed these summits—even the mighty Mount Foraker. We were simply thousands of feet above their summits. It felt amazing.

After eating and resting a little, the common down-climb neurosis kicked in. If I felt this exhausted, how did the less experienced climbers feel? The team's fatigue concerned me. I prayed fervently for a safe descent and for total safety for everyone on the mountain.

We retraced our route and, slogging down the mountain, stumbled into High Camp without incident fifteen and a half hours after undertaking our summit bid in the early morning. I crawled into my tent, dragged myself into my bag, and barely got my zipper closed before I fell dead asleep.

The next morning, a howling blizzard greeted me. This was bittersweet, as there is a desire to just get off the mountain once the summit has been bagged. Even so, being stuck in the tent forced us to rest. Still, in a blizzard, the rest is of low quality, and the frustration of being stuck in our tents again taxed everyone.

A sixty-mile-per-hour gale, with gusts of up to ninety miles per hour, battered our tents and our psyches. It never fails to amaze me how the tents are rugged enough to keep from being ripped to shreds in these blizzards . . . but I would never say this will never happen. And as much as sleep is needed, it is nearly impossible to sleep deeply when the winds rage like that. Most of the time, napping means existing in the state where you are between consciousness and sleep, similar to how you might be on a plane. You aren't quite asleep, and you aren't quite awake. The problem is, this means you are not getting sufficient rest and are perpetually exhausted.

To make matters worse, I felt the beginnings of a cold, so every moment became miserable. It is mind-numbingly boring but, at the same time a little (okay, maybe a lot) terrifying since in the back of your mind, there is always the nagging feeling your tent is about to be ripped from its stakes and carried down the mountain. The other thing you do is try to keep melting enough snow to stay hydrated. But drinking melted snow means you have to pee, which in turn means going outside the tent in a howling blizzard. My solution on these climbs is to carry a Nalgene bottle I have marked as my "pee bottle," so I can use it and just dump it outside the tent without having to venture into the storm. This is simple but effective. Being stuck in a blizzard after summiting can be tough, but thankfully, on Denali I had a great tentmate.

Glenn was a stockbroker from Chicago. He truly had an adventurous spirit, as he had hiked the famous Appalachian Trail, river-rafted in Africa, and completed a number of marathons all over the world. Glenn had given triathlons a shot but just couldn't deal with training in a cold pool in the early mornings. Feeling blessed to have him as my tent mate, we spent some of the time cooped up in the storm by regaling each other with tales of our worldwide travels. Glenn, too, had a competitive streak, which meant when we ran out of stories we had some knock-down, drag-out card games. He confessed to being an avid Chicago Cubs, Bears, Bulls, and Blackhawks fan and stated his greatest fear was dying without seeing the Cubs end their curse and win a World Series. I really hoped he would see his dream come true.

The next day, the weather mercifully cleared enough to resume our descent. After waking, we scrambled out of our tents and stretched our legs and backs. After breakfast, we down-climbed all the way from High Camp to the camp at 11,000 feet, picking up cached items along the way. Enduring another long day, with meticulous caution we regarded our footing as we followed Arlo's exact steps. The risk of misstepping on ice or loose rock and losing our footing is always greatest on the way down any mountain. This is because you get more momentum from gravity going downhill, you are tired, and you tend to be less focused. And there's still the chance of stepping into a crevasse or—heaven forbid—setting off an avalanche. We spent the night at 11,000 feet, which should have been my second-to-last night on the ice. The next morning, we planned to head to base camp and then, weather permitting, I'd take a quick flight out to Talkeetna the following day and soon arrive home to the dry warmth of Phoenix.

I started down that morning roped to two other climbers, Glenn and Steve. The team had been roped together for almost the entire time as a constant precaution and a reminder of the danger of crevasses on the glacier. Steve led, I was second in line, and Glenn brought up the rear. It had snowed lightly overnight, and the gray and misty morning made visibility poor. About two hours into the trek, daydreaming, just trudging down the mountain, not truly present, I absently hiked down, pulling my sled behind me. It's entirely likely my thoughts revolved around the stack of work piling up on my desk and mentally trying to anticipate what my priorities would be upon my return.

Then it happened.

Steve, also absentmindedly, wandered slightly off Arlo's path. Suddenly, he stepped through a thin layer of snow that had camouflaged a huge crevasse. Steve dropped like a stone, disappearing in an instant as the rope between us snaked away down the crevasse. We had practiced the response numerous times, so almost immediately, my muscle memory kicked in. I fell with all my weight, chest first, onto my ice ax, plunging it into the ice. Glenn, thankfully, did the same thing a split second after me.

Our ice axes pegged deep into the ice just as the rope between Steve and me sprung taut as Steve jerked to a halt inside the crevasse, swinging into its wall. Thankfully, he couldn't fall more than a rope's length into the chasm. This meticulously drilled response ultimately saved Steve's life.

The guides rushed over to help and secured the line as everyone cautiously gathered around the edge to call down to Steve. Crevasses can be extremely dangerous, with spires, icicles, and spikes jutting out from all angles, so we wanted to be sure Steve hadn't sustained any unexpected injuries. After a minute or so, Steve gathered enough strength to use the rope to climb out of the crevasse. Amazingly, except for some bumps and bruises, he was okay. His heavy, down-climbing gear had cushioned his bang against the crevasse wall.

Unfortunately, the same could not be said for me.

I had fallen so hard on my ice ax, I cracked two ribs and hyper-extended my knee. I wasn't sure at the time that I'd broken my ribs, but I took the searing pain seriously because each breath took effort. But I didn't say anything. I didn't want to burden the team with what could be just serious bruising. Steve had almost lost his life and making sure he was okay took priority. Although well-intentioned, I made a serious mistake by not telling the guides about my injuries. After about fifteen minutes, the shock and adrenaline of the incident wore off. Everyone got reoriented, and we continued heading down, albeit much, much more alert.

Soon I realized I could no longer pull the sled with just my body. Instead, I had to grab the rope and pull it with my arm to relieve some of the pressure the rope placed on my waist because it sent sharp, dagger-like pain through my ribs with each step. I began to suffer badly. To make the situation worse, I had developed a full-blown cold. This meant every time I sneezed or coughed, my ribs erupted in pain. Before long, I started to become delirious and wanted to lie down on the snow beneath me, curl up in a ball, and just go to sleep, never to awake. Physically, mentally, and emotionally exhausted, this was one of the rare times on a mountain I wanted to quit. This is a precarious place to find yourself in while you're on a world-class mountain, as the risk level for you and others spikes exponentially.

I had entered what I have mentioned climbers call "the pain cave," and this was the most lethal kind. The inky-black darkness of the pain cave engulfed me, and this time I had no idea how to escape.

Before long, our guides noticed my rope adjustment and wilting energy. I admitted I might have broken a rib or two falling on my ice ax. When they saw my face, they stopped the party and jumped to my aid. They checked my ribs and agreed they were probably broken. The pain from even a gentle touch on the ribs is indescribable. After some friendly chiding, asking why I hadn't said anything, they insisted on taking the gear off my sled and redistributed my load amongst the other people's sleds. They did the same with my backpack.

Maybe because I'd sat down for a while, or maybe because my pain was out in the open, I told Arlo I was done. I couldn't stand up, let alone go on. I told him to just leave me on the snow; it would be fine. I had made peace with my demise.

Something I have learned is spending time in the pain cave doesn't apply only to climbing high mountains. The pain cave is a real and frequent place in the corporate world, too. Everyone's pain cave is different in terms of cause, intensity, and duration, but what is not different is that we all eventually find ourselves there. I will share something from my Denali climb that may have saved my bacon on that mountain and has helped me in the corporate world more than I can explain. It is, by far, the most important lesson from Denali and one of the most important lessons I could ever impart. It comes from a simple question Arlo asked when I told him I could not continue.

As a leader, whenever you or your employees enter that pain cave, ask yourself, "Are you hurt, or are you just hurting?" If I'd been truly hurt to the point I couldn't physically go on, Arlo would have, without hesitation, requested a rescue helicopter to make a risky attempt up the mountain to get me off. Doing that would endanger both me and the helicopter pilot but would be necessary if I was truly disabled. If, however, I was just *hurting*—deep in the pain cave from a Denali summit, a full-blown cold, and two broken ribs—but could keep down-climbing, if I could somehow dig deeply enough into my mental fortitude . . . well, then I should keep going.

It is moments like this that show you what you're made of. I could have easily told Arlo I needed that chopper. No one would have thought one iota less of me for doing so, and Arlo would have radioed it in within seconds, but I would have known in my heart that I had given up. The team would have had to wait for me to be air-lifted out. I knew that despite being deep in the pain cave, I could keep going, especially without my pack and sled. So that is exactly what I did. Slowly, painfully, methodically, I pulled myself up to my feet, told them "let's go", and proceeded to place one foot in front of the other to continue down the mountain.

To this day, when I face a difficult situation at work

or in my personal life, I always think back to Arlo's words on the mountain and ask myself, "Are you hurt, or just hurting?" I then act accordingly.

When I went through my "real-life pain cave" in Ridgecrest, I ended up working at that credit union for two years. For the first twenty-two months, I resisted being there and refused to accept it. I kept applying for HR jobs all over the country, trying to escape, but to no avail. I found myself still sitting in the pain cave.

Finally, for whatever reason, I had an epiphany and decided I would accept where God had placed me and try to bloom where I had been planted. Mentally, I finally made peace with living in Ridgecrest, and began to be grateful for some of the good things about living there. Being a small town, that meant no traffic. I could even walk to work. Close to the Eastern Sierras, the area experienced 355 days of sunshine a year, and I had an easy, non-stressful job that never exceeded forty hours a week.

Within a month of having that epiphany and coming to peace with my situation, something amazing happened. A friend I hadn't talked to in a couple of years emailed me about a good HR job in Tucson. My friend had applied for the job but did not land it, so he encouraged me to apply. They hired me within a week with only two phone interviews. This was the quickest and easiest job application process I had ever experienced, and within three weeks, I left Ridgecrest and headed to Tucson.

The real question, of course, is "Am I totally out

of this pain cave?" Yes, and no. The thought of all the money I lost is still a raw wound that may be there for the rest of my life. But a priceless lesson I learned was when things spiral downward in life, just as they can on a mountain, you may have to go into that pain cave and persevere and accept that God has you in that place for a reason, even though you may not understand it.

I also know that eventually you will come out on the other side, but it will be in His time, not yours. Trust me, the sooner you can accept that, the better off you will be.

We made it all the way down to the Kahiltna Glacier to a waiting EMT and plane that would fly me off the mountain to the nearest hospital in Fairbanks. I lay on the stretcher in that plane, disappointed about leaving the mountain that way, but happy my friend hadn't died and that I had made it down to at least the base camp. At the hospital, they X-rayed me and confirmed I had broken a couple of ribs. Everything else checked out okay, but they kept me overnight just to be sure there was no internal bleeding.

Unfortunately, there isn't much you can do for broken ribs, so they wrapped my torso, but it didn't help. The thought crossed my mind that if I came down with the flu, causing me to cough or sneeze constantly, I would sincerely ask them to just shoot me to put me out of my misery. Rib pain is brutal.

After my brief hospital stay, the guide company assisted me in changing my flights so I could fly out of Fairbanks instead of Anchorage. Although grateful for this, it also bummed me out to be unable to have a celebratory dinner with my team (I hadn't forgotten about that cheeseburger in Talkeetna). It especially disappointed me that I couldn't say goodbye to my new friends in person.

As I made the long, sometimes painful journey back to Phoenix, I thought about the climb on Denali and about goals in general. When you set a goal, there may be unexpected pain in attaining it. There certainly was on Denali, from miserable weather, to bone-chilling cold, to pushing through exhaustion and making the summit, then descending safely down, only to break two ribs and still have to hike a few miles more to get out. There may be times when going after a goal requires you to not only accept the pain but also embrace it to reach your goal.

I made up my mind to always push through the pain if I was only *hurting*.

I had also wondered why—despite my prayers for protection—unlike on most other climbs, God had allowed me to be injured. Then it dawned on me. Sometimes there is a lesson to be learned, a point we never knew we could push past. Yes, breaking my ribs at the tail end of a seven-summit climb is something I never want to experience again in a million years, but I had found a new boundary of endurance, a new limit I knew I could push to.

At that moment, I became immensely grateful to God for not only allowing me to participate in the unexplainably magnificent Denali experience but also for allowing me to learn this invaluable valuable lesson.

CHAPTER 21

Summit Fever

IN THE SUMMER OF 2008, MY OLD FRIEND TODD AND I decided to do a Colorado road trip to climb some fourteeners. We hit the southwest corner of the state and headed up to an old mining town called Lake City, which we used as a base for the next few days.

There are fifty-four peaks that stand over 14,000 feet in Colorado, and I have been blessed to climb all of them at least once. Each peak has its own personality, attractions, and dangers. My favorite fourteener *trail* is the Barr Trail on Pikes Peak, my favorite fourteener is my beloved Longs Peak, and for an overall hiking experience, the most enjoyable fourteener is Uncompahgre Peak—the highest point in southwest Colorado's San Juan Range at 14,309 feet.

I love hiking up Uncompahgre because a national forest flourishes on the lower part of the mountain, making the views so spectacular they are literally postcard and calendar material. At the higher elevations, it is an often snowy, alpine climate (meaning no tree growth).

I enjoy this hike so much I have done it six times. Most of these times I've gone solo, but I was looking forward to Todd's company. This trip, however, would be different from my previous climbs. I'd trained as a Wilderness First Responder a few years before, but a few years is a long time when a crisis is thrust upon you.

The Wilderness First Responder Training is comprehensive and teaches a non-medical or layperson to deal with a range of injuries or ailments that can be encountered in the wilderness. This includes basic life support, responding to signs of circulatory shock, soft tissue injuries, such as burns or wounds, dealing with bone and joint injuries, such as fractures, sprains, strains, and dislocations, and management of suspected head and/or spinal injuries, among other skills.

We climbed several fourteeners over the next few days, thoroughly enjoying each climb. With great weather for the most part, and views that are so stunning and mountain air that's so refreshing and exhilarating, the feeling of being there can't quite be put into words. It's something you just have to experience. Finally, on our last day, the time arrived for my favorite climb—Uncompahgre.

In our high-clearance, four-wheel-drive truck, we drove up to Uncompahgre on a rough road, making it all the way to the trailhead. Even the drive up was beautiful, and as a bonus, this saved us eight miles of hiking. We started out in the gorgeous forest, but within a half-mile, we were above timberline, overlooking the lush valley. Wildflowers abound on this landscape, which made the colors and beauty utterly spectacular. I couldn't have been any happier if I'd been on the Matterhorn.

We continued on the scenic main trail for the next couple hours. The trail wound its way up Uncompahgre's south ridge until we reached the crest at about 13,800 feet. At the top of this ridge, we realized we hadn't been paying attention to the weather. I felt a flutter of disquiet in my stomach as I tried to assess the situation. Serious storm clouds were building to the east. I wondered how long it would take them to reach our position if the storm headed our way at all.

Maybe because we'd just hiked several other fourteeners without incident, and Uncompahgre is not a technical peak, we'd let our attention slip, but not paying attention to the weather is a mistake that experienced climbers should not make.

Todd immediately said he wanted to head back.

I rubbed my jaw in frustration, trying to figure out what I wanted to do. I felt annoyed at myself for not noticing the clouds. The dangers of exposure in a storm are many on a mountain: slipping and falling, losing your way, tumbling rock, and lightning, to name a few. I had climbed Uncompahgre many times, so I knew the trail pretty well. The storm clouds appeared ominous, but the wind didn't seem to be blowing super hard in our direction. I figured—worst case—I could most likely make it back into the timberline before the storm really hit. This would mean I'd at least have some cover and solid footing.

I probably wouldn't have admitted it at the time, but I had a touch of summit fever. Since Uncompahgre is my favorite hike and the crescendo of our trip, I wanted to finish well and make it to the top. I decided to continue. Todd said he'd head back down. Before he did, he asked me if I was sure. I smiled and said, "Yeah, I'll be fine." He nodded and told me to be careful and started back down the mountain.

I continued on, and soon reached the crux of the climb—150 feet of steep, loose rock below the upper slopes. I had done this scramble before, so I knew the best path. I ascended it as quickly as I could, making sure I didn't slip. I cleared the section before long, then started up a well-defined trail that leads up the last few feet to the summit. Despite darkening skies, the beautifully scenic climb up the last stretch made it seem worthwhile. I took all the beauty in and soon reached the summit. I grinned with satisfaction over having conquered Uncompahgre again.

Well, almost. I still had to descend.

I turned around and looked back over the valley. It surprised me to see how much closer the clouds had come. I hadn't expected this. I felt a sudden twinge of anxiety. I knew I had to hightail it off the summit, especially to get past the loose rock slope. The thing about Uncompahgre is that the rock in the region is full of iron ore. This meant I'd be pretty much scrambling down a lightning rod.

I ran down the trail and soon made it to the rocky slope. The darkest clouds were now near the forest and closing in rapidly. Although dangerous to go too fast on loose rock, I scrambled down as quickly as I could without taking a fall. I guess I did it a little too quickly because about two-thirds of the way down I lost my footing and rolled my ankle. *Dang it!* I thought, as I sat for a minute rubbing my ankle. *This is all I need right now.* Suddenly, I saw a bright flash of lightning and heard the subsequent peal of thunder not far behind.

I realized then I had been foolish to insist on summiting. I got up quickly and began to, somewhat gingerly, make my way down toward the timberline. I prayed I could get to the trees safely without being hit.

I reached the main trail and saw another bright flash and heard a loud clap of lightning. *That was* much *closer!* I thought. I picked up the pace as much as I could, making a beeline for the trees. There are different kinds of exposure on a mountain. Climbing an icefall with an ice ax in the Himalayas is one kind; pulling yourself up fixed-lines is another. Running down a rocky slope during a lightning storm is an entirely different level of dread since you have zero control over when you might be struck.

Then I saw him.

Down below me, another climber was making his way *up*. I could see it wasn't Todd by his clothing and gait, so this dumbfounded me. *Why is this guy still going up when lightning is flashing all around us?* I knew he had to be inexperienced, so I continued going down as fast as I could. I planned to do everything in my power to convince this guy to turn back.

I was still about 200 yards above him when it happened: an immensely bright flash of light, followed by an instant, thunderous roar. I nearly jumped out of my skin and instinctively hit the ground. After a few seconds, I rose to my knees and, realizing (thankfully) I hadn't been hit, looked down to check on the other climber. *Oh my God!* Adrenaline surged through my body. He lay on the ground and wasn't moving.

I couldn't tell if he'd taken a direct hit or if the lightning bolt struck close to him, but I sprinted down to his position. As I approached, it relieved me somewhat to see him on his back and moaning. *At least he is breathing!* The guy looked to be in his early twenties; just a kid, really. "It's gonna be okay, buddy." I tried to reassure him, but I wasn't sure if he could hear me. I frantically struggled to remember my First Responder Training.

Since he was still breathing, I didn't need to bother with CPR. Then I remembered the first thing to do is to stabilize the head in case of spinal injury. I placed my hand in a way that kept his head from moving, then checked for any visible injuries on his body, also feeling underneath him for any bleeding. I then rolled up some of my rain gear and placed it around his head to keep it from moving. He continued to moan incoherently in pain, so I kept trying to reassure him in as soothing a way as possible.

Then it started to rain.

With the addition of cold rain, I knew the danger of hypothermia and shock setting in, so I took off my rain shell and covered him. I had to get help. No way could this guy recover soon enough to climb back down, and if hypothermia set in, he was as good as dead.

I always carry an emergency satellite transponder when I am in the backcountry, but I had never activated it before. For a long, frustrating few seconds, I couldn't remember how to do it. Finally, I figured out you just open up the antennae, set it in a place where it has clear access to the sky (above timberline, this wasn't an issue), and hit the activate button. Because I had no way of knowing whether a satellite had picked up the signal, I decided I needed to make a call as a backup plan.

Our location had no signal, so after making sure I had the guy as stable as possible, I headed back up the mountain to see if I could get a signal. This was hair-raising—not literally, as that actually means you're about to be struck by lightning, but it was really scary. As I made my way back up, checking the bars on my phone, lightning kept flashing with a loud clap, and then peals of thunder followed close behind. The storm had thankfully, however, moved away from my location a little. I ended up having to climb all the way back to the top of the south ridge before I could get a signal. I quickly dialed 9-1-1 and reported what happened. They assured me help was on the way.

I hiked back down to the stricken climber. He had quieted down, which at first scared me until I verified that he was still breathing. I had practiced CPR in my Wilderness First Responder Training, but I wasn't confident in my practical ability, so I prayed this dude just kept breathing. From what I could tell, it did not look like the climber had taken a direct hit since I didn't see any burn marks or scorched skin. It must have been close, though, because he'd clearly taken an indirect hit.

An indirect lightning strike can either travel through a ground current, flowing into nearby objects (or people), or it can travel through what is known as a side flash. This is when the lightning seems to "jump" through the air from one object to another, but it's actually the charge seeking to expend the rest of its energy through a new path. Indirect strikes still carry more than enough amperes to kill.

The guy began to shiver, which indicated shock. I covered him with everything I had, then sat down in front of his head to keep it steady with my hands. I'd reached the limit of my first aid knowledge in the situation. I had lost all concept of time, so I just started to pray for him, and I prayed the rescuers would arrive soon. Between praying, I kept speaking soothing words to him.

I have no idea how much time passed, but eventually, I saw Todd come rushing back up the trail as fast as he could. I felt so grateful to see him, especially since it seemed the danger had mostly passed. He told me he had been waiting at the truck when the Search and Rescue team arrived. He said his heart sank until he spoke to them and discovered it wasn't me who was down. He immediately set up the trail, though, while Search and

Rescue geared up. He estimated they were about a half-hour behind him.

Todd wisely brought all the rain gear and clothing he had, and we packed it on the kid. I took Todd's rain shell, as I had started to get cold, too. Todd took over for me, holding the guy's head, which allowed me to do a few pushups and jumping jacks to get my blood flowing and warm my body up. Todd's estimate proved correct, as about thirty minutes later, I saw a party of six men hiking up the route, carrying a gurney.

As soon as they reached us, we let them take over. We kind of just stood around and watched. They quickly took the kid's vitals and gave him a shot of something as they readied him to be placed on the gurney. I could see they were adept at keeping his head from moving. Soon they had him strapped down and were ready to go.

Todd and I volunteered to help the team carry the gurney down, which they gratefully accepted. This allowed for two of us to rotate out every so often, giving our arms a chance to rest. We made our way through the forest and down the main trail, rotating gurney bearers all the way down the mountain.

By the time we finally made it down to the trailhead, the kid's vitals were weak, but thankfully, he'd never stopped breathing. He never did fully regain consciousness. The rescue team loaded him up into an ambulance and transported him back down the mountain to Lake City. From there, a helicopter waited to transfer him to a hospital in Pagosa Springs. I prayed again for his full recovery.

Todd and I both felt mentally and physically drained. Todd, being in slightly better shape, drove us down the mountain. We had planned to drive to Durango that night to make the next day's drive back to Phoenix much shorter, but being completely wiped out from the experience, we stayed in Lake City.

The next morning, we checked with the head of Search and Rescue to see if they had any word about the climber (we later found out his name was Blake). We were told he was in stable condition, but they didn't know anything more. I thanked God and thought of how blessed Blake was that he hadn't taken a direct hit from the lightning bolt, and that even though I had broken several of my leadership and climbing rules, it seems God had orchestrated for me to be on the trail to help a fellow climber. I shudder to think of anyone alone on a mountain after being hit by a lightning strike.

A simple but profound lesson came out of this experience: never become complacent in your vigilant assessment of the risks. And more important, even in our greatest, strongest moment, we are utterly insignificant compared to God and His creations. Ultimately, it's God working in you Who gives you the ability to withstand all the threats life poses.

As I mentioned in a previous chapter, summit fever is similar to the "deal fever" companies can fall into when they become enamored with completing an acquisition with which they have no business being involved. You see, companies totally ignore or skew their due diligence to fit the narrative that it will be a good deal because *they want it to happen so badly.* So often, they go ahead, and it turns into a disaster. I think the statistics are that about seventy percent of acquisitions ultimately fail. I believe this "deal fever" is a huge reason why.

As mentioned in the Denali chapter, when I bought an existing doggie daycare franchise, I didn't do the proper due diligence. I got caught up in the dream of owning my own business, helping shelter dogs, and I thought I would make a good deal of money, too. When reality hit, I realized I'd inherited a business with a horrible, financially untenable lease situation. Because of my overriding desire to buy this business at all costs, I lost over $300,000.

On the mountain, my exuberance to make the summit of Uncompahgre at all costs could have cost me my life.

Corporations do the same thing when they put blinders on because they want something so much.

As I pondered the gravity of these thoughts, I again thanked God that Blake didn't die and that I did not get hit myself after the foolishness of my summit fever. I also gave thanks for the Search and Rescue people. As it turned out, my satellite transponder did work, and they received that alert before my phone call.

I had witnessed the immense, raw power of God's creation in the form of this lightning storm and summarily felt humbled by this experience. I had seen firsthand how the tremendous power of electricity is neutral in its regard for life: it can be harnessed to improve life, or it can take life in a moment. Thankfully, everyone made it off the mountain alive this time.

I wish, with all my heart, I could say the same for my climb up Mount Aconcagua.

CHAPTER 22

Pride Before a Fall

MY FAVORITE MOUNTAIN OF ALL THE SEVEN summits also happens to be the highest mountain in the world outside of the Himalayas. The mighty Aconcagua looms tall and proud at 22,834 feet above sea level, on the border of Argentina and Chile. The mountain is part of the epic Andes Range, but its tall, iconic pyramid stands out clearly from the rest. Even though an average of three people die each year on this mountain, I love it because of its beauty. I also knew the ascent would be a great physical challenge, but well within my capabilities. First summited in 1897 by a climber named Matthias Zurbriggen, Aconcagua has many tricks up her sleeve.

A few days after Christmas in 2008, I flew from Phoenix to Miami, Miami to Lima, Peru, and then from Lima to a small Argentine city called Mendoza.

Mendoza is gorgeous, lazily picturesque, and known as the gateway to the Argentine wine country. Arriving there seemed like a welcome reward for flying all night.

After arriving at my hotel around noon, I had just settled down to take a nap when my phone rang. The rest of my climbing team had arrived, and they were all meeting downstairs to get acquainted. I had contracted with Tusker (the same company as I used on Aconcagua), who had, in turn, subcontracted with a local company, which meant both of our guides—Carlos and Ernesto— were Argentinian.

Ernesto, our lead guide, looked like a Latin movie star, but his appearance belied his humility. Waiting in the lobby, he welcomed me with a warm smile when he met me and introduced me to Carlos and the rest of my team.

Three of the climbers were from California. Two guys named Jimmy and Patrick were best friends and planned to do the Inca Trail after Aconcagua. Alan and Vicki hailed from the United Kingdom, worked for the same bank, and had just started dating each other. Dave, like me, was climbing solo, so it made sense that he would be my tent mate.

The last member of our crew was an attractive, yet bold and brash Israeli lady named Merka. Merka had medium-length blonde hair, and she became the immediate focus of every single guy on the team. She told us she had successfully summited Kilimanjaro and felt up to climbing Aconcagua. I nodded and smiled, hoping this would prove true. It seemed to be a good, fun group.

Despite my lack of sleep, the rush of a new adventure surged through me.

We spent the next two days in Mendoza enjoying the city, especially the food. Argentina is known for its high quality of beef, and I have to say the reputation is well deserved. The steaks were *incredible*. The relaxed Latino lifestyle that permeates this city is, however, what really struck me. I absolutely loved it.

We did our obligatory gear check, renting whatever we didn't have, and on our third day got ready to depart. We each had to possess a climbing permit for the mountain, so we went to an administrative office in downtown Mendoza to purchase them. There are always extra costs and red tape like this when doing these expeditions, and even though it is frustrating, it is a necessary and understandable evil of gaining access to the mountains. We all piled into a van and headed into the Andes.

We drove until we reached a small ski resort called Penitentes, which rests at 8,500 feet. We spent the night in dorm-style bedrooms. The next morning, we got off the highway and headed into the park. We stopped at the trailhead and prepared to hike into the Vacus Valley, through which flowed the Rio de Vacus.

Fortunately, I had brought along a large duffel bag because I'd been told we would carry our gear up the valley by mules. Each duffel bag could weigh up to forty-four pounds, with each mule carrying a maximum load of 132 pounds Guys called *muleteers* drove the mules.

Finally, we were ready to start. We faced a three-day hike up desert terrain to base camp, hiking about ten miles a day. Ernesto and Carlos kept a slow yet steady pace to aid our acclimatization. We planned to camp each night at an official site monitored by park rangers.

On day one, we had a tricky crossing of a creek swollen with melted snow. We risked injury and losing gear to the creek if we fell in, but our guides searched for an easy route to cross. Finally, they found a route that we could cross while staying dry if we had decent balance. Everyone made it across, and then I went for it. Immediately, I realized how slick the rocks were. The current pushed hard and fast against my legs. Placing one foot on a rock, I slid, and the current pushed me the rest of the way, causing me to fall into the creek. Fortunately, I gained my feet quickly and made sure I had all my gear intact. I did a check for physical injuries.

Thankfully, only my pride had been wounded.

Making good time, we reached our campsite and set up our own tents, while Ernesto and Carlos cooked for the team. I liked my tent mate, Dave, and found him easy to talk to. We quickly became friends. Dave, despite not being a climber, had decided he wanted to do Aconcagua and Denali. He reasoned if he could successfully make this climb, he would attempt Denali the next year. I liked that he aimed big with little experience.

We woke up the next day and followed the same routine, making good time again. On the third day, however, a new challenge arose—we had to cross the Rio de Vacus. Far too wide and too deep to risk crossing on foot, we had to ride mules across. I had never been on a horse or mule in my life, so it would be a new experience. Nervous about the prospect, I naturally had trouble getting on the mule. After a few tries, though, I managed to climb on his back and quickly crossed the river without incident. I had a new experience to write home about.

At this point, we had our first view of the snow-covered Aconcagua in the distance. I had read about this mountain for so long; it was awe-inspiring to finally see it in person. I immediately noticed the strong winds on the summit. Even from a distance, I could see snow blowing off the summit like spindly white clouds. My climber's sense went on alert.

Aconcagua has an iconic cross on the summit that I had seen in pictures. The cross is made from black tubes and is brightly decorated. I wondered what it would feel like when I, at last, got to see that cross. It seemed so far off. I prayed for safety for myself and my team, as I knew we had a significant challenge ahead, and the weather on Aconcagua could change rapidly.

About ten minutes later, as if in response to my sober prayer, we heard the familiar *whomp-whomp* of rescue helicopter rotors before we saw the choppers soaring up the mountain to evacuate someone. I prayed they were okay.

We made base camp around 3:00 p.m. The camp, named Campo Argentina, looked enormous, with various expeditions set up around the site. A large dining tent, complete with a dining table, chairs, and tablecloths, stood as the camp's central focus. To my amazement, a tent with computer equipment where you could check email, stood nearby. We rested the following day and had a mandatory check-in with the camp doctor, where he took our pulse, blood pressure, and oxygen saturation levels. My readings looked fine, so he cleared me to go higher on the mountain. Merka's oxygen saturation levels read a little low, but not low enough to call off her climb. I had noticed she'd slowed down a bit, and I hoped she'd be okay.

I've climbed enough high mountains to recognize good leaders and not-so-great ones. One key of leadership on the mountain is noticing the little things that add up to significant red flags. In many ways, it is like the proverbial frog in the boiling pot, blissfully unaware as the water is slowly warmed, then heated, then finally boiled. The frog doesn't realize he is boiling until it is too late.

Paying attention to the little signs that things are not going well is crucial for anticipating disaster, instead of reacting to it. The driving force behind this sort of blindness is focusing too much on the goal—the summit—and not on the journey. When you focus on the journey, you naturally pay attention because there exists far less cognitive dissonance between the reality of your situation and reaching your objective at any cost.

Ernesto and Carlos appeared to be seasoned, methodical climbers and patient, detailed guides. If anything went wrong, heaven forbid, I trusted them completely, and I believed they would make good decisions.

We rested the following day at Camp Argentina, then hiked up to see a strange snow formation. I haven't seen anything like it anywhere else except on Aconcagua. The formation is called Penitentes Ice and looks like elongated, thin blades, or sometimes cones, of ice, three-feet to five-feet tall. To me, the ice almost resembles fields of mini, white Christmas trees, since they are closely spaced together in vast numbers and generally point up at the sun. My guess is that the Penitentes Ice requires the dry, desert-like air of this region, with plenty of sun and a high altitude to form. The ice fields possessed a unique beauty, and I felt privileged to see them.

One of the best things about climbing is hanging out at base camp, meeting other groups of climbers. This time of social relaxation is always a welcome relief from the grind of the climb. On this trip, it pleased me to meet the first Canadian to climb Everest. He was a fascinating individual who has made a career of linking the challenges of climbing to the challenges encountered in business. I definitely "got" him, since our philosophies were so similar. He had a lot of great qualities, including being articulate, humble . . . and *much* faster than any of us going up or down this mountain. I truly felt honored to meet this gentleman.

We also met a funny and boisterous Italian team. One night we shared the dining table with their crew: Giuseppe, Luca, Angelo, Gianna, and their guide, Stefano. Gianna, a petite twenty-something, with long, dark hair, seemed quite sweet. Surprisingly (for an Italian), she was soft-spoken. She shared that she loved the outdoors, and despite her gentle exterior, I recognized a fiercely resolute glint in her eye. In fact, she outright told us of her determination to hold her own with all the men in her group. I liked her immediately.

The three guys paid a ton of attention to Merka. Giuseppe, probably thirty years old, and typically Italian in his confidence of his abilities with women, appeared to be quite taken with Merka. For most of the conversation, he focused on and flirted with her. He mentioned he lived in the Tuscan region and he appeared to not see much value in work, so I guessed he came from money. Giuseppe had an infectious laugh which he loudly bellowed often, and he clearly lived life with a passion.

Luca, slightly more demure than Giuseppe, also appeared to love life. He seemed to me to be a genuinely nice guy. He'd also become smitten with Merka, but he didn't have the boldness of Giuseppe. The group attested to the fact that he was a powerful climber and the strongest of their group. If I recall correctly, he mentioned being from Rome and said he and Angelo were longtime friends who had climbed all over the Alps together.

Angelo told us he was married with kids, and it was evident he was completely devoted to his family. Also a friendly guy, he seemed to be closest to Gianna. Angelo had such a warm heart and friendly nature, no one could fail to like him immensely.

Their guide, Stefano, looked clean cut and,

unfortunately, seemed exceedingly cocky. Although friendly, he engaged in a somewhat condescending, arrogant sort of way. I got it that the guy had supreme confidence, but he also had an edge of hubris that concerned me a little. Everyone enjoys a bit of friendly banter and competition, but where Ernesto and Carlos demonstrated their competence through their actions, Stefano appeared to demonstrate his competence through his words. Nevertheless, I liked the guy and enjoyed his tall tales.

We had a roaring good time with the Italians and shared stories and laughter way into the night. We stayed up far too late, but eventually reached the point where we knew it would ruin our climb the next day and had to call it a night. Our team, especially, had a big day starting the next morning.

I knew I would stay in touch with my new Italian friends, and I hoped to see them higher up on the mountain.

CHAPTER 23

Fatal Leadership

A FTER OUR LATE NIGHT WITH THE ITALIAN TEAM, I woke up feeling great and chipper—a good thing because we had our first climb up to Camp 1 at over 16,000 feet to drop off a load of our gear. With the sun out and the brisk air, I felt incredibly strong. That day became one of the best climbing days I have ever had in my life. I surged past everyone even though I paid attention to the magnificent views far more than usual. Climbing is weird sometimes; some days you're strong, and other days not at all.

Our guides told us this day would be a good test for going higher on the mountain where we'd face a thirty-degree scree slope. I scrambled up the loose rock like a mountain goat, despite potent gusts of wind blasting us now and then. Looking back occasionally, I saw Merka struggling, falling farther and farther back at the end of our line. I had been feeling concerned about her, but the decision to turn back belonged to her and the guides. Eventually, we all made it up the slope, and that familiar feeling of being close to the top of the world returned. I was in my element!

Camp 1 had a few tent sites, curiously walled in by rocks. I quickly understood why when a powerful gust of wind picked me off my feet. That experience is way more terrifying than it sounds because I could have been close to a ledge. I decided to steer clear of any sheer drop-offs.

Speaking of sheer drop-offs, Camp 1 also had a uniquely interesting feature—a toilet sat outside of the camp on the edge of a ridge, so you could look 12,000 feet down a valley as you were doing your business. We all had to carry waste bags, which you just clipped in while you sat there on this "throne" admiring the view. I prayed fervently a gust of wind would not carry me to my untimely and embarrassing doom.

We stayed at Camp 1 for about an hour, then headed back to base camp to spend another rest day hanging out with the other climbers to play cards and relax. Although bummed knowing the Italians would not be there since they were taking a different route up the south face, I still had a good time just chilling with my group and with the many other climbers that day.

The next day, we headed back up to Camp 1. We practiced crampon techniques the day after that, but the wind at Camp 1 blew stronger than ever. The fear of a gust of wind taking me to my death stayed constant—that and the biting cold during the two nights we stayed at Camp 1 kept me eager to leave. Fortunately, my down sleeping bag, rated to minus-thirty degrees Fahrenheit, made the nights tolerable.

Eventually, we hiked up to what we called Camp 1.5 at 17,500 feet and spent the night there, but the wind gusted even worse than at Camp 1. It whipped the tent around with near-animalistic howls and made sleep difficult. I figured if I could survive hearing what truly sounded like a yeti on Ama Dablam at midnight, I could survive a bit of wind.

The next morning, we headed back down to Camp 1 to spend one more night, following the "climb high and sleep low" credo for acclimatization. In layman's terms, we did this to create more oxygen-carrying red blood cells in our bloodstreams to avoid altitude sickness and either of the dreaded edemas.

The next day broke sunny with a little less wind, which didn't mean much as I'd made up my mind that Aconcagua would always be windy. We started trekking up to Camp 2, the high camp. I would describe the trail from Camp 1 to Camp 2 to be more like high-altitude hiking than high-altitude climbing. By the time we reached Camp 2, however, the wind howled ferociously around us, and setting up tents became super difficult.

Ernesto and Carlos took our oxygen readings, just like they had been doing every day or two since the doctor's first check at base camp. Everyone's readings registered okay—even Merka's—so we relaxed a little . . . which wasn't easy because of the news we received that day.

Besides the altitude, what makes Aconcagua a dangerous mountain is the weather. The peak is less than a hundred miles from the Pacific Ocean, so terrible Pacific storms come inland rapidly, battering the mountain. Thankfully, our guides always stayed in radio contact with their "home base," where they got the latest updates on any weather systems moving in.

After they checked in that day, they told us a major storm front was supposed to hit the mountain the following evening. It would be perilously risky to be caught near the summit when the storm hit. Snow-covered crevasses, exposure to the elements, losing our way . . . I didn't want to even think about the list of perils. After some deliberation, the guides moved our plan to leave Camp 2 for the summit at 2:00 a.m. up to 11:30 p.m.

This meant little or no sleep.

Aconcagua began to feel more and more like Everest.

We wanted to reach the summit no later than 8:00 a.m. so we could be well down the mountain if the storm hit the following evening. The team had "dinner" at around 4:00 p.m., but even that didn't provide any comfort. Most of the meals on the trip all had some sugar in them, and as I've mentioned, I'm severely allergic. A few days prior, I had to miss three meals in a single day. If I consume even the slightest amount of sugar, I get nauseous instantly. The stuff just tastes terrible to me.

We all headed for our tents and tried to sleep. I think I dozed a little, but I talked to Dave for a good deal of the time as he couldn't sleep, either. We were going to make the summit bid on one of the mightiest mountains in the world on little to no sleep. Add in the chance that we'd catch at least part of a major blizzard and I again asked myself, *Why do I do this?*

Carlos roused us at 10:45 p.m., and we began to don our gear. At that point, we did not need crampons, but I put on all my cold-weather gear: heavy Gore-Tex pants, down jacket, thermal underwear, multiple layers, mitten liners, Gore-Tex mittens, a balaclava to protect my face, and ski goggles to protect my eyes. We ate a little food, then it was time to rock.

Ernesto maintained his usual slow but steady pace, using the "rest step" as we headed up the hill. The trail, once again, seemed more like hiking than climbing, and we made steady progress throughout the night. Overhead, one of my favorite parts of high climbs shone brilliantly. It seemed like I could almost reach up and run my hand through a million twinkling stars in the obsidian sky. The icy cold air—below zero for sure—made me grateful for my warm gear, but mercifully, the wind had died down. As long as we kept moving, I felt okay.

Soon it became clear that Merka couldn't handle the altitude. She had been struggling since we climbed above Camp 1, and as our team stopped after slowing a good deal to accommodate her, she finally had to admit she physically could not keep going. We all encouraged Merka, telling her she'd get it next time, then Carlos left with her and took her back down the mountain.

We continued our steady pace through the night

and watched in bated anticipation as the dawn cracked through a dark sky in the East. As the sun slowly rose, Aconcagua cast a gigantic pyramid-shaped shadow across the entire landscape to the west. I had to take a moment to appreciate the splendor of a site so few on a planet of over seven billion people get to witness—the shadow of a mammoth mountain, long and intimidating, yet one of the thousands God created. I worshiped Him in quiet reverence as my eyes drank in the sight.

After another hour or so, we reached the base of a gully called the Canaleta and stopped to take a break. Sleep-deprived and physically tired, we couldn't help but think about the toughest part of the climb that lay ahead. The final 1,000 feet is straight up the Canaleta. I had read about the challenges of this gully, a spot alleged to be filled with loose scree.

That rumor turned out to be true.

As many mountains do, Aconcagua had saved her toughest feature for the end. Our pace up the steep slope slowed to a crawl due to the loose rock. The route wandered aimlessly back and forth across the slope, with our sole encouragement being a view of the summit. Even this seemed bittersweet, as a few climbers who were a little faster had already summited, and we could see them celebrating. As our muscles burned and our feet ached, the site of them felt both infuriating and motivating.

Finally, after what seemed like half the day but more likely equaled about an hour and forty-five minutes, we reached the top of this interminable gully. I didn't even wait to rest for a minute after cresting. I just marched straight up to the summit.

Within minutes, I joined the other climbers we'd seen celebrating.

I had summited Aconcagua!

I walked up to the colorful, iconic tube cross I had seen in so many pictures and was a little . . . underwhelmed. To be honest, even though seeing the cross had been important to me, in actuality, it appeared much smaller than I thought and much less spectacular. Still, I took many pictures, which I suspected would look more glamorous than in real life as well.

From the top, I could see Chili, Argentina, and Aconcagua's deadly, imposing south face. Normally you can see the Pacific Ocean, but it was covered in a rolling tempest of clouds that were quickly moving towards us. The lack of snow on the summit surprised me. It's hard to believe you can be at almost 23,000 feet of elevation with zero snow, but the winds are so strong on Aconcagua, the summit is constantly wiped clean. I realized I had seen very little snow on the entire climb up, which is rare for such a big mountain.

Because of the impending storm, Ernesto only let us chill on the summit for an hour. After resting and snapping the obligatory pictures and poses, we gathered our gear to head back. Only after we started down did Ernesto tell us that, for our safety, we would not only have to descend beyond Camp 2 but continue down a different route to a base camp on the south side called the Plaza de Mulas. This route had proven to be more difficult and more treacherous. Still, we had no choice because we couldn't risk being a few hours off in the estimation of when the storm might hit the west face.

Our long day on no sleep just got much, much longer.

Ernesto pushed the pace as much as possible on the way down, and even though exhaustion flooded our weary bodies, we made decent time. There are few motivators like a life-and-death scenario to convince someone to dig deep. This is one of the many things I love about mountain climbing.

On our way down, it stunned me when we passed our Italian friends and their guide, Stefano. Even more shocking, *they were still heading up.* We crossed paths with them around noon, and they still had a good three to four hours to go before reaching the summit. Although well aware of the storm front coming in, they were determined to summit that day.

We all protested vehemently, telling them they were crazy to try to summit with a storm coming in. They stuck to their guns. Ernesto attempted to discretely reason with Stefano, but the Italian guide's uber-confident swagger took control, and he assured Ernesto they would be fine. I decided to talk to Gianna, hoping to reason with her, since she seemed the most levelheaded of the group.

"Gianna, you have to persuade them to turn back!" I held back none of the urgency I felt.

"I think we'll be okay, Mark." She smiled. "Stefano is a good guide. He knows what he is doing."

I rubbed my face in frustration. "Gianna, it's crazy.

The storm is going to hit while you're on the top of the mountain! There is no doubt about that."

"Bro," Angelo interjected, but not without hostility, "we'll be good. We're going fast. Gianna is as strong as all of us, and we'll be back down before the storm fully hits. We can handle a bit of snow. We'll just catch the end."

I shook my head. My pleas would have been more effective to a brick wall.

There is an element of excessive self-confidence in summit fever. I have been guilty of it and, fortunately, have never paid a steep price. *Many* climbers are not so blessed. More often than not, summit fever leads to fatal consequences. Even the most experienced and powerful climbers in the world have paid the ultimate price because they didn't turn back when they should have.

The trouble is, it's understandable.

One doesn't always make good decisions on the mountain. You've been climbing for days and you've sacrificed tens of thousands of dollars, physical effort, and months of planning. You know there is no second chance to redo it—at least not in the short term. It feels like pure, soul-crushing failure. Make no mistake, turning back from a summit is gut-wrenching.

But it usually means life over death.

The stubbornness of the Italian team meant they would not listen. It dismayed me that they wouldn't even listen to Ernesto. They hung back as he desperately pleaded with them to not continue. All to no avail.

Strangely, their attitudes reminded me of myself not long before. I bought a business in my own stubbornness, despite many friends, whom I consider wise, telling me the risk outweighed the opportunity. So certain I could make it work—even in the worst-case scenario—I ignored solid advice. The problem is cognitive bias.

Powerless to change their minds, we said goodbye to our friends and continue our descent. I whispered silent prayers for their safety as I trudged down the steep south face.

Twenty hours after we left Camp 2, we dragged our exhausted bodies into the Plaza de Mulas. The weather had begun to turn really bad, and we were way too tired to fight the wind and snow blasts to struggle with securing our tents. We wearily greeted Merka and Carlos and briefed them about the Italian team. Merka's eyes widened in fright, as they had already been concerned about us, and we were almost a half day ahead of the Italians.

We just threw our sleeping bags on the floor of one of the dining tents and fell asleep without even eating dinner.

The next day, Ernesto woke us with grim news. Stefano and the Italian team had summited at around 3:00 p.m., but the storm swept in soon after, as predicted. The team quickly became disoriented and took the wrong route off the summit.

Luca subsequently fell into a crevasse, but Stefano somehow managed to rescue him and saved his life. Stefano had, however, expended a tremendous amount of energy in the process.

Gianna had fallen into another crevasse and died.

Stefano and the others were still somewhere on the mountain at about 22,000 feet, and a rescue attempt was being organized.

We were all too stunned to speak. Our worst fears had been realized.

January 6, 2009 had started out to be such a great day for the six of us as we had summited Aconcagua, but we now forever think of it as the day Gianna died. Sweet, quiet, fiercely determined Gianna. I didn't even want to think about where her final resting place might be.

We barely ate breakfast and, like zombies, packed our gear to get ready to leave the camp. The conditions were still terrible, so instead of hiking, Ernesto arranged for us to ride on short-footed mules down the trail to the next camp. Although not thrilled with this, I had no choice.

Nobody said much on the way down. All we could do was pray for Stefano, Giuseppe, Matteo, and Angelo, as Ernesto gave us updates throughout the day. The rescue operation couldn't make much headway because of the weather and because it seemed to be somewhat disorganized.

Before long, unaccustomed to the jostling and bouncing of the mule as it slowly lumbered down the snow-covered trail, terrible pain set into my hips and thighs.

Through blowing snow, we rode twelve miles down on the mules to Confluenza Camp. When at last I could get off my mule, every part of me ached and a deep weariness had set in.

The rescuers had still not reached the Italian team by the end of that day, January 7th.

We stayed that night at Confluenza Camp at 11,500 feet. Grief for Gianna and concern for our friends still on the mountain hung silently in the air. Again, despite expending so much energy over the past two days, we could eat only a little, and everyone went to bed early.

The next morning, we set off again. After another difficult day in terrible weather, we finally made it off the mountain and back to Mendoza late on January 8th.

That night, we heard conflicting accounts of what happened, but what we knew for sure Stefano Campanini, aged thirty-one, had perished. They had rescued the other three. A *YouTube* video of Stefano's last moments would later surface. The video may still be on the web, but I have never watched it, and I will not. I have heard his rescuers screamed and tried every way possible to get him up and moving, but he just couldn't go any further. I've heard they tied a rope around his upper torso to assist him and force him up. He would walk a few steps, then collapse again, taking his final few breaths in his last resting spot on the mountain. Stefano died of pulmonary edema.

Shocked with grief, and the reality that the mountain we had just climbed had claimed the lives of two friends, we all said our goodbyes with a little more heartfelt emotion than usual. Suffering always bonds people, as does trauma and grief. We vowed to stay in touch.

Somber and pensive, I flew home, considering the nature of life and death on these mountains. I had seen dead bodies on mountains before—and had even found one on Blanca in Colorado—but I had never had people I knew and had connected with die on a mountain. I truly wondered if I would ever climb again. I needed time to process what happened. I needed to pray, and I needed to grieve.

I knew Stefano and Gianna died loving what they did, but sitting in that plane, it all seemed so pointless. The inevitable question popped up: *Why does God allow tragedies to happen to good people?* To me, the answer, in this case, seemed simple. *Poor decisions were made, and untenable risks were taken, so I don't think God carries any blame in this situation.* He allows us to make our own decisions, no matter how ill-advised they may be.

Stefano had been so maddeningly stubborn. He shouldered the responsibility of knowing they wouldn't be able to outrun the storm, and he bore the responsibility to listen to our more experienced, local guides. Still, the man's heart was good, as he basically sacrificed himself for one of his team. Had he not used so much energy rescuing Luca, he would almost certainly be alive. Any climber knows the odds of survival in a storm are greatly diminished once you expend that amount of energy. Stefano died with honor. . . but it was still so avoidable.

My thoughts eventually drifted back to work and daily life, but even those thoughts were colored by my regret over this tragedy. I knew I had tried everything to persuade my friends to turn back, but part of me still felt guilty. This likely is the driving force, at least in part, of one of my heart's deepest desires in leadership coaching—teaching people to turn away from crazy decisions.

I desperately want to show the executive who has a sudden midlife crisis, to heed his spiritual advisors and check that impulse to trash his marriage for the hot, twenty-five-year-old new hire. I want to encourage the director, whose husband has been laid off and is suffering from depression, to avoid bailing for alleged greener pastures. I want to warn the global account manager, who has been with the company for twenty-five years and believes she knows what is best for her customer accounts to listen to her manager's warnings about her performance and behavior so she can turn things around before she is terminated.

As usual, our team from Aconcagua stayed in touch frequently for a few months, but then we all gradually moved on with our lives. That's how it goes, I guess; out of sight, out of mind. Even after many years have passed, though, I am still so saddened by what happened. We tried so hard to get them to turn around, but ultimately, they made the decision to continue. I would like to say the experience cured me of ever having my thoughts clouded by summit fever again, but I truly don't know—and won't know—until I am faced with that decision on a mountain.

All we can do is pray for wisdom and try to discern God's voice through the pain.

CHAPTER 24

The Great Trek

MOUNT EVEREST, THE HIGHEST SUMMIT IN THE world—29,029 feet of raw beauty, wonder, and danger. The ultimate prize for most climbers . . . the pinnacle of my lifelong dreams. At the turn of the century, I decided, "What better new century's resolution than to summit the mother of all mountains?" Since my overarching goal had always been to climb the seven summits, I figured, "Why wait to tackle the queen?"

In 1999, I worked for Motorola when our division was spun off into a new company. They gave all employees founder's stock, which I decided gave me the perfect opportunity to cash in to afford the outrageous price of a good Everest guide company. At the time, the trip cost over $40,000. Today, an expedition up Everest will cost upward of $75,000 with a reputable guide company.

This is purely based on supply and demand economics. Nepal and Tibet grant only so many climbing permits per year, as more and more people want to undertake the challenge, despite the gravity of the risks. It is big tourism for such small countries.

Climbing the Nepal side, which has its unique pros and cons, appealed to me. I planned to fly to the legendary capital city of Kathmandu to start my journey in late April 2000. I planned to make a summit attempt a few weeks later in mid to late May. The vast majority of (sane) Everest summit attempts take place in this small window since this is the only time of the year the Himalayan jet stream moves away from the mountain. Yes, Everest is so high it pierces this jet stream—a narrow, high-speed, westerly flowing air current *in the troposphere.*

Most of the year, the summit is blasted by the jet stream, making the winds far too strong for climbing. Every year in May, the jet stream shifts north and makes the summit potentially accessible. In June, the monsoon season starts and heavy rains assault Nepal from India in the south, making the weather too volatile for any summit bid. The result is a two-week weather window during this time in May, where you will see hundreds of climbers making attempts at the summit from both sides of the mountain. Even during this sliver of opportunity, winds can reach up to 110 miles per hour.

Nepal has long fascinated the world with its beautiful and dramatic landscapes, but the tiny country has only been open to the west since 1951. Despite the veneer of westernization in certain areas, it remains a traditional society steeped in religion. The majority of people are Hindu, although there is a strong Buddhist presence as well. The country, however, is a mosaic of cultures with over forty ethnic groups, each with a unique language and tradition.

Although Nepal is a small country, it contains a huge variation in altitude from the lowland region of the Terai near sea level in the south, to the summit of Everest in the north—the highest point on Earth. From south to north, you cross tropical jungles through the terraced Himalayan foothills, up through pine and rhododendron forests, to the peaks and glaciers of the Great Himalayan Range which form Nepal's northern border with Tibet. This great range, which runs from Pakistan through India, Nepal, Tibet, and Bhutan, is the result of the tectonic collision between the main Asian continent and the Indian sub-continent. Nepal bears the brunt of this collision, resulting in the string of great peaks that run almost *500 miles* in length. Of the world's fourteen peaks over 8,000 meters, eight are in Nepal. These are Everest, Kanchenjunga, Lhotse, Makalu, Cho Oyu, Dhaulagiri, Manaslu, and Annapurna-1.

My flight from Phoenix to Kathmandu took over thirty hours, including layovers in Los Angeles and Bangkok. When I arrived at the Kathmandu Airport, I couldn't help but compare this third-world airport with those I'd just passed through. A representative of the guide company worked his way through all the bustle to take me to Hotel Shanker, where I would be staying.

Hotel Shanker is a beautiful, four-star facility with strong colonial décor, blended with authentic Nepali authenticity. The rich wood and metal carvings add to the mystical "feel" of the region. One is immersed in the culture right away, and the atmosphere is both tranquil and energizing.

After my long flight, I slept like a baby.

I awoke the next morning in time for our guides to run through an orientation and review our gear. Anything we didn't have we bought at various climbing stores in the city. That afternoon, I thoroughly enjoyed a guided tour of Kathmandu, which has more World Heritage sites than any other city in the world. These include ancient, ornate temples, royal palace complexes, housing mounds for sacred relics, and much more. The culture and tradition are beautiful, and one has to wonder how many secrets the ancient walls, roads, and countryside hold. Sadly, many of the sites were damaged or destroyed in the terrible Gorkha earthquake that rocked the region in 2015. Over 9,000 people died in that tragedy.

The time arrived all too soon the next day for an epically hair-raising part of the expedition—the flight from Kathmandu to Lukla's Tenzing-Hillary "Airport." I use quotes because this airport, despite how busy it is in the climbing season, is just a tiny landing strip on a plateau carved into the mountain. All climbers going into the Everest region must travel to Lukla by either plane or helicopter. Arriving at, or departing from, the Tenzing-Hillary Airport is not for the faint of heart.

The landing is one of the most dangerous in the world because the runway, at only 547 meters, is twice as short as it should be, making landing a procedure requiring pinpoint accuracy. Add high wind gusts, and you have an experience that will rattle the most seasoned climbers.

To accommodate the short strip, the runway slopes upward 11.7 degrees into the side of the mountain. This incline helps slow landing aircraft so they don't barrel into the mountain (although it happens occasionally if the winds are strong behind the craft). This incline serves the dual purpose of giving a speed boost to aircraft as they're taking off. This is crucial because pilots get just one chance to get off the ground. Once the strip runs out, it is a free-fall into the deep valley below. If you ever wish to attempt climbing any mountain in this range, I strongly recommend never watching YouTube videos of landings and takeoffs from Tenzing-Hillary.

We flew in a Yeti Airlines Twin Otter—a typical aircraft for this sort of trip. The bright side is the thirty-five-minute flight through the Kathmandu Valley into the Himalayan Range provides jaw-dropping scenery. Soon after we took off, the jagged snow-dusted crags of the Himalayan Range came into view. I marveled at their setting against a crystal clear, blue backdrop of sky with zero pollution. The whole scene looked like a painting crafted by the hand of God Himself. God's presence filled the cabin around me.

The mountains loomed larger, and more vivid, until we flew into the heart of the range, cruising between the ashy-green slopes and valleys of the lesser peaks. The plane climbed and climbed, passing hills and slopes, flying between walls of rock and vegetation. Suddenly, Lukla appeared. I could not believe we'd be able to land on the alarmingly short runway without plowing into the mountain to our doom. Anxiety sprang into my belly, and as I gripped my armrest, I realized the term "white-knuckling it" had to have first been coined on a flight into Lukla.

The Otter began its descent, as my lunch threatened an ascent. A gust of wind bounced us to the right, after which the Nepali pilot barked a terse order to his copilot. Levers were pumped, dials adjusted, and the plane banked left. Suddenly, the pilots drastically decelerated. It felt like we were about to drop out of the sky. This may not seem that scary unless you're approaching the crest of a ridge on top of a sheer cliff face. One small miscalculation and the plane could smack into a wall of rock with a burst of flame and smoke that would be featured on the Nepalese evening news. (Yes, it has happened. More than once.) I could hear my heart pounding over the roar of the Otter's twin engines.

The plane dropped from the sky as the ridge of the runway rushed up to meet us. The pilot kept his eyes glued to the landing strip, while we all held our breath. The cliff face loomed in front of us. At the last second, the pilot yanked up the steering yoke. I literally rose a little off my chair and gritted my teeth instinctively, sure the landing gear would clip the ridge. At the same time, the stall horn screeched, signaling the engines were about to stall. With a loud thud, we hit the runway, bounced a few times, and coasted to a stop. We were safe. We had landed. All the passengers on board erupted in a roar of applause.

Whew. I shuddered. *I wonder if I'll have any adrenaline left to deal with the climb.*

Now for the eight-day trek to Everest's base camp. We all donned our packs soon after landing and began to walk. We'd only have about four miles to cover, while gaining only 650 feet in elevation, which meant an easy hiking day. After the crazy landing, I didn't need anything else to tax my nerves.

Each night, we slept in a teahouse. Teahouses are basically rudimentary hotels with a dining room, bedrooms, and communal bathrooms. Teahouse guests are generally trekkers, heading into the Everest region. The closer we got to base camp, however, the more primitive the accommodations became.

Day two, although one of the hardest of the trek, felt rewarding, as we hiked over six miles but gained over 2,700 feet. Our walk took us along the Milk River, which originates at Everest's base camp. Along the way, we passed through several small villages. Gorgeous wildflowers dotted the countryside when we reached the pretty village of Namche Bazaar at 11,300 feet. Namche Bazaar's little blue- or red-roofed buildings curve around a sort of amphitheater in the side of the mountain and provided a welcome sight to weary travelers. It felt good to stop for some rest in such idyllic scenery.

Namche Bazaar is a bustling village of about 2,000 people, and it's the spot where climbers can get their first view of Everest in the morning—if the day is clear. Namche is also the main trading hub for the Khumbu region and includes a police garrison, post office, and even a bank. It also holds the headquarters for Sagarmatha National Park, which is one of Nepal's great attractions. If you forgot to buy something in Kathmandu, you could probably get it in Namche, but at about three times the price.

Anytime I think back to my entire Everest experience, I have to say the most enduring memories I hold are of the Nepalese people. In every village, smiling locals greeted us, calling out "Namaste," the universal Nepalese greeting. These people are physically strong and always helpful and humorous and maintain an incredibly positive attitude toward life. I'm not sure if their friendly, humble dispositions are due to their primitive and rugged existence in the mountains of Nepal, or if they exist despite it. Regardless, it enables them to endure the requirements of this harsh, unforgiving environment.

This is one of the things I just love about climbing— the people you meet are at all levels of the socioeconomic strata. Some are rich, but most are just middle class. The Sherpas and locals are extremely poor, but everyone is equal on the mountain. That is, except for the Sherpas and the guides, who are the leaders.

That night I experienced the Nepalese staple of "dal bhat" for the first time. This is a delicious mixture of steamed rice, lentil soup, and vegetable curry. There is a Nepali saying, "Dal bhat power, twenty-four hour," which means each meal of dal bhat will provide the energy to trek for twenty-four hours. This is far more than a cute saying to the porters and guides, who eat dal bhat three times a day during expeditions.

Sure enough, the next morning, we could see Everest peeking up behind Lhotse. A lump rose in my throat at such beauty. There she was! The mother of mountains . . . the queen of peaks. So close I could almost touch her. My heart raced in anticipation and I couldn't stop staring at her.

Day three of the trek served as an acclimatization day; we climbed 1,000 feet up to the village of Khumjung to visit a local school and monastery. We then hiked back to Namche and spent another night to further our acclimatization. On an Everest climb, this is especially critical. If you ascend too rapidly, you can develop Acute Mountain Sickness (AMS), which means you need to either stay put and not go any higher or descend if AMS is severe. If you continue to ascend with AMS, you risk high-altitude cerebral or pulmonary edema. Either of these is typically fatal.

Day four would be a long one, as we would trek from Namche to a village called Tengboche. It would be about a seven-mile hike, with an elevation gain of 1,500 feet. We got up at 6:00 a.m. and had our usual breakfast of porridge, toast, potatoes, and black tea. We looked down at spectacular views from our spot high over a river valley. We could see the Himalayas off in the distance, while our destination—Tengboche—rested majestically on a hilltop. We also passed several Buddhist temples, which are always fascinating for me to see. At this point, Everest was in full view. Every time I looked up, I again experienced the novelty of seeing her soaring peak.

Everything delivered beyond Namche needed to be carried by porters or yaks. Men hiked past us carrying huge sacks of food, cases of soda and beer, furniture, clothing, pots, pans, and even *doors*. They carried each load on their back, with a strap around their head to help distribute the weight. Like so many of the porters on mountains around the world, these people humbled and astounded me. They are such simple yet happy men, carrying these crazy-heavy loads up these high-altitude, rocky trails.

I, too, began to feel strong at this point, and everything around me gave me a near-constant pleasure. So far.

At Tengboche, our teahouse overlooked a lovely, ornate Buddhist monastery, which exuded the sort of calm and peace these monks embody. What a real treat to see them in meditation or practicing their martial arts movements in the gardens. That night, I began to feel how much colder the air had become as we moved north. All electricity north of Namche is generated either by water, wind, or solar power, so access to electricity is limited. As such, a central fireplace heated the dining room of the teahouse, but our host did not use wood for fuel. They burned *yak dung patties*—disks of yak dung, shaped by hand and allowed to dry on the stone walls. As you can imagine, this filled the teahouse with an "earthy" scent.

Every trip has a new experience.

Day five had us hiking from Tengboche, gaining 2,000 feet of elevation to Dingboche. This meant we hit 14,000 feet. Everyone started to feel the altitude. In fact, we passed several climbers already struggling with it, and we hadn't even reached the actual climb yet. Our breath became shorter, muscles received less oxygen, everything took a little more effort, and for some . . . the headaches started.

My day, fortunately, began only with a sense of excitement because I got an up-close view of one of the most beautiful mountains in the world—a pyramid of snow and ice standing at over 22,000 feet called *Ama Dablam*. This mountain reminds me of the Matterhorn with its striking lines and angles, and the story of the glacier hanging around the "neck" of the mountain, becoming its namesake, is one that always fascinates me.

We arrived in Dingboche at 14,500 feet and settled in. The accommodations grew worse and worse each day, and Dingboche would make anyone disgusted. Understandably, the buildings had been constructed with the bare minimum of materials, but that didn't make it any easier. Walls and doors consisted of paper-thin plywood, and the windows would not shut completely. I could hear every word of conversation in adjoining rooms, and when someone woke to use the bathroom at night, the entire house could hear them. Horrible bathrooms with overflowing toilets created an unbelievable stench. Our overall comfort, due to the much colder weather as we got higher, coupled with zero insulation in any of the buildings and the abhorrent conditions, quickly deteriorated.

The bitter side of the expedition had arrived, but I knew this was child's play compared to what lay ahead. I tried to maintain my positive attitude, focusing on the summit goal. Even as a somewhat seasoned climber, though, I had no idea what I'd face.

Day six of the trek we acclimated as we hiked 1,000 feet up to a little village named Chukhung. We then trekked back down to Dingboche, continuing the universal strategy of "climb high and sleep low," even on days when we rested our bodies. We slept in the stinky, paper-thin teahouse again and woke early.

Our next-to-last day of the trek involved a five-mile hike from Dingboche up to 16,100 feet of elevation, where we stopped at a small town called Lobuche. There were maybe twelve buildings in the town, including our teahouse. Many of the trekkers at the teahouse began to complain about a constant, low-grade headache that no amount of Ibuprofen would kill. This is an inevitable part of any high-altitude climb. Some handle altitude better than others, but on Everest, it is always just a matter of time before the headaches start.

Thankfully, I hadn't experienced them yet, but my knee, on the other hand, pained me more than usual. I have a condition called Calcium Pyrophosphate Dihydrate Deposition Disease (CPPDD) which, in layman's terms, is called pseudogout of the knee. What this means is that my body produces excess calcium crystals, which are similar to gout crystals. These crystals pool in the knees, causing extreme pain somewhat like that from rheumatoid arthritis. Unfortunately, these crystals are not tied to diet like regular gout crystals. The result is my knees continuously ache, and there really isn't a lot I can do about the pain but take Ibuprofen. This is the biggest "pain cave" issue I have to deal with. And Everest seemed to have really set it off.

After a fitful night of sleep, day eight dawned, which meant we would finally finish our great trek and arrive at Everest Base Camp that afternoon. We climbed slowly up to the village of Gorek Shep, which would be our northernmost stop on the way to base camp. From there, we turned toward the infamous Khumbu Glacier, walking parallel to it. We began to pass huge, manmade piles of rocks as high as my head. When I inquired about these, our Sherpas explained they were monuments to fallen Everest climbers.

As we trekked to base camp, I couldn't help but have the reality roll around in my mind that an average of three strong climbers lose their life each year on this mountain. I pushed these thoughts out of my mind, focusing instead on the interesting section of this journey. We could see the camp up ahead, even though we had two more hours of climbing. This is because of the many rolling hills of boulders and rocks to traverse before we arrived.

Eventually, we made it to base camp, and I marveled at the number of tents and people already there. Music blared, and laughter rang out from every corner of the camp. It seemed so strange to see what felt like a festival or camping party set up in this rocky, barren area at the base of the Khumbu Icefall in the Himalayas. I could not see Everest from base camp, but I knew I would get my fill soon enough so in the meantime I'd enjoy the festive atmosphere.

We had climbed to over 17,000 feet. With fifty percent less oxygen than at sea level, breathing felt entirely different—and the air would only get thinner.

We set up our tents and settled in for our first night at base camp. Our group had our own dining tents with tables and chairs and even our own cook. Base camp also has a medical tent, staffed by a camp doctor who is there for the entire climbing season. The doctor checks oxygen saturation levels and can treat many climbing injuries.

The next morning, however, our first order of business was to undergo the Puja, a local cleansing and protection ceremony. As we approached the site, I saw and smelled smoke billowing up from burning fir boughs at the Puja altar. A local lama (holy man) awaited us and asked us to gather around the firepit. We stood around in silence, and although I am a Christian, I showed proper respect for the tradition and appreciated the culture of the ceremony. The lama then prayed in Nepalese for our safety on the mountain and wafted smoke over each of us. The warm and touching gesture affected us all.

At last. Time to go.

From the start, Everest presents you with a serious challenge. That morning, we took our first trip into the notorious Khumbu Icefall to practice crossing crevasses on metal ladders. The Khumbu Icefall is at the head of the Khumbu Glacier, which is located right above base camp. This part of the glacier is characterized by rapid ice flow, which unfortunately means a heavily crevassed surface. Here, the movement of the ice is faster than elsewhere on the glacier, which causes the ice to fracture, creating huge cracks in the ice and ice towers called *seracs*. These towers stretched up to fifteen stories high. When they sway in the wind, they can suddenly collapse, crushing everything and everyone in their path.

Aside from the seracs and crevasses, large blocks of ice can spontaneously break off this part of the glacier and tumble down the mountain. These blocks range from the size of cars to the size of large houses. All this makes crossing the icefall one of the most dangerous aspects of climbing Everest. As always, in any icy climb, the best time to cross the icefall is before sunrise, when temperatures are at their lowest. The route from base camp to Camp 1 goes directly through the icefall, as Camp 1 sets just above it. Most climbers can get through the icefall in three to five hours, but naturally, that varies with each climber.

Because of my acrophobia, I didn't look forward to this part of the climb. A key aspect of going through the icefall is climbing across and up wobbly metal ladders strung across the many crevasses. Ice screws and ropes secure the ladders, and there can be over twenty ladders throughout the icefall. They call certain Sherpas "icefall doctors" and those Sherpas specialize in installing and maintaining these ladders in a constantly changing environment. The guides warned us to practice diligently and stay focused, since some sections have as many as four ladders strung together, making for an unsteady, nerve-wracking crossing.

Thankfully, parallel fixed-lines are strung above each ladder, allowing the climber to clip in with carabineers. If you fall off the ladder, the ropes will keep you from plunging to the bottom of the crevasse, but you never really want to entrust your life to metal and ropes. Besides, odds are you'll get banged up if you fall, which will kill your summit bid. It is not uncommon for the ladders to twist or sway as you cross. I cannot explain how unnerving this is—you are tired, cold, the air is thin, and you have to cross two or even three shaky ladders roped together, wearing *crampons,* while fifty-foot ice towers sway around you.

But at this point, I was officially climbing Everest.

The Khumbu Icefall is a trial by . . . well, not fire, but ice, which, in this case, seemed far more treacherous. I had to keep reminding myself, "This is what you want. Focus on the goal. Focus on the summit. The reward will outweigh the cost."

I had to believe my own words . . . unless the cost became my life.

CHAPTER 25

Among the Stars

I HAD TRAINED FOR THESE LADDER CROSSINGS AS BEST I could by putting a metal ladder up on cinder blocks and stringing a fixed rope across my garage. I wore my crampons and carefully practiced walking on the sideways steel rungs. I don't have great balance, so this aspect of the icefall worried me.

On the first day, we went a little way into the icefall to work on our ladder crossing. Grateful that I had improvised the situation in my garage, I had at least a little experience. The key is being careful where you point the crampons on the rungs. Once you master this, it is not that difficult, but it's still essential to concentrate on every single step and be as precise as possible.

After practicing on a few smaller crevasses, the time arrived for me to cross my first big crevasse in the icefall. Despite the Sherpa's warning not to look down,

I did. I gasped and froze in terror; the crevasse looked bottomless. Seeing what happened, one of the Sherpas called out and encouraged me to keep walking and focus on him. Shaking, I looked up as the ladder wobbled and shook. I tried to watch where I put my feet and took one scary step at a time. My heart raced, and fear gripped my entire body.

I kept walking. One step. Two steps. Three steps.

Eventually, I stepped off on the other side of the giant crevasse. The Sherpa chuckled and patted me on the back. "If you look down deep into a crevasse," he said, smiling, "you can probably see all the way to America." I tried to smile back.

The more crevasses we crossed, the easier it became, and by evening, we could cross the ladders easily. The next day, we went through the entire icefall for the first time as we headed up to Camp 1 at 19,500 feet. Besides crossing the ladders, going through the icefall stretched all my alpine climbing skills and made me glad for my experiences on Mont Blanc and Mount Rainier.

It took me about four-and-a-half hours to make it through the icefall the first time, and I breathed a huge sigh of relief, gleefully expressing my gratitude to God when I finished.

We reached Camp 1 and spent two nights there. Camp 1 sits in the Western Cwm (pronounced koom), which is a large valley surrounded by three of the world's highest mountains: Everest, Lhotse, and Nuptse. We slept in heavy North Face tents, built to withstand the rigors of extreme high-altitude conditions.

These tents offered a far better experience than the northernmost teahouses.

The next day, we climbed through the Western Cwm, halfway up to Camp 2, to acclimate. The Western Cwm is also known as the Valley of Silence. The shape of this land feature acts as a massive solar oven, and curiously, there is virtually no sound except for climbers crunching their crampons on the ice. The topography seems to stifle all the wind and there are no signs of life.

To me, the Cwm felt like a house of mirrors, as the sun's intense, ultraviolet rays glared off the ice, which, even when the temperature is below freezing in the Cwm, felt searing hot. Many people don't realize the sun's rays in the thinner atmosphere at high altitudes can far more easily burn the skin and eyes, causing snow blindness and blisters on the skin. We had also reached the altitude where subfreezing temperatures, exacerbated by perpetually strong winds, cause frostbite, killing the skin and the underlying tissue, especially on one's extremities.

The following day, we climbed all the way through the snowy Cwm to reach Camp 2. Despite the magnificent weather, the sun's reflection off the snow meant I had to cover my entire body to avoid sunburn. This overheated me, so staying hydrated, though challenging to do, became critical. The goal: to drink *six liters* of liquid per day.

Camp 2 lies at 21,000 feet and is referred to as "Advanced Base Camp." Nestled in a rocky ravine, there's always a crowd. Most of the expeditions station full-time cooks here because of the many trips they'd need to make back and forth. This results in a lot of large, diamond-shaped dining tents.

Although the food at Camp 2 tasted good, I still had a hard time eating. One of the first things to break down at altitude is your appetite, so as we got higher it became harder and harder to eat. On average, climbers lose between fifteen to thirty pounds of weight on Everest. I lost muscle mass in my shoulders, back, and legs, despite trying to consume 6,000 calories a day. The danger is that once a climber is above the Death Zone at 26,000 feet, it is easier for the body to consume muscle mass than to digest new food. At that altitude, if you run out of muscle mass, your body collapses, and dies.

We were doing an extreme form of "climb high and sleep low," forcing our bodies to acclimatize to higher and higher altitudes. To reiterate, this strategy causes the body to create more red blood cells to carry more oxygen to the muscles and organs as the air becomes thinner and thinner. Overall, I felt okay. My body seemed to acclimatize well, and I felt optimistic about my chance at summiting. I say "my chance" because once in the Death Zone, although you are part of a team, it is a cold fact that many will have to turn back. I knew the climb ahead wouldn't be easy, but if determination factored into the success, I knew I'd be one of the people on the team to make it.

We spent two nights at Camp 2, then headed back down to base camp, making another trip through the icefall.

We stayed at base camp for a night, then made yet another trip through the icefall, spent four nights at

Camp 2, and climbed back up to Camp 3 for one night. Every time I went through the icefall, I prayed constantly for the safety of myself and everyone on the mountain. Each time I crossed the icefall it felt like playing Russian roulette, as I knew an ice block could break off at any time and crush me. The icefall had claimed more lives than any other section, but my prayers helped to calm me, knowing God's providence surrounded me.

The real test of the expedition began with the climb to Camp 3. Aside from parts of the icefall, this is where actual ice climbing began, as we had to go up Lhotse's face from 21,500 feet to almost 24,000 feet. If you struggle here, it's likely you won't make it to the summit. It involves ice climbing on twenty-five- to fifty-degree slopes, with an occasional seventy-degree bulge. The climb is physically and mentally exhausting, and the exposure is constantly stressful on the mind.

Looking up at Lhotse's face is also dizzying. The face is so dangerous, being clipped into the fixed-lines is crucial as you just assume you will slip at some point. In places, crude steps are carved out, but most of the time, we had to be razor-focused about where we placed our feet. There is just no other option but to gain maximum purchase on the rock-hard ice. I found myself already having to dig deeper into my psyche to find the determination to keep going.

I'd completely stepped into the pain cave.

Despite how tiring it is, the climb itself isn't technically difficult. Basically, it involves sliding your jumar up the fixed-line while you stamp your crampons into the ice. The jumar is an instrument that grips the fixed-line, which you hold on to and then move up the line as you climb. Once you slide your jumar up, you stamp one foot into the ice, then you raise your other foot and repeat the process. At this point, my extremities felt frozen and my muscles burned constantly. It took any remaining effort just to breathe as I tried to extract every precious molecule of oxygen out of the icy-thin air. If I breathed too rapidly, I would expel too much carbon dioxide, which impacts the acidity of the blood and could cause me to faint.

As one's breathing quickens, so does your heart rate. You can sustain this for short periods, but over a longer stretch, this creates hypoxia, which means low oxygen in the blood. Hypoxia can cause organ damage minutes after onset, so even though your body is screaming to breathe faster, it is literally a life or death issue for you to take measured, controlled breaths.

After a grueling climb, we made it to Camp 3, which I noticed had different levels spread out on the slopes. With little wind, the sun beat down on the Lhotse face, so with relief, I stumbled into the tent. The whole of Camp 3 lay at a steep angle, which requires fixed-lines set up between all the tents. Our guides emphatically reinforced that we had to clip in whenever we were out of the tents, especially in the middle of the night if we got up to relieve ourselves. They told us that failure to clip in at Camp 3 had resulted in several deaths when climbers had gotten up in the middle of the night, slipped, and ended up falling down the entire Lhotse face. I made a mental note and prayed I remembered to do so if I woke in a sleepy stupor.

Bedtime came early at 7:00 p.m. As wiped out as I felt, I hoped for some solid sleep, but that wasn't going to be the case. At about 7:30, the winds picked up, and within another hour or two, hurricane-force gales battered our poor little tents for the entire night. At this height and incline, this was *terrifying*.

Twice, the wind picked up our tent, making me and my tent mate scramble to adjust our weight so the tent would remain flat on the ground. We shared a concern that the poles would break, and our tent would collapse. In the middle of the night, when you're so tired and emotionally beat anyway, this hammers on your mind to the point that you think you cannot take another hour of it. It seemed like the night would never end.

Despite being so exhausted, I got maybe an hour or two of sleep, which made it one of the most miserable nights of my life.

Mercifully, our tent held, and at about 6:00 a.m. the winds died down. After breakfast, we prepared to head back down the mountain to base camp. If I'd had some sleep, I might have enjoyed the down-climb, but the incredibly slick ice going to Camp 2 drained me even further. I knew I had to maintain focus, but that effort seemed almost impossible. My joints and muscles ached, breathing remained a labor, and in addition, my head had started to ache. Also, people were coming up the fixed-lines, which meant we had to figure out how to pass each other, unclipping and clipping back on to the fixed-lines. To lose a moment's focus could mean slipping and tumbling down the mountain. Every effort became excruciating.

And we still had to cross the icefall.

When we reached Camp 1, I didn't feel well at all and knew I could not face the icefall without extreme risk. The challenge is not just pushing the limits of one's body, but the mind begins to wilt as well. The mountain, for that period, has become your home—your entire life. You have this desperate mission to reach the summit, but you must approach it in slow, painstaking steps. Patience is a virtue anytime, but on Everest it is a life or death necessity. I discussed the situation with my guide, who agreed I should stay a night in Camp 1. I collapsed in a tent and thankfully got some desperately needed sleep.

The next day, I made it back to base camp with a Sherpa, where we rested for another few days. One day, I hiked down to the little village of Gorek Shep, mainly out of boredom. This monotony is something one must deal with on long expeditions. You have rest days and days when the weather keeps you inside your tent. All you can do is read and maybe play cards. It can grind you down mentally.

At base camp, besides resting, we also waited for a prediction of several days of clear weather to make our attempt on the summit. Finally, on May 13th, we heard there should be four consecutive days of clear weather.

Time for the summit push!

We packed our gear and made another journey

through the icefall to Camp 2. We spent two nights there with one rest day, then made the treacherous climb back up to Camp 3. I had to admit, I felt much stronger at the start of that trip. *The acclimatization is having an impact.* The wind, however, gusted even stronger during the second time on the Lhotse face, so even though I felt more physically able my time up to Camp 3 took longer. Pushing through the wind tired me, zapping my strength enough to slow me down. *So much for any sliver of advantage.*

By the time we made it back to Camp 3, my body ached to the point of misery. I desperately needed the rest, as we had to make it to Camp 4 on the South Col the following day. If the weather held, we would summit in less than two days.

That night, I used oxygen for the first time in an attempt to sleep. Wearing a mask over your face is insanely uncomfortable. I couldn't sleep on my back, but when I turned on my side, the mask would push away from my mouth. The night consisted of constant tossing and turning, trying to adjust and readjust. When the mask slipped off, a desperate shortness of breath followed, waking me instantly.

The truth is, it is just difficult to sleep at high altitudes. And the worst was yet to come. In the area between Camp 4 and the summit, the scarcity of oxygen and unforgiving conditions quickly kill those who remain in the Death Zone for too long. Because the altitude increases, atmospheric pressure decreases, reducing oxygen. The body tries to compensate by sending more blood to the brain, which causes swelling and the inevitable headaches. And we know the real risk of this swelling is cerebral edema—excess fluid on the brain. The body is also fighting to send more blood to the lungs, which could cause the dreaded pulmonary edema. The first symptoms are coughing and respiratory problems.

My sleep could not be measured in hours, but minutes. I became anxious about having the strength to summit without getting anywhere close to enough sleep. I felt trapped in the Catch-22 of the more I worried about getting sleep, the less sleep I got. After a long, brutal, near-sleepless night, our guide came and told us to get up and get ready for the climb to Camp 4.

I sighed and shook my head in frustration. I hadn't imagined everything going this way.

Despite this being the first day to use oxygen, the climb to Camp 4 took even more effort than the climb to Camp 3. We started out by climbing another few hundred feet up the Lhotse face, then we turned left and traversed what is called the Yellow Band. The Yellow Band is a forty-foot-high wall of dolomite and limestone that encircles Everest's summit, sort of like a golden wedding band. The Band is not difficult to traverse, but it is tiring as it involves rock climbing with about a hundred meters of rope. A feature called the Black Turtle is a raised bump on the Yellow Band that you have to scuttle across as well.

After passing the Yellow Band, we continued upward to the anvil-shaped Geneva Spur, which is a large, rock buttress that provides access to the South Col and Camp 4. "Col" is a Welsh word for saddle or pass. South Col had been named by a British Reconnaissance Expedition in 1921. The South Col is the barren saddle between Everest and Lhotse, with little more than boulders scattered around.

We arrived where the fixed ropes had been placed on the Spur so climbers could clamber up the steep, snow-covered rock. The route took us up the lower part and required we rock-climb about fifty-feet, almost straight up. At that altitude, it slowed everyone down, which caused a long queue of climbers to form as they waited to go up. Every minute waiting meant a minute of used oxygen and biting cold.

I began to get concerned because I could feel my body beginning to rapidly break down—and we hadn't even reached Camp 4. I felt I was a strong climber, but this mountain posed a challenge like nothing I'd ever faced before. I had to dig deep—deeper than I ever had—and tell myself *the Spur is just the last significant hurdle before reaching Camp 4. I'll rest when I get there.* I told myself I would figure out how to sleep with the oxygen mask, and within one day I would have conquered Everest's summit.

Eventually, the time came for our group to make our way up the Spur. I took a deep, measured breath and forced myself to pull my jumar, take a step, pull my jumar, take another step. I just repeated and breathed, repeated and breathed. My lungs burned, and my legs shook, despite being nearly numb. Bitter, merciless cold bit into my toes, fingers, and face. Pull, step. Readjust. Pull, step

After what felt like an eternity, I crested the Spur. Just a simple hike up to Camp 4 on the South Col remained.

Welcome to the Death Zone.

We arrived. I collapsed into my tent. After resting for at least thirty minutes, I forced down some noodles, then went straight to bed. To my astonishment, I slept for a few hours. Then I awoke and anxiety rippled through my body. *Do I have enough strength left? Do I have enough muscle mass? Will I make it? Or will I be another casualty, forever embalmed in ice, the harsh wind whipping at my clothes?*

On the doorstep of outer space, I marveled at where I lay. Literally at the edge of Earth's atmosphere, the surrounding sky glowed a strange, endless, deep blue. I lay in the infamous Death Zone at 26,300 feet above sea level. In the deathly still air, I quietly thanked God for taking me safely to this point. I prayed a long, solemn prayer for safety for the remaining and most difficult part of the journey. A single day remained before I could stand atop Mount Everest, the highest peak on Earth . . . the ultimate prize for most climbers. The pinnacle of my dreams.

• • •

Long before dawn, we donned our gear to begin our summit push. *This is it*, I told myself as I began to move. All I want to do is make the summit and get off this mountain. My head is pounding.

Up and up and up we climb. The ice turns slick, hard, scary. The cold, long since making it through my clothing, saturates my muscles, soaks into my bones. I long for the searing, uncomfortable heat of the Western Cwm. We cross a small desert of ice, flanked by deep crevasses. The path takes us up a steep, rocky incline until we arrive at a tiny plateau on the mountain. We have reached the Balcony. My Sherpa changes both of our oxygen bottles, and we set our sights on the Southeast Ridge—1,000 feet of climbing up an entirely exposed fin that leads to the South Summit.

But before that, I must face the notorious Hillary Step.

My knees are stiff and in agony. My fingers and toes are numb and ache from the subzero bite. Many of the climbers around me have developed coughs—a precursor to pulmonary edema. I've heard stories of some people coughing so hard they break ribs. I know I have to compartmentalize the pain. I cannot let this pain become my primary focus. I acknowledge the pain, even embrace it, but I do not dwell on it. Well, at least not all the pain at once. If my knees are in excruciating agony, I think about my altitude-induced headache. This takes my mind off my knees. If my toes are in searing pain, I focus on my knees. I have to trick myself.

Only for a few more hours. That is all I can afford, anyway.

The trip from Camp 4 to the summit and back should take no more than eighteen hours—twelve hours to ascend, six hours to descend. The general rule of thumb is that you should be descending no later than noon. If you have not summited, you should turn back. Extended exposure can be deadly, not only due to the finite supply of oxygen bottles and the onset of altitude sickness, but because afternoon weather on Everest is nearly impossible to predict.

The first rays of dawn break through, and I am blessed with a tiny surge of energy. We crest a ridge, and suddenly, right above us, emerges the majestic South Summit. I look down to see how far we've come, and I notice ominous clouds beginning to swirl, thousands of feet in the valley below. I know we are pushing the limit of our window before a storm arrives. For some reason, I see the vacant, upward stare of the fallen climber we found on Blanca. My mind reels.

What do you have left, Mark?

I know Everest's true summit is just around the corner, only 300 vertical feet above us. But this is the most difficult part of the climb. Between me and the summit towers is the infamous Hillary Step—a forty-foot vertical rock climb at 28,800 feet. We hike through a half tunnel and climb up onto a knife-edged ridge. n one side, Nepal lies 8,000 feet below; on the other side, Tibet at 10,000 feet below. *Don't step wrong, Mark.* The urgency of this induces more mental strain.

We approach the Hillary Step. Something is wrong. Many climbers are standing below the Step, and when I inquire, I am told the Sherpas who were supposed to secure the lines were late. This has delayed everything, and I am far back in the queue. We now stand, waiting, and the cold feasts on the opportunity. Now, not only my fingers and toes are numb, I've started to shiver. Frostbite is a real possibility. *Darn it!* I grit my teeth. *Not now, not now.* I need to stay warm but doing jumping jacks on ice while attached to a fixed-line is not a good idea for many reasons, but most of all, I can't afford the energy burn. The clouds seem to swirl thicker and faster below.

In an instant, a climber in front is done. For reasons unknown, he turns back, and we do our one-two-you-go-I-go dance, clipping and unclipping. It is impossible to not be mentally shaken. After several minutes, I look up, and to my joy, I see climbers finally beginning to climb the Step. My joy is short-lived, as I know my turn is still a good way off. I am now shivering uncontrollably and am, without a doubt, in the first stages of hypothermia.

What follows will be incoordination, confusion, weakness, and apathy.

I picture the two bodies I have seen today, eternally embalmed in the ice along the route. One was in a state of undress. Disoriented, numb, and confused, a hypothermia-related phenomenon on mountains is climbers will shed their clothing, believing they are overheating, instead of slowly dying from cold.

I am engaged in the greatest mental battle I have ever faced. I have come this far . . . the pinnacle of my dreams . . .

The pinnacle of my *suffering.*

Do I truly have the strength left to summit Everest? Or

will it cost me my life?

More importantly, do I even care?

And just like that, something clicks in my mind. *Is that God speaking to me, or my own will?* I have no idea, but what I know is that my summit bid is over. I am too cold, too oxygen deprived, and too focused on dying to think about the consequences of my decision. That comes later. Much later. Although it is guaranteed I will replay, analyze, and reanalyze this moment over and over and over. But right now, I have nothing left. Just the determination to get off this mountain.

I let my Sherpa know I am heading back, and he confirms he will go with me. He has no expression—not surprise, disappointment, or relief. He merely acknowledges me and begins to lead me back down the knife-edged ridge. He has been here many times before with many other climbers.

Soon we are back at the Balcony, heading down toward the South Col. I pass climbers still going up, and like others did to me, I wish them "good luck." But I am in a trance. Only one hazy thought fills my entire consciousness: *Get back to your tent on the South Col.*

I habitually glance at the clouds below. *Did they stop rising? Did I worry about them for nothing?*

Several hours later, we arrive at Camp 4. I climb into my tent and collapse, too exhausted to think, too exhausted to care about anything except rest. I force down some hot tea but cannot make myself eat. I remove my boots, fearing my toes are black from frostbite, but in sheer relief, I see they are okay. Unbeknownst to me at the time, I have minor frostbite on three fingers of my right hand but considering how long I stood around at the Hillary Step, I am blessed this is all that happened.

I close my eyes and sleep. Nothing matters except sleep.

•   •   •

The storm didn't happen. Later in the day, the clouds dissipated; all my worry was for naught. Most of my team summited successfully, and while pleased for them, I felt a deep emptiness inside. In that moment, I wished I had not read *Into Thin Air*. Maybe then I wouldn't have been so worried. I tried not to think about it as we headed down the mountain for the final time, but the obsessing had begun. Still, I tamped my thoughts down so I could focus and get off the mountain.

I took extra care during my descent of the Lhotse face. I really didn't want to slip on this final trip down. My fears rose again as we approached the Khumbu Icefall. I prayed God would help me with safe passage through the icefall as I played Russian roulette for one last time.

When I took the final steps out of this ice chamber, I thanked God with all my heart. Base camp sat a few hundred yards away, and I knew I was finally safe. I also knew I would be going home. My mind remained numb about the decision I had made because I purposely did not want to think about it.

It only took three days to make the trek back to Lukla. Unfortunately, this gave me more than enough time to think about what I had done. I began to go back to that moment at the Hillary Step when I decided to turn back. *What happened?* The decision came over me so quickly. One moment I stood waiting, mind dulled, numb, wondering what to do, then an instant later, the decision to descend became clear. My Everest dreams died. At least for that year. I wanted to believe God spoke to me. But did He? I really don't know.

The thing about climbing, in both success and defeat, is it teaches you that you cannot control what life offers; you can only control how you respond. You have to adapt and keep going. I came to realize the ultimate goal of summitting might not have been the best goal. The best objective, really, is to live and enjoy another day's adventure.

As the years have passed, the pain of not making it to the summit has not diminished, but with time comes perspective. Before I began the expedition, I told myself, and my family, that safety came first; that coming down safely from the mountain would be my highest priority— much higher than successfully reaching the summit. I had held true to that priority. I had no way of knowing the clouds below would not continue rising and create the same kind of blizzard that killed the climbers in 1996. I also knew the first stages of hypothermia had set in and my extremities were bordering on frostbite. As much as I wanted to reach the summit, I didn't want it badly enough to lose any fingers or toes.

Still, my decision continues to haunt me.

Obviously, I have thought countless times about going back to Everest to try again. The financial cost is prohibitive. I could buy a small house for what it now costs to do an Everest attempt. I also think about one climber I follow. He is the oldest American to summit K2, also known as Mount Godwin-Austen, the second-highest mountain in the world at 28,251 feet. It took him four attempts before he successfully summited Everest. I wince at the thought of how much money he must have spent just on this one mountain alone. What if I spent close to $100,000 to go back to Everest and, once more, didn't succeed?

One thing that consoles me is that I moved on. I set a big, hairy, audacious goal to climb all of the seven summits—the highest mountain on every continent—and despite my failure on Everest, I have continued on and succeeded at my goal of summiting the other six. I kept going; I kept plugging away.

If you want a leadership lesson from these two final chapters, I guess there it is: When you set a huge goal for yourself, you might not make it to the exact place you hoped to be, but if you keep going and keep persevering, even if you fail, where you end up will be pretty darn great.

Besides, I figure I have successfully climbed the seven summits minus only the last 300 vertical feet on Everest. That is not half bad.

I shot for the moon, and even though I missed by just a bit, I still ended up among the stars.

Thanks for reading my story. I pray you have been able to take something valuable with you.

Mark

I hope you enjoyed the book. If you are interested in learning more about how you can hire Mark for speaking engagements or as an executive/leadership coach please visit my website at
www.summitparadigm.com
or email me at
mark@summitparadigm.com

For bonus chapters about my climbs on Mount Fuji and Mount Kinabalu, go to
summitparadigm.com/bonus.

Appendix

THE VISION I HAD FOR MY LIFE WAS TO LIVE ONE of adventure, travel, and seeing the world's natural beauty. The vehicle I used to attain that vision was my mountain climbing. In many ways, climbing can be a metaphor for achieving any important vision in your life, as climbing is all about pushing through difficulties and having faith that when all is said and done, you will have reached your dream, conquered the summit, and safely arrived back at your base camp.

People often ask me how to realize their own vision, especially leaders with a vision for where they want to take their teams, departments, and organizations. My response is *it will not be easy*, but even if you only follow the summarized advice in this appendix, you can push through the difficulties, and it will be worth the effort.

All of us lead busy and sometimes stressful lives, and it can be hard to remain focused and motivated enough to achieve a vision. There are many days I struggle with what I believe is my God-ordained vision, and so this quote from the book *Visioneering*[4] by Andy Stanley really speaks to me:

> *"If you are consumed with tension between what is and what could be, if you find yourself emotionally involved—frustrated, brokenhearted, maybe even*

4 Stanley, Andy. *Visioneering*. Multnomah; Annotated edition, 2005.

angry—with the way things are, and if you believe God is behind your anguish, then chances are you are on the brink of something divine. Something too important to walk away from."

He goes on to say,

"Everybody has a mental picture of what could and should be for his life. But not everybody will pay the price to turn that mental image into reality. Pay the price. Embrace the vision. After all, everybody ends up somewhere in life. You have the opportunity to end up somewhere on purpose."

Are you willing to pay the price? Are you willing to climb the metaphorical high mountain that embodies your vision? In the end, it will be worth it, but it will require faith. Sometimes strong faith. As Stanley puts it,

"Pursuing a vision requires faith. Pursuing a great vision requires great faith. Pursuing a vision will test, stretch, and at times exhaust your faith. And while you are pulling your hair out down here, God revels in the glory He receives."

I hope that in the chapters of this book I conveyed my own struggles, fears, and how I achieved victory so many times. I have always told people that at its core, climbing is about suffering and about pushing through that suffering to achieve the goal you have set for yourself.

There's one final quote from Stanley's book I want

to share with you. I wrote this quote on a small piece of paper and many times when I lay in my tent on some mountain or trail, cold and lonely, I would take out this piece of paper and read this quote. It always brought me tremendous comfort.

> *"So be encouraged. The agony you are experiencing is normal. The loneliness you feel is to be expected. The sleepless nights when you stare up at the ceiling and think, 'What have I gotten myself into?' are part of the process. All of those experiences will ultimately lead you to the conclusion, 'God, if You don't come through, I'm sunk!' And that is exactly where He wants you to be—and stay. For this reason, men and women of vision are men and women of faith. And through their faith, God is honored."*

Summary
of Leadership Lessons

CHAPTER 1
The Mother of Mountains

1. Embrace your desire to live an extraordinary life.

2. Take the leap of faith instead of
   living with regret.

CHAPTER 2
Embrace The Challenge

1. Envision your lifelong dream. Be specific.

2. In the middle of crazy fear, numbing pain, exhaustion,
   and even unpreparedness, your vision will help you dig
   deep to steel your resolve.

3. You have to want it so badly that you will push
   through all fears and pain.

4. Slow and steady is better than fast and erratic.

CHAPTER 3
No Man Is an Island

1. Solo journeys are risky journeys.

2. Working with a team is most often a better choice.

3. Self-awareness is key.

4. Teamwork protects the individual and the team.

CHAPTER 4
Touching the Sky

1. Do what scares you in little doses.

2. This is called *systematic desensitization,* and it will help
   you overcome your fears.

3. Slowly build confidence, and you will realize you can
   do more than you think.

CHAPTERS 5 & 6
Russian Hospitality
& Overcoming Challenges to Take on Your Primary Challenge

1. Sometimes you will need to overcome challenges to take on your primary challenge.

2. Don't let anyone deter you from achieving your goals.

3. There will always be people who try to stand in the way of you living an extraordinary life. Sidestep them and keep moving forward.

CHAPTER 7
Finding Strength in Weakness

1. Learn to be comfortable being uncomfortable.

2. Determination is the key.

3. Find the beauty of life. It is present even in the midst of trials if you look for it.

4. There is power in the team.

5. A leader has to be aware that people are always watching to see how they react to adversity. As a leader, you must model what you preach.

CHAPTER 8
The Mountain I Did Not Want to Climb

1. Embrace challenges you dread or ones that are inconveniently thrust upon you.

2. Look for and remember the success in your efforts.

CHAPTER 9
The Forty Percent Rule

1. Do what you have to do to get the job done.

2. Sometimes you just have to grind through suffering to achieve your goal or not let your team down.

3. When you think you have nothing left, you really have sixty percent left.

CHAPTERS 10 & 11
The Wonder of Embracing a Challenge
& The Cradle of Life

1. Good leaders spend quality time with all levels of the organization. They walk the floor, get to know the people, and take an interest in staff at every level.

2. If you want to be energized as a leader, spend more time with those lower levels and treat them with the utmost dignity and respect, because they have wisdom, they have experience, they have ideas, and they can teach you many things.

3. You can learn how to be excellent. Sometimes that's discovered in unusual places.

4. Never approach people in a more vulnerable position with arrogance. You will ultimately harm yourself.

5. Embrace life wherever you are and be grateful every day for the blessings provided.

CHAPTER 12
The Silent Climb

1. You do not have to strive to reach your goals alone.

2. A life worth living sometimes involves risk.

3. What are you passionate about? Is it possible God has put that calling in your heart?

CHAPTER 13
The Frozen Moment

1. Whether in climbing or in business, risk exists. You can minimize risk by being prepared.

2. In business, proper due diligence is like wearing a climbing helmet—it minimizes the risk.

3. Never approach a decision with "Ready, fire, aim."

4. Take the time to prepare, do your due diligence, prepare some more, and then "Ready, aim, fire."

5. Avoid "deal fever." It is as dangerous as summit fever.

CHAPTER 14
The Greatest Day of My Life

1. When you work hard, take calculated risks, and put the effort in, sometimes it all comes together to fulfill your wildest, childhood dreams.

2. Keep chasing your dream, and you will reach that moment where you feel the dream has coalesced around you.

CHAPTERS 15 & 16
Mother's Necklace
& Matthew 19:26

1. Ask yourself, "Is it hard, or is it impossible?" More often than not, if you're honest, you'll find it is merely hard. Hard is doable.

2. Hebrews 12:1 says, "With God all things are possible." God can empower you.

CHAPTER 17
Hubris at 15,774 Feet

1. Never assume you know more than anyone else or that nobody can teach you anything.

2. Understand your team's limitations and never push anyone past what they are capable of achieving.

3. Have a solid understanding of what will make a venture successful.

4. Share information and do not hoard power.

CHAPTER 18
Servant Leadership on a Stratovolcano

1. Work towards serving others with humility, skill, and servant leadership. Never ask your team to do anything you wouldn't do.

2. Be visible in appropriate ways.

3. Besides trust and respect, being friendly and fun is important.

4. Create the vision for your team and lead by example.

CHAPTERS 19 & 20
The Cost of the Summit, Part I & Part II

1. Sometimes you have to push through extreme situations to come out on the other side.

2. Know that eventually you will come out on the other side, but it will be in God's time and not yours, and the sooner you can accept that, the better off you will be.

3. Decide to bloom where you are planted, and before long you will be promoted out of that situation.

4. How much are you willing to pay to accomplish your dreams? Embrace the pain to reach the goal.

5. People learn more from watching what you do than they do by hearing what you say.

6. In business, respect is currency.

CHAPTER 21
Summit Fever

1. *Deal fever* is as common as it is dangerous. Avoid it at all costs.

2. Never become complacent in your vigilant assessment of the risks.

3. Even in our greatest, strongest moment, we are utterly insignificant compared to God and much of His creation.

CHAPTERS 22 & 23
Pride Before a Fall
& Fatal Leadership

1. Be friendly and embrace humanity—the people you meet will lift your vision. As Mark Twain wrote, "Travel is fatal to prejudice."

2. Stubbornness can be fatal.

3. Check your impulses, especially when under duress. Impulsive decisions can cost you everything.

4. Consider the proverbial boiling frog—watch for the little signs that things are not going well.

5. Anticipate instead of reacting.

6. We often focus too much on the summit and not enough on the journey. Appreciate the journey to understand there will be another day to tackle the summit again.

CHAPTERS 24 & 25
The Great Trek
& Among the Stars

1. Recognize that there sometimes is a point of no return and respect that boundary. There is great danger in not respecting the window to turn around.

2. When situations aren't the way you envisioned, adapt, and keep going. Live to enjoy another day's adventure.

3. You may experience bitter disappointment right before the summit of your lifelong goal, but don't let one failure (or several) stop you.

4. Always keep going. You will find yourself among the stars.

Mark Carr:
Transformation Speaker, Author,
Leadership Coach

MARK CARR is a speaker, writer and certified leadership coach. He is also an elite adventurer and mountain climber and has worked as a professional outdoor adventure guide in the Grand Canyon and Yosemite. He has climbed mountains all over the world and has successfully summited the highest peak on six of the seven continents. Additionally, he has climbed all the 14,000-foot peaks in Colorado, as well as such iconic summits as the Matterhorn, the Eiger, and Mt. Blanc.

As a sought-after keynote and workshop presenter, he shares pictures, stories and leadership lessons from his climbs and translates those lessons to the corporate world through his passion to positively impact others by instilling quality leadership principles that can transform the employee experience. He also speaks about overcoming fear and adversity, again weaving in riveting pictures and stories from his adventures around the world. He has spoken at conferences and seminars for international companies such as Motorola, Celestica, Deutsche Telecom and T-Systems.

He is a Fortune 200 Human Resource Executive with almost 25 years experience in human capital management, including employee engagement, strategic workforce planning, succession planning, leadership assessment and mergers and acquisitions. He has a Master's degree in Business Administration from the University of Arizona, and a Master's degree in Clinical Psychology (concentrating in Forensic Psychology) from Arizona State University. As an undergraduate, Mark played Division 1 varsity baseball, and was an Academic All American his senior year of college. Mark is certified in both DISC and the Meyers Briggs Type Indicator.

Mark is the founder and president of THE SUMMIT PARADIGM (www.summitparadigm.com). He can be reached at mark@summitparadigm.com.